"Just a fantastic talent …

spectacular, brutal, uncompromising, captivating**"**

Ian Rankin

GB
DAVID PEACE
84

"Just as James Ellroy retold the story of the JFK years as a menacing tale of corruption and abuse of power in **American Tabloid**, so Peace has spun a disturbing re-imagined history from the Thatcher years. GB84 is utterly masterful and easily David Peace's best work to date**"**

Yorkshire Post

www.faber.co.uk

ff

GRANTA 85, SPRING 2004
www.granta.com

EDITOR   *Ian Jack*
DEPUTY EDITOR   *Matt Weiland*
MANAGING EDITOR   *Fatema Ahmed*
ASSOCIATE EDITOR   *Liz Jobey*
EDITORIAL ASSISTANT   *Helen Gordon*

CONTRIBUTING EDITORS   *Diana Athill, Sophie Harrison, Gail Lynch, Blake Morrison, Andrew O'Hagan, John Ryle, Sukhdev Sandhu, Lucretia Stewart*

ASSOCIATE PUBLISHER   *Sally Lewis*
FINANCE   *Geoffrey Gordon, Morgan Graver*
SALES   *Frances Hollingdale*
PUBLICITY   *Louise Campbell*
SUBSCRIPTIONS   *John Kirkby, Darryl Wilks, Anna Tang*
PUBLISHING ASSISTANT   *Mark Williams*
ADVERTISING MANAGER   *Kate Rochester*
PRODUCTION ASSOCIATE   *Sarah Wasley*

PUBLISHER   *Rea S. Hederman*

Granta, 2–3 Hanover Yard, Noel Road, London N1 8BE
Tel 020 7704 9776 Fax 020 7704 0474
e-mail for editorial: editorial@granta.com

Granta US, 1755 Broadway, 5th Floor, New York, NY 10019-3780, USA

TO SUBSCRIBE call 020 7704 0470 or e-mail subs@granta.com
A one-year subscription (four issues) costs £26.95 (UK), £34.95 (rest of Europe) and £41.95 (rest of the world).

Granta is printed and bound in Italy by Legoprint. The paper used in this publication meets the minimum requirements of American National Standard for Information Sciences—Permanence of Paper for Printed Library Materials, ANSI Z39.48-1984.

Granta is published by Granta Publications.
This selection copyright © 2004 Granta Publications.

Design: Slab Media.

Cover photograph: © Powerstock

Acknowledgements are due to the following publishers for permission to quote from:
'Whatever You Say Say Nothing' by Seamus Heaney from 'New Selected Poems 1966–1987' reprinted by permission of Faber and Faber Ltd and Farrar, Straus & Giroux.

ISBN 0-903141-67-1

THE PRESIDENT OF GOOD AND EVIL

TAKING GEORGE W. BUSH SERIOUSLY

Peter Singer

A penetrating examination of Bush's ethics by one of the most controversial and influential living philosophers.

'Very well-researched and timely. The ethical judgements make a welcome change from the idea that profit and loss are the only valid criteria for assessing what is good and what is bad'
Tony Benn

'A screamingly funny,
genre-defying feat
… sublime'
**Maggie O'Farrell,
Books of the Year,
Daily Telegraph**

CHANGE YOUR MIND

GRANTA 85

Hidden Histories

London Review Bookshop

14 Bury Place, London WC1A 2JL
Telephone: 020 7269 9030   Fax: 020 7269 9033
email: books@lrbshop.co.uk

Looking for Granta titles? Look no further than the London Review Bookshop

The President of Good and Evil – Taking George W. Bush Seriously
by Peter Singer
£8.99 ISBN 1862076936
Published 17 April

The Smoking Diaries
by Simon Gray
£12.99 ISBN 186207688X
Published 17 April

Both of these titles are featured in our Spring 2004 catalogue, containing around 200 of the best new books published this spring.

Simon Gray is one of the many authors taking part in the London Review Bookshop's ongoing programme of literary events. He will be reading from **The Smoking Diaries** at 7pm on Thursday 22 April.

Tickets £4 from the shop or by phone (020 7269 9030) or by e-mail from **events@lrbshop.co.uk**

A RELIGIOUS CONVERSATION

Orhan Pamuk

TRANSLATED FROM THE TURKISH

BY MAUREEN FREELY

'Hello, sir. Do you recognize me?'
'No, I'm afraid I don't.'

'That's what I thought you'd say, sir. Because we haven't ever met. I did try to come and see you last night and then again this morning. Yesterday the police turned me away from the school doors. This morning I managed to get inside but your secretary wouldn't let me see you. I wanted to catch you before you went into class. That's when you saw me. Do you remember me now, sir?'

'No, I don't.'

'Are you saying you don't remember me, or are you saying you don't remember seeing me?'

'What did you want to see me about?'

'To tell you the truth, I'd like to talk to you for hours, even days, about everything under the sun. You're an eminent, enlightened, educated man. Sadly, I myself was not able to pursue studies. But there's one subject I know backwards and forwards. And that's the subject I was hoping to discuss with you. I'm sorry, sir. I hope I'm not taking too much of your time?'

'Not at all.'

'Excuse me, sir, do you mind if I sit down? We have a great deal of ground to cover.'

'Please. Be my guest.' (The sound of someone pulling out a chair.)

'I see you're eating a pastry with walnuts. We have lots of walnut trees in Tokat. Have you ever been to Tokat?'

'I'm sorry to say I haven't.'

'I'm so sorry to hear that, sir. If you ever do come to visit, you must stay with me. I've spent my whole life in Tokat. All thirty-six years. Tokat is very beautiful. The rest of Turkey is very beautiful, too. But it's such a shame that we know so little about our own country, that we can't find it in our hearts to love our own kind. Instead we admire those who show our country disrespect and betray its people. I hope you don't mind if I ask you a question, sir. You're not an atheist, are you?'

'No, I'm not.'

'People say you are, but I myself would find it hard to believe that a man of your education would—God forbid—deny God's existence. But you're not a Jew, either, are you?'

'No, I'm not.'

'You're a Muslim.'

'Yes. Glory be to God. I am.'

'You're smiling, sir. I'd like to ask you to take my question seriously and answer it properly. Because I've travelled all the way from Tokat in the dead of winter just to hear you answer this question.'

'How did you come to hear of me in Tokat?'

'There has been nothing in the Istanbul papers, sir, about your decision to deny schooling to girls who cover their heads as dictated by their religion and the Holy Book. All those papers care about is scandals involving fashion models. But in beautiful Tokat we have a Muslim radio station called Flag that keeps us informed about the injustices perpetrated on the faithful in every corner of the country.'

'I could never do an injustice to a believer. I too fear God.'

'It took me two days to get here, sir. Two days on snowy, stormy roads. While I was sitting on that bus I thought of no one but you, and, believe me, I knew all along that you were going to tell me that you feared God. And here's the question I imagined asking you next, sir. With all due respect, Professor Nuri Yılmaz—if you fear God, if you believe that the Holy Qur'an is the Word of God, then let's hear your views on the beautiful thirty-first verse of the chapter entitled "Heavenly Light".'

'Yes, it's true. This verse states very clearly that women should cover their heads and even their faces.'

'Congratulations, sir! That's a good, straight answer. And now, with your permission, sir, I'd like to ask you something else. How can you reconcile God's command with this decision to ban covered girls from the classroom?'

'We live in a secular state. It's the secular state that has banned covered girls, from schools as well as classrooms.'

'Excuse me, sir. May I ask you a question? Can a law imposed by the state cancel our God's law?'

'That's a very good question. But in a secular state these matters are separate.'

'That's a good, straight answer, sir. May I kiss your hand? Please, sir, don't be afraid. Give me your hand. Give me your hand and watch how lovingly I kiss it. Oh, God be praised. Thank you. Now you know how much respect I have for you. May I ask you another question, sir?'

'Please. Go right ahead.'

'My question is this, sir. Does the word "secular" mean "godless"?'

'No.'

'In that case, how can you explain why the state is banning so many girls from the classroom in the name of secularism, when all they are doing is obeying the laws of their religion?'

'Honestly, my son. Arguing about such things will get you nowhere. They argue about it day and night on Istanbul television, and where does it get us? The girls are still refusing to take off their headscarves and the state is still barring them from the classroom.'

'In that case, sir, may I ask you another question? I beg your pardon, but when I think about these poor, hard-working girls of ours who have been denied an education, who are so polite and so diligent and who have bowed their heads to God-only-knows how many decrees already... The question I cannot help asking is: how does all this fit in with what our constitution says about educational and religious freedom? Please, sir, tell me. Isn't your conscience bothering you?'

'If those girls were as obedient as you say they are, then they'd have taken off their headscarves. What's your name, my son? Where do you live? What sort of work do you do?'

'I work at the Happy Friends Teahouse, which is just next door to Tokat's famous Mothlight Hamam. I'm in charge of the stoves and the teapots. My name's not important. I listen to Flag Radio all day long. Every once in a while I'll get really upset about something I've heard, about an injustice done to a believer. And because I live in a democracy, because I happen to be a free man who can do as he pleases, I sometimes end up getting on a bus and travelling to the other end of Turkey to track down the perpetrator wherever he is and have it out with him, face to face. So please, sir, answer my question. What's more important, a decree from Ankara or a decree from God?'

'This discussion is going nowhere, son. What hotel are you staying at?'

'What—are you thinking of turning me in to the police? Don't be afraid of me, sir. I don't belong to any religious organizations. I despise terrorism. I believe in the love of God and the free exchange of ideas. That's why I never end a free exchange of ideas by hitting anyone, even though I have a quick temper. All I want is for you to answer this question. So please excuse me, sir, but when you think about the cruel way you treated those poor girls in front of your institute—when you remember that these girls were only obeying the Word of God as set out so clearly in the "Confederate Tribe" and "Heavenly Light" chapters of the Holy Qur'an—doesn't your conscience trouble you at all?'

'My son, the Qur'an also says that thieves should have their hands chopped off. But the state doesn't do that. Why aren't you opposing that?'

'That's an excellent answer, sir. Allow me to kiss your hand. But how can you equate the hand of a thief with the honour of our women? According to statistics released by the American Black Muslim Professor Marvin King, the incidence of rape in Islamic countries where women cover themselves is so low as to be non-existent and harassment is virtually unheard-of. This is because a woman who has covered herself is making a statement. Through her choice of clothing, she is saying, "Don't harass me." So please, sir, may I ask you a question? Do we really want to push our covered women to the margins of society by denying them the right to an education? If we continue to worship women who take off their headscarves and just about everything else, too, don't we run the risk of degrading our women as we have seen so many women in Europe degraded in the wake of the sexual revolution? And if we succeed in degrading our women, aren't we also running the risk of—pardon my language—turning ourselves into pimps?'

'I've finished my croissant, son. I'm afraid I have to leave.'

'Stay in your seat, sir. Stay in your seat and I won't have to use this. Do you see what this is, sir?'

'Yes. It's a gun.'

'That's right, sir. I hope you don't mind. I came a long way to see you. I'm not stupid. It crossed my mind that you might refuse to hear me out. That's why I took precautions.'

'What's your name, son?'

'Vahit Süzme. Salim Fesmekkan. Really, sir, what difference does it make? I'm the nameless defender of nameless heroes who have suffered untold wrongs while seeking to uphold their religious beliefs in a society that is in thrall to secular materialism. I'm not a member of any organization. I respect human rights and I oppose the use of violence. That's why I'm putting my gun in my pocket. That's why all I want from you is an answer to my question.'

'Fine.'

'Then let us go back to the beginning, sir. Let's remember what you did to these girls whose upbringing took so many years of loving care. Who were the apples of their parents' eyes. Who were so very intelligent. Who worked so hard at their studies. Who were all at the top of the class. When the order came from Ankara, you set about denying their existence. If one of them wrote her name down on the attendance sheet, you'd erase it—just because she was wearing a headscarf. If seven girls sat down with their teacher, you'd pretend that the one wearing the headscarf wasn't there, and you'd order six teas. Do you know what you did to these girls? You made them cry. But it didn't stop there. Soon there was another directive from Ankara, and after that you barred them from their classrooms. You threw them out into the corridors and then you banned them from the corridors and threw them out into the street. And then, when a handful of these heroines gathered trembling at the doors of the school to make their concerns known, you picked up the phone and called the police.'

'We weren't the ones who called the police.'

'I know you're afraid of the gun in my pocket. But please, sir, don't lie. The night after you had those girls dragged off and arrested, did your conscience let you sleep? That's my question.'

'Of course, the real question is how much suffering we've caused our womenfolk by turning headscarves into symbols—and using women as pawns in a political game.'

'How can you call it a game, sir? When that girl who had to choose between her honour and her education—what a tragedy— sank into a depression and killed herself. Was that a game?'

'You're very upset, my boy. But has it never occurred to you that foreign powers might be behind all this? Don't you see how they might have politicized the headscarf issue so that they can turn Turkey into a weak and divided nation?'

'If you'd let those girls back into your school, sir, there would be no headscarf issue.'

'Is it really my decision? These orders come from Ankara. My own wife wears a headscarf.'

'Stop trying to mollify me. Answer the question I just asked you.'

'Which question was that?'

'Is your conscience bothering you?'

'My child, I'm a father, too. Of course I feel sorry for those girls.'

'Look. I'm very good at holding myself back. But once I blow my fuse, it's all over. When I was in prison, I once beat up a man just because he forgot to cover his mouth when he yawned. Oh yes, I made men of all of them in there. I cured every man in that prison wing of all his bad habits. I even got them praying. So stop trying to squirm out of it. Let's hear an answer to my question.'

'What did you ask, son? Lower that gun.'

'I can tell you what I *didn't* ask. I didn't ask if you had a daughter, or if you felt any remorse.'

'Pardon me, son. What *did* you ask?'

'Don't think you have to butter me up, just because you're afraid of the gun. Just remember what I asked you.' (Silence.)

'What did you ask me?'

'I asked you if your conscience was troubling you, infidel!'

'Of course it's troubling me.'

'Then why do you persist? Is it because you have no shame?'

'My son, I'm a teacher. I'm old enough to be your father. Is it written in the Qur'an that you should point guns at your elders and insult them?'

'Don't you dare let the word "Qur'an" pass your lips. Do you hear? And stop looking over your shoulder like you're asking for help. If you shout for help, I won't hesitate. I'll shoot. Is that clear?'

'Yes, it's clear.'

'Then answer this question: what good can come to this country if women uncover their heads? Give me one good outcome. Say something you believe with all your heart. Say, for example, that by uncovering themselves they'll get Europeans to start treating them like human beings. At least then I'll understand what your motives are and then I won't shoot you. I'll let you go.'

'My dear child, I have a daughter myself. She doesn't wear a headscarf. I don't interfere with her decision, just as I don't interfere with my wife's decision to wear a headscarf.'

'Why did your daughter decide to uncover herself? Does she want to become a film star?'

'She's never said anything of the sort to me. She's in Ankara studying public relations. But she's been a tremendous support to me since I've come under attack over this headscarf issue. Whenever I get upset about the things people say, whenever I am slandered or threatened, whenever I have to face the wrath of my enemies—or people like you—who have every right to be angry, she calls me from Ankara and...'

'And she says, "Grit your teeth, Dad. I'm going to be a film star."'

'No, son, she doesn't say that. She says, "Father dear, if I had to go into a classroom full of covered girls, I wouldn't dare go in uncovered. I'd wear a headscarf even if I didn't want to."'

'So what if she didn't want to cover herself—what harm could come of it?'

'Honestly, I couldn't tell you. You asked me to give you a reason.'

'So tell me, infidel, was this your thinking when you allowed the police to club these devout girls who have covered their heads at God's command? Are you trying to tell me that you drove them to suicide just to please your daughter?'

'There are plenty of women in Turkey who think as my daughter does.'

'When ninety per cent of women in this country wear headscarves, it's hard to see who these film stars think they're speaking for. You might be proud to see your daughter exposing herself, infidel, but get this into your head. I might not be a professor, but I know a lot more about this subject than you do.'

'My good man, please don't point your gun at me. You're very upset. If the gun goes off, you'll live to regret it.'

'Why would I regret it? Why would I have spent two days travelling through this miserable snow if not to wipe out an infidel? As the Holy Qur'an states, it is my duty to kill any tyrant who visits cruelty on believers. But, because I feel sorry for you, I'm going to give you one last chance. Give me just one reason why your conscience doesn't bother you when you order covered women to uncover themselves and I swear I won't shoot you.'

'When a woman takes off her headscarf, she occupies a more comfortable place in society and gets more respect.'

'That might be what that film-star daughter of yours thinks. But the opposite is true. Headscarves protect women from harassment, rape and degradation. It's the headscarf that gives women respect and a comfortable place in society. We've heard this from so many women who've chosen later in life to cover themselves. Women like the old belly-dancer Melahat Şandra. The veil saves women from the animal instincts of men in the street. It saves them from the ordeal of entering beauty contests to compete with other women. They don't have to live like sex objects, they don't have to wear make-up all day. As Professor Marvin King has already noted, if the celebrated film star Elizabeth Taylor had spent the last twenty years covered, she would not have had to worry so much about being fat. She would not have ended up in a mental hospital. She might have known some happiness. Pardon me, sir. May I ask you a question? Why are you laughing, sir? Do you think I'm trying to be funny?' (Silence.) 'Go ahead and tell me, you shameless atheist. Why are you laughing?'

'My dear child, please believe me, I'm not laughing! Or, if I did laugh, it was a nervous laugh.'

'No! You were laughing with conviction.'

'Please believe me, I feel nothing but compassion for all the people in this country—like you, like those covered girls—who are suffering for this cause.'

'I told you, kind words will get you nowhere. I'm not suffering one bit. But you're going to suffer now for laughing about those girls who committed suicide. And now that you've laughed at them, there's no chance you'll show remorse. So let me tell you where things stand. It's quite some time now since the Freedom Fighters for Islamic Justice condemned you to death. They reached their verdict in Tokat five days ago and sent me here to execute the sentence. If you hadn't laughed, I might have relented and forgiven you. Take this piece of paper. Let's hear you read out your death sentence...' (Silence.) 'Stop crying like a woman. Read it out in a good, strong voice. Hurry up, you shameless idiot. If you don't hurry up, I'm going to shoot.'

'"I, Professor Nuri Yılmaz, am an atheist..." My dear child, I'm not an atheist.'

'Keep reading.'

'My child, you're not going to shoot me while I'm reading this, are you?'

'If you don't keep reading it, I'm going to shoot you.'

'"I confess to being a pawn in a secret plan to strip the Muslims of the secular Turkish Republic of their religion and their honour and thereby to turn them into slaves of the West. As for the girls who would not take off their headscarves, because they were devout and mindful of what is written in the Qur'an, I visited such cruelty on them that one girl could bear it no more and committed suicide..." My dear child, with your permission, I'd like to make an objection here. I'd be grateful if you could pass this on to the committee that sent you. This girl didn't hang herself because she was barred from the classroom. And it wasn't because of the pressure her father put on her, either. As the MİT has already told us, she was suffering from a broken heart.'

'That's not what she said in her suicide note.'

'Please forgive me, but my child, I think you should know—please lower that gun—that even before she got married, this uneducated girl was naive enough to give herself to a policeman twenty-five years her senior. And—it's an awful shame—but it was after he'd told her he was married and had no intention of marrying her...'

'Shut up, you disgrace. That's something your whore of a daughter would do.'

'Don't do this, my son. My child, don't do this. If you shoot me, you're only darkening your own future.'

'Say you're sorry.'

'I'm sorry, son. Don't shoot.'

'Open your mouth. I want to shove the gun inside. Then put your finger on top of mine and pull the trigger. You'll still be an infidel, but at least you'll die with honour.' (Silence.)

'My child, look what I've become. At my age, I'm crying. I'm begging you, take pity on me. Take pity on yourself. You're still so young. And you're going to become a murderer.'

'Then pull the trigger yourself. See for yourself how much suicide hurts.'

'My child, I'm a Muslim. I'm opposed to suicide.'

'Open your mouth.' (Silence.) 'Don't cry like that. Didn't it ever cross your mind that one day you'd have to pay for what you've done? Stop crying, or I'll shoot.'

(The voice of the old waiter in the distance.) 'Should I bring your tea to this table, sir?'

'No, thank you. I'm about to leave.'

'Don't look at the waiter. Keep reading your death sentence.'

'My son, please forgive me.'

'I said read.'

'"I am ashamed of all the things I have done. I know I deserve to die and in the hope that God Almighty will forgive me..."'

'Keep reading.'

'My dear, dear child. Let this old man cry for a few moments. Let me think about my wife and my daughter one last time.'

'Think about the girls whose lives you destroyed. One had a nervous breakdown, four were kicked out of school in their third year. One committed suicide. The ones who stood trembling outside the doors of your school all came down with fevers and ended up in bed. Their lives were ruined.'

'I am so very sorry, my dear, dear child. But what good will it do if you shoot me and turn yourself into a murderer? Think of that.'

'All right. I will.' (Silence.) 'I've given it some thought, sir. And here's what I've worked out.'

'What?'

'I'd been wandering around the miserable streets of Kars for two days and getting nowhere. And then I decided it must be fate, so I bought my return ticket to Tokat. I was drinking my last glass of tea when...'

'My child, if you thought you could kill me and then escape on the last bus out of Kars, let me warn you: the roads are closed due to the snow. The six o'clock bus has been cancelled. Don't live to regret this.'

'Just as I was turning around, God sent you into the New Life Pastry Shop. And if God's not going to forgive you, why should I? Say your last words. Say, "God is great."'

'Sit down, son. I'm warning you, this state of ours will catch you all. And hang you all.'

'Say, "God is great."'

'Calm down, my child. Stop. Sit down. Think it over one more time. Don't pull that trigger. Stop.'

(The sound of a gunshot. The sound of a chair pushed out.)

'Don't, my son!'

(Two more gunshots. Silence. A groan. The sound of a television. One more gunshot. Silence.) □

ALIVE, ALIVE-OH!
Diana Athill

She thought of herself as a rational woman, but while she could sleep alone in an empty house for night after night without worrying, there were other nights when her nerves twitched like a rabbit's at the least sound. On the many good nights and the few bad the chances of a burglar's breaking in were exactly the same: the difference was within herself and signified nothing which she could identify. And she had always been like that over the possibility of pregnancy.

For several months it would not occur to her to worry, and in another she would be convinced, perhaps as much as a fortnight before the month's end, that this time it had happened. The anxiety seemed in itself an indication: why this sudden fret if there were no reason? She would start working out how to find the money for an abortion, or whether she was capable of bringing up a child single-handed, and when the anxiety proved groundless she would feel foolish as well as relieved.

This last month had been an easy-minded one. She happened, for once, to know the date on which, in this sense, it should have ended, having filled an idle moment by marking little crosses in her diary some way ahead; but although she was often a few days early and never late, she was so far from worrying that she hardly noticed when the day came and went. Six more days passed before she said to herself: 'Hadn't you better start acknowledging this? The curse is six days overdue and your breasts are hurting.'

Rational? How did she square that with the fact that in spite of the fluctuations in anxiety she had taken no precautions against pregnancy for almost two years? From time to time, at the end of an anxious month, she had thought of it: 'If I'm let off this time I'll never be such a fool again.' But she never did anything about it. 'Not today', 'Not this week', 'Another time', or even, 'What's the point? I'll only put the damned things in a drawer and forget to use them.' The mere thought of it seemed too tedious to bear. Although she had twice become pregnant in the past, that was now such a long time ago and surely she had reached an age when it was less likely? After all, month after month had gone by to confirm her optimism.

If anyone had said to her: 'There can be only one reason for an unmarried woman in her early forties to ignore good sense so stubbornly: she does it not from an optimistic belief that she will not conceive, but because of an exactly opposite subconscious optimism; deep inside herself she wants a child,' she would have answered, 'Of course she does. I do know that, really. I suppose I must have been choosing to ignore it.' But although she had not been able to prevent her subconscious from undermining her reason, she saw nothing against putting it in its place. She had overruled it twice before and had felt no ill effects. 'All right, so you want a baby. Who doesn't? But as things are you can't have one—I'm sorry but there it is, too bad for you.' Neither time had it put up any fight. It had accepted its frustration placidly—and placidly it had resumed its scheming.

She had once met a man who had been persuaded to consult an analyst about, of all things, his constipation. He had found the experience interesting and beneficial, and summed it up in words that delighted her: 'It is fascinating to learn what an old juggins one's subconscious is.' That was what she now felt: what an old juggins! What a touching and in some ways admirable old juggins! She saw her subconscious plodding along, pig-headed, single-minded, an old tortoise lumbering through undergrowth, heaving itself over fallen branches, subsiding into holes full of dead leaves. Sometimes, no doubt, the obstacles had been almost too much for him and he had lain panting slightly, staring up at the sky and blinking in apparent bewilderment, but then a blunt foreleg would begin to grope again, his toes would scratch for purchase and on he would go. The question was this: did she slap her subconscious down again by finding the necessary cash and the obliging doctor from the past (if he was still taking such risks), or did she capitulate and have this child?

The reasons against it were these: she was unmarried, forty-three years old and had no private income. She lived comfortably on what she earned, and could do things she enjoyed, such as travelling, with the extra money she had recently begun to earn by writing which, at present, was well within her energies. She would like to preserve these conditions.

The reasons for it were these: if she did not have a child now she would never have one, and she loved its father.

This child's father was married—well married, to an admirable woman who had done him no wrong and to whom he owed much. He had begun an affair simply because he had been married for seven years, was no longer romantically in love with his wife, and was polygamous by nature. He had come to take the affair seriously because the two of them suited each other in every way, one of their strongest bonds being that neither of them was possessive. He might have been described as sitting pretty, married to a good, dependable wife without whom he could not imagine himself, and in love with a good, dependable mistress to whom he could turn whenever he wished. But it was more complex than that. She was nine years older than he which, together with her nature, had given her a certain authority over the situation. He saw her as having *chosen* this form of relationship rather than having been persuaded or manoeuvred into it, and he was right: there was no reason why he should develop a sense of responsibility towards her except in their own terms of honesty and tenderness. It was a perfect situation for him, since he had no money and was trying to live by writing; but that one partner is well suited does not necessarily mean that the other is ill-used. She herself might have condemned some other woman's lover in a similar situation, but she knew him and herself too well to condemn him. He was what he was: the person with whom, *being as he was*, she was most at home. What, then, would be the point of wishing him otherwise?

And could she make him otherwise, if she wanted to? No. And she didn't mind that because she was perfectly willing to accept that they, as they both were, were each other's unexpected bonus from life. It was this that had established so much ease and sweetness between them. If, when she told him she was pregnant, he were to offer to leave his wife and come to her, she would be quite as anxious as she would be happy. She would not, whatever she decided, try to make him do that. Perhaps this was cowardice—a fear of actually facing a lack of success which she thought she could envisage with equanimity. Or perhaps it was vanity—a desire to go on representing freedom, pleasure, stimulation, all the joys of love rather than its burdens. Or perhaps it was really what she would like it to be: the kind of respect for another person's being that she would wish to have paid to her own. But there was no doubt that, if she was pregnant, life would be a great deal easier if her lover and her love were otherwise than they were.

So it would be sensible to have an abortion. In her experience it was not a profoundly disagreeable thing to have. The worst part of the operation, performed under a local anaesthetic, was the grotesque position into which one is trussed on the table. The last time she found that she could see a tiny but clear reflection of herself in the globe of the lampshade above her, and at that she almost lost grip but screwed her eyes shut instead. There is this humiliating ugliness, and there are sounds, and for a few moments there is a dim sensation of pain. If the doctor is businesslike and kind, treating one (as hers had done) like an ordinary patient, there is no sinister or shaming atmosphere to contend with. One is simply having a quick little operation for a sensible reason... So it was odd that she should start to shiver slightly as she thought about it. No, she did not feel that murder is committed during that operation. She would go so far as to say that she was sure it was not: no separate existence, at that stage, was being ended, any more than when a sperm was prevented from meeting an egg. But that old juggins, the pinheaded, pig-headed tortoise behind her reason: he was tough, he was good at recovering from setbacks, but at the prospect of yet another of them he was showing signs of turning into a porcupine. He wanted her to have this child.

Having acknowledged the situation, she found herself no nearer a decision, only slightly more aware of reluctance towards either course. It was still early. She could have an abortion, if she so decided, at any time within the next three months. So the best thing to do seemed to her to be nothing: go blank, drift for a week or so, think about it as little as possible and see what happened. Perhaps she would wake up one morning knowing what she wanted to do.

The next two weeks dragged. She managed to keep her mind on other things for much of the time, but the fact of pregnancy was always there, lying in wait for any unoccupied moment. It seemed common sense not to begin worrying again at least until she had missed her second period, but long before that date came she felt that her condition had endured for months. Each morning, when she awoke, she would lie still for a minute or two trying to overhear her state of mind, but all she picked up was irritation and depression at being in this quandary. About ten days after the start of her 'truce' she spent a weekend in the country with her mother, and the depression increased: supposing she had the child, how appalling the family explanations would be, how impossible it was to imagine the degree of consternation such a decision would raise in her mother and the rest of the family. In the train on the way back to London she looked up from her book and bumped, as usual, into 'What am I going to do?' Oh god, she thought, I do wish *it would all go away*.

Well, she thought next morning, if that's the best I can do I suppose I had better *make* it go away: get the money in, anyway. There was a sum waiting for her in New York, where she had planned soon to spend a holiday. If she used half of that, would there be enough left for the holiday? Probably not. Resentment and disappointment were added to the depression, but she told her agent a story of unexpected bills as a result of moving house, and he cabled her the money at once. That done, she had only to call the doctor— his number, on a grubby scrap of paper, discreetly minus his name, still lurked at the back of a drawer in her dressing table after all those years. 'I'll do it soon,' she thought. 'Next week, perhaps. I've got the money and that's the main thing.' She spent a couple of days in a rage at missing her first chance to visit New York, and a couple more arguing that she needn't miss it after all: if she spent only three weeks there instead of four, and lived very cheaply, she could manage. If that were so she was not only being sensible, but was not going to suffer for it, so there was nothing to be depressed about any more.

It was on the fifth morning after the arrival of the money—a morning in April—that she awoke congratulating herself on living in her new flat and opening her eyes in her new bedroom. It was the top floor of a house which might almost be in the country, the last house in a short street which projected like a little promontory into a park. All the windows looked on to trees and grass, and her bedroom window had gardens as well, the long range of gardens behind the houses of the street at right angles to hers. Cherry and pear trees were in flower, and a fine magnolia; daffodils and narcissi twinkled in the grass. Soon the lilacs would be out, and the hawthorns, and the irises—it was a galloping spring after a mild winter. The sun shone into her bedroom window, and the birds were singing so loudly that they had woken her before her alarm clock went off: each garden seemed to have its own blackbird. She got out of bed to lean out of the window and sniff the green smells, and found herself saying, 'What a morning for birds and bees and buds and babies.'

This sentence was still humming in her mind as she walked to the bus stop, past the walls of more gardens, not high enough to conceal the trees and shrubs behind them. During the previous winter, before moving into the flat, she had thought as she walked this way: 'This will soon be my part of London—I shall see that pear, that crab apple tree in flower, and then heavy with dusty summer green, and then with hard little London fruit on their branches— they will be familiar landmarks.' And here they were, going into their spring performance with abandon against a brilliant blue sky, part of her daily walk to the bus. 'It is a lovely place to live,' she thought. 'I suppose I *am* going to have this baby after all.'

She was late, she had to run for a bus, those words evaporated and no thought of her predicament disturbed her morning's work. Then her business partner came into her room, to spring on her a discussion of long-term plans for the firm. Someone might be persuaded to join them and, if he did, shares would have to be re-allocated, certain changes of status would have to be made. 'It concerns you, too,' he said, 'so you must think it over.' She had a slight sensation of breathlessness and could feel her face flushing, but she made no decision to say what in fact she did say: 'I don't know that it *will* concern me. I may not be here then. I'm going to have a baby.' And inside saying: 'Oh lord, now I've done it!'—but the dismay was a laughing dismay, not a horrified one.

Perhaps her mood would not have held if her news had been received differently. As it was, her partner, a very old friend, said, 'You mean you're pregnant *now*?'

'Yes.'

'Have you seen a doctor?'

'Not yet...of course it may be a mistake, but I'm sure it's not.'

'Well then, are you mad?' he said, sitting down on the radiator, frowning. 'How do you think you're going to support the child if you don't stay on here?'

'Oh somehow—people do manage. And I thought it might be a bit embarrassing in the office...'

'Good God! If anyone's embarrassed they can bloody well get out!'

Then, dropping his poker face, he asked if she had really thought he would expect her to leave, and she answered that of course she hadn't, but it had seemed that it would be such an imposition...each of them slightly awkward at being pitched so suddenly into full awareness of their long and usually taken-for-granted affection for each other, and she the more so for having to produce thoughts which she had not yet formed on the practical side of this pregnancy. Then he kissed her and said that he was happy for her, and she was left grinning across her desk like the Cheshire cat, established in her full glory as an Expectant Unmarried Mother.

After that she was happy. She was quite often frightened too, but on a level superficial compared with that of the happiness. The birth would be easy. She could take as much time off as she needed, drawing her salary all the while, and for so long as she could stay at home all would be simple. The house in which she had her flat was owned by a close friend who herself lived in the rest of it, and who, from the moment she knew of the pregnancy, was eager to help. Neither woman had much money—she herself had to let one of the rooms in her flat to help pay its modest rent—so she was anxious not to become a financial burden on her friend, but it was reassuring to know that if the worst came to the worst she would never be chased for the rent. But she could not take advantage of that reassurance for more than a short time, and didn't want to do even that. And in addition to her usual living expenses she would have to pay for someone to care for the child while she was working, and for its food and clothes, and for its education—no, it would go to a state school, of course, there was a good one near by—but for its bicycle and its roller skates and its holidays by the sea... Year after year of financial strain stretched ahead. Financial strain and, to start with at any rate, physical exhaustion: office all day, child for every other minute—would she ever again be free to write? Not for years, anyway.

And no less frightening was the thought of the gap in the child's life where a father ought to be. Material considerations could be smothered by 'I'll manage somehow—people do'—of course she would manage when she had to. But the argument advanced by her more sober-minded friends, and by her own mind as well, that one has no right to wish this lopsided upbringing on any child—that was less easy. Surely only an exceptional woman could reasonably expect to steer her child comfortably through the shoals of illegitimacy, and could she make any claim to be exceptional? To this question she could make no answer. She could only say: 'Whatever happens, whatever the child itself may one day say (and there probably *will* come a time when it will say "I never asked to be born"), I believe that it will prefer to exist rather than not.' But the real answer was not in those words, nor in any others that she might think up. It was simply that now it was beyond her to consider an abortion. When she tried to force herself to think about it she felt as though something physical happened in her skull, as though an actual shutter came down between the front part of her brain, just behind her eyes, where the thought began, and the back of her brain into which it would have to go if it were to be developed.

The biggest immediate worry was how to tell her mother whose outlook would make it very hard for her to accept such news. She veered between a desire to get the worst over by writing at once, and a longing to put it off for ever. Her lover advised her to put it off for a month or so, just in case something went wrong, and finally she agreed, though her itch to tell made her write in advance the letter she would send later, choosing a time to post it just before one of her visits home so that her mother could get over the worst of the shock before they discussed it. She enjoyed writing that letter: putting into words how much she wanted a child and how determined she had now become to have this one. She found her letter so convincing that she couldn't believe her mother would not agree.

The longing to tell everyone else was strong. She scolded herself, arguing that when she began to bulge would be soon enough; people *did* have miscarriages, and no discreet woman would announce a pregnancy before the fourth month. But as each day passed, discretion became less important, jubilation grew stronger, and she had soon told everyone with whom she was intimate and some with whom she was not. Almost all her friends appeared to be delighted for her, and their support gave her great pleasure. Sometimes they said she was brave, and she enjoyed that too, in spite of knowing that courage did not come into it. The interest and sympathy that seemed to surround her was like a good wine added to a delicious dinner.

The child's father was, in a detached way, pleased. The pregnancy made no difference to the form of their relationship, but it did deepen it: his tenderness and attention were a comfort and a pleasure. She wondered, sometimes, what would happen about *that* once the child was born: would an 'uncle' in its life instead of a father be a good thing or a bad one? They would have to see. She knew that if it proved a bad thing she would have to lose her lover—would lose him without hesitation however great the pain—but for the present having him there was a large, warm part of the happiness which carried the anxieties like driftwood on its broad tide.

She felt gloriously well, hungry, lively and pretty, without a single qualm of sickness and with only a shadow of extra fatigue at the end of a long day, from time to time. 'Well, *you* seem to be all right,' they said to her at the hospital clinic which she began to attend. During the long waits at this clinic she watched the other women and thought that none of them looked so well or so pleased as she did. At her first visit she kept quiet, half anxious and half amused as to how her spinsterhood would be treated by the nurses and doctors, but once she discovered that it was taken not only calmly but with extra kindness, she relaxed. One of the other expectant mothers, very young, was like herself in having suffered nothing in the way of sickness or discomfort, and the two of them made an almost guilty smug corner together. She contrived to read details about herself over the shoulder of a nurse who was filling in a form about her, and glowed with ridiculous pride at all the 'satisfactories' and at 'nipples: good'.

However simple and quick the examination itself, the clinic proved always to take between two and three hours, so she arranged to see her own doctor regularly instead. As she left the clinic for the last time she happened to be thinking about the problem of the child's care while she was at the office, when a man leaned out of the cab of a passing truck and shouted at her, 'That's right love—keep smiling!' She may have been worried, but there was still a smile on her face.

Those weeks of April and May were the only ones in her life when spring was wholly, fully beautiful. All other springs carried with them regret at their passing. If she thought, 'Today the white double cherries are at their most perfect' it summoned up the simultaneous awareness: 'Tomorrow the edges of their petals will begin to turn brown.' This time a particularly ebullient, sun-drenched spring simply existed for her. It was as though, instead of being a stationary object past which a current was flowing, she was flowing with it, in it, at the same rate. It was a happiness new to her, but it felt very ancient, and complete.

One Saturday, soon after her last clinic, the child's father came to see her at lunch-time. She had got up early and done a big shop, but not a heavy one, because a short time before she became pregnant she had bought a basket on wheels (was it coincidence that several of her purchases just before the pregnancy were of things suited to it: that basket, the slacks which were rather too loose round the waist, with the matching loose top?). She left the basket at the bottom of the stairs for him to bring up, because strong and well though she felt, she was taking no foolish risks. They ate a good lunch, both of them cheerful and relaxed. After it he was telling her a funny story when she interrupted with, 'Wait a minute, I must go to the loo—tell me when I get back,' and hurried out to have a pee, wanting to get back quickly for the end of the story. When she saw blood on the toilet paper her mind went, for a moment, quite literally blank.

So she got up and went slowly back into the sitting room, thinking, 'To press my fingers against my cheek like this must look absurdly over-dramatic.'

'I'm bleeding,' she said in a small voice.

He scrambled up from the floor, where he'd been lying, and said, 'What do you mean? Come and sit down. How badly?'

'Only a very little,' she said, and began to tremble.

He took her by the shoulders and pulled her against him, saying quieting things, saying, 'It's all right, we'll ring the doctor, it's probably nothing,' and although she didn't know she was going to start crying, she felt herself doing it. She had not yet been able to tell what she was feeling, but suddenly she was having to control herself hard in order not to scream. 'The important thing,' he said, 'is to find out.' He went to fetch the telephone directory and said, 'Come on now, ring the doctor.'

The telephone was near her chair, so she didn't have to move, which she felt was important. The doctor was off duty for the weekend, but a stand-in answered. Any pain? No. How much bleeding? She explained how little. Then there was nothing to be done but to go to bed at once and stay there for forty-eight hours. 'Does this necessarily mean a miscarriage?' she asked. No, certainly not.

How would she know if it turned into one? It would seem like an exceptionally heavy period, with the passing of clots. If that happened she must telephone again, but otherwise just stay lying down.

Her lover ran out to buy her sanitary towels, alerting her friend downstairs as he went. During the few minutes she was alone she found herself crying again, flopped over the arm of her chair, tears streaming down her face, saying over and over again in a sort of whispered scream, 'I don't *want* to have a miscarriage, I don't *want* to have a miscarriage.' She knew it was a silly thing to be doing, and when her friend came she was relieved to find that she could pull herself together, sit up and talk.

They put her to bed, and there she lay, the bleeding almost imperceptible, feeling perfectly well. They reminded each other of women they knew about who had bled during pregnancy with no ill effect, and she soon became calm. During the next two days the bleeding became even less, but it did not quite stop, and over the phone her doctor repeated his colleague's words: no one could do anything, it was not necessarily going to be a miscarriage, she would know all right if it became one, and she must stay in bed until it stopped. She was comfortable in her pretty bedroom, reading Jane Austen almost non-stop for her calming quality (she reread the whole of *Mansfield Park, Northanger Abbey, Persuasion* and *The Watsons* in four days), listening to the radio and doing a little office work. By the fourth day her chief anxiety had become not the possibility of a miscarriage, but the fear that this slight bleeding might tie her to her bed not for days but for weeks. A bedridden pregnancy would be bad enough for anyone, but for her, entirely dependent as she was on friends who all had jobs or families... How could they possibly go on doing as much as they were doing now?

She was lucky in one way: anxiety, fear and certain kinds of misery always had an almost anaesthetic effect on her, making her mind and feelings sluggish. Under such stresses she shrank into the moment, just doing the next thing to be done, and sleeping a lot. So those four days passed in a state of suspended emotion rather than in unhappiness—suspended emotion stabbed every now and then with irritation at the absurdity of having to fear disaster when she was feeling as well as ever. It was ridiculous!

Diana Athill

During the night of the fourth day she came slowly out of sleep at three in the morning to a vague feeling that something was amiss. It took her a minute or two of sleepy wondering before she identified it more exactly. Not since she was a girl had she suffered any pain during her period—she had almost forgotten what kind of pain it was—but now...yes. In a dim, shadowy way it was that old pain that was ebbing and flowing in her belly. When it ebbed she thought, 'Quick, go to sleep again, you were imagining it.' But it came back, its fluctuations confirming its nature. More numb than ever, barely awake, she got up, fetched a bucket from the kitchen and a newspaper to fold and use as a lid, and a big towel from the linen cupboard. She arranged all this beside her bed and went to sleep again.

When she woke an hour and a half later it was because blood was trickling over her thigh. 'This is it': dull resentment was what she felt. She hitched herself out of bed and over the bucket—and woke with a cold shock at the thudding gush, the sensation that a cork had blown. 'Oh god oh god,' she thought, 'I didn't know it would be like this.' Blood ran fast for about half a minute, then dwindled to a trickle. Swaddling herself in the towel, she lay back in the bed, telling herself that no doubt it had to be fairly gruesome to start with.

After that the warning trickle came every ten or fifteen minutes, out over the bucket she went, terrified that she might overturn it with a clumsy gesture as she removed and restored the newspaper lid. The gush was never as violent as the first one, but each time it was violent and it did not diminish. She tried not to see the dark, clotted contents of the bucket—it was only when she saw it that she almost began to cry. There was a peppery smell of blood, but if she turned her head in a certain way she could catch a whiff of fresh air from the window which lessened it. It was already light when she woke the second time, and soon after that the first blackbird began to sing. She lay still between the crises, watching the sun's first rays coming into the room and trying to make out how many blackbirds were singing behind the one in her own garden.

Her friend would be coming up to give her breakfast. She usually came at eight—but it might be later. 'If she doesn't come till late...' she thought, and became tearful. Then she decided to wait until seven-thirty, by which time the bleeding would surely be less, and telephone her—with the towel between her legs she would be able to get to the sitting room where the phone was. The thought of telephoning the doctor herself was too much because if his number were engaged or he were out she couldn't bear it, her friend must do it. Time was going very fast, she noticed, looking at the alarm clock on the corner of the chest of drawers. That was something anyway.

She had come out in a heavy sweat after the first flow, and at about six-thirty it happened again. The sweat streamed off her and she was icy cold, and—worse—she began to feel sick. The thought of having to complicate the horror by vomiting into that dreadful bucket put her in a panic, so when the sweating was over and the nausea had died away, immediately after another violent flow, she knew she must get to the telephone now. She huddled the towel between her legs, stood up, took two steps towards the door, felt herself swaying, thought quite clearly, 'They are wrong when they say everything goes black, it's not going black, it's disappearing. I must fall on to the bed.' Which she did.

The next hour was vague, but she managed to follow her routine: use bucket, put paper back, lie flat on bed, wrap dressing gown over belly. She began to feel much iller, with more sweating, more cold, more nausea. When she heard her lodger moving about in his room next door she knew she had to call him. He knew nothing of her pregnancy—thought she had been in bed with an upset stomach— and they were so far from being intimate that it had not entered her head to call him earlier. Perhaps she had even forgotten he was there. Now she tapped on the wall, and called his name, but he didn't hear. A little more time passed, and she heard him in the passage outside her door and called again. This time he heard, and answered, and she told him to go downstairs and fetch her friend. 'You mean now?' came his startled voice through the door. 'Yes, quickly.' Oh that was wonderful, the sound of his feet hurrying away, and only a minute or two later her door opened and in came her friend.

One look and she ran for the telephone without saying a word. She caught the doctor in his surgery, two minutes before he went out on a call. He arrived so soon that it seemed almost at once, looked into the bucket, felt her pulse, pulled down her eyelid and left the room quickly to call an ambulance and alert the hospital.

She felt hurt that neither he nor her friend had spoken to her, but now her friend said could she drink a cup of tea and she felt it would be wonderful—but couldn't drink it when it appeared. The relief of not having to worry any more would have been exquisite, if it had not given her more time to realize how ill she was feeling. The ambulance men wrapped her in a beautiful big red blanket and said not to worry about bleeding all over it (so *that* was why ambulance blankets were usually red). The breath of fresh air as she was carried across the pavement made her feel splendidly alert after the dreadful dizziness of being carried downstairs, so she asked for a cigarette and they said it wasn't allowed in the ambulance but she could have one all the same and to put the ash in the sick bowl. One puff and she felt much worse, so that her friend had to wipe the sweat off her forehead with a paper handkerchief. There was a pattern by then: a slowly mounting pain, a gush of blood, the sweating and nausea following at once and getting worse every time, accompanied by a terrible feeling that was not identifiable as pain but simply as *illness*. It made her turn her head from side to side and moan, although it seemed wrong to moan without intolerable pain.

The men carried her into a cubicle in the casualty department, and she didn't want them to leave because they were so kind. As soon as she was there the nausea came again, stronger than ever so that this time she vomited, and was comforted because one of the men held her head and said, 'Never mind, dear.' A nurse said brusquely, while she was vomiting (trying to catch her unawares, she supposed), 'Did you have an injection to bring this on?' Her 'No' came out like a raucous scream, which made her feel apologetic so she had to gasp laboriously, 'I wanted most terribly to have this baby.' The man holding her head put his other hand on her arm and gave it a great squeeze, and that was the only time anyone questioned her.

Her head cleared a bit after she had been sick. She noticed that the nurse couldn't find her pulse, and that when the doctor who soon came was listening to her heart through his stethoscope he raised his eyebrows a fraction and pursed his lips, and then turned to look at her face, not as one looks at a face to communicate, but with close attention. She also noticed that they could never hear her answers to their questions although she thought she was speaking normally. 'They think I'm really bad,' she said to herself, but she didn't feel afraid. They would do whatever had to be done to make her better.

It went on being like that up in the ward, when they began to give her blood transfusions. Her consciousness was limited to the narrow oblong of her body on the stretcher, trolley or bed, and to the people doing things to it. Within those limits it was sharp, except during the recurring waves of horribleness, but it did not extend to speculation. When a nurse, being kind, said, 'You may not have lost the baby—one can lose a great deal of blood and the baby can still be all right,' she knew that was nonsense but felt nothing about it. When a doctor said to someone, 'Call them and tell him he must hurry with that blood—say that he must run,' she saw that things had gone further than she supposed but did not wonder whether he would run fast enough. When, a little later, they were discussing an injection and the same doctor said, 'She's very near collapse,' she thought perfectly clearly, 'Near collapse, indeed! If what I'm in now isn't collapse, it must be their euphemism for dying.' It did, then, swim dimly through her mind that she ought to think or feel something about this, but she hadn't the strength to produce any more than, 'Oh well, if I die, I die,' and that thought, once registered, did not set up any echoes. The things which were real were the sordidness of lying in a puddle of blood, and the oddness of not minding when they pushed needles into her.

She also wanted to impress the nurses and doctors. Not till afterwards did she understand that she had slipped back into infancy; that the total trust in these powerful people, and the wish to make them think, 'There's a good, clever girl,' belonged in the nursery. She wanted to ask them intelligent questions about what they were doing, and to make little jokes, provided she could do so in not more than four or five words, because more would be beyond her. It was annoying that they seemed not to hear her little mumblings, or else just said, 'Yes dear', looking at her face as they said it with that odd, examining expression. She made a brief contact with one of the doctors when he told them to do something 'to stop her from being agitated'. What she wanted to say was: 'Don't be silly, I can't wait for you to get me down to the theatre and start scraping,' but all that came out was a peevish 'Not agitated!' to which he replied politely, 'I'm sorry, of course you're not.' The only words she spoke from a deeper level than these feeble attempts at exhibitionism were when someone who was manipulating the blood bottle asked her if she was beginning to feel sleepy. It was during a wave of badness, and she heard her own voice replying hoarsely: 'I'm feeling *very ill*.'

She had always dreaded the kind of anaesthetic one breathes, because of a bad experience, but when she understood that they were about to give her that kind and began to attempt a protest, she suddenly realized that she didn't give a damn: let them hurry up, let them get that mask over her face and she would go with it willingly. This had been going on much, much too long and all she wanted was the end of it.

The operation must have been a quick one, under a light anaesthetic, because when she woke up to an awareness of hands manipulating her back into bed she was confused only for an instant, and only as to whether this was happening before or after the operation. That question was answered at once by the feeling in her belly: it was calm, she was no longer bleeding. She tried to move her hand down to touch herself in confirmation, and a nurse caught it and held it still—she hadn't realized that there was still a transfusion needle taped into the back of it. Having moved, she began to vomit. She had a deep-seated neurotic queasiness about vomiting, a horror of it, and until that moment she would never have believed that she could have been sick while lying flat on her back with the bowl so awkwardly placed under her chin that the sick went into her hair, and felt happy while doing it. But that was what was happening. An amazing glow of relief and joy was flowing up from her healed belly. 'I AM ALIVE.' It was enough. It was everything. It was filling her to the brim with pure and absolute joy, a feeling more intense than any she had known. And very soon after that she was wondering why they were bothering to set up a new bottle of plasma, because she could have told them that all she needed now was to rest.

So if she were pinned down to the question 'What did you feel on losing your child?' the only honest answer would be 'Nothing'. Nothing at all, while it was going on. What was happening was so bad—so nearly fatal—that it eclipsed its own significance. And during the four days she spent in hospital she felt very little; no more than a detached acknowledgement that it was sad. Hospital routine closed round her gently, isolating her in that odd, childish world where nurses in their early twenties are the 'grown-ups', and the exciting events are visiting time and being allowed to get up and walk to the lavatory. When it was time to go home she was afraid that she would hate her bedroom, expecting to have a horror of the blackbird's song and perhaps of some little rusty stain on the blue carpet, but friends took her home to an accompaniment of flowers, delicacies and cheerful talk, and she saw that it was still a pleasant room, her flat still a lovely place to live.

There was even relief: she would not now have to tell her mother anything, and she would not have to worry about money any more than usual. She could spend some on clothes for her holiday as soon as she liked, and she saw that she would enjoy the clothes and the holiday. It was this that was strange and sad, and made her think so often of how happy she had been while she was expecting the child (not of how unhappy she was now, because she wasn't). This was what sometimes gave her a dull ache, like a stomach-ache but not physical: that someone who didn't yet exist could have the power to create spring, and could then be gone, and that once he was gone (she had always thought of the child as a boy) he became, because he had never existed, so completely gone: that the only tears shed for him were those first, almost unconscious tears shed by her poor old tortoise of a subconscious rather than by her. 'I *don't want* to have a miscarriage.' Oh no, no, no, she hadn't wanted it, it was the thing she *didn't want* with all her heart. Yet now it had happened, and she was the same as she had always been...except that now she knew that, although if she had died during the miscarriage she would hardly, because of her physical state, have noticed it, the truth was that she loved being alive so much that not having died was more important to her by far than losing the child: more important than *anything*.

I lost that child forty years ago. Much has changed since then. Nowadays, if you want an abortion it is not necessary to know of a doctor willing to risk his career by breaking the law; and although the mother of a woman in her early forties would be unlikely to rejoice on learning that her unmarried daughter planned to have a child, she would be less shocked at such news than mothers used to be. The surroundings of the event would now be different. But the event itself—that would be the same.

Diana Athill

After the miscarriage, I scribbled some notes to rid my mind of it and forgot all about them. Recently, when I was hunting for something in a rarely opened drawer, I found them under a pile of other old papers. My sense of recall as I read them was sharp, yet the woman to whom this happened, though not exactly a stranger—I knew her well—was no longer me. Retelling this experience in the third person is my way of acknowledging the difference between 'her' and me.

I think now that, if the child had been born, my lover would have been a devoted father; over the years I have seen how much he enjoys children. As for me, I suppose—I hope—that I would have loved the child wholeheartedly; but the truth is that in forty years I have hardly ever thought about it, and never with anything more poignant than painless speculation as to how it would have turned out.   □

EIGHT PIECES FOR THE LEFT HAND

J. Robert Lennon

One

Autumn, once the most popular season in this town of tall trees, is now regarded with dread, thanks to the bitter athletic rivalry between our two local high schools. The school in the neighbourhood commonly called the Flats is attended by the children of the working class, who are employed by the town's restaurants, motels, gas stations and factories, and who live in those low-lying areas most frequently plagued by pollution, flood and crime. The school in the Heights, on the other hand, is populated by the children of academics who live on wooded hillside lots that offer panoramic views of our valley. Students at the Flats consider students at the Heights to be prissy, pampered, trust-fund halfwits, while Heights students regard Flats students as mustachioed, inbred gas huffers. Historically, these class tensions were brought to bear in the annual football game, played at our University's enormous stadium the last weekend in October.

Five years ago, however, some Heights players spray-painted ethnic slurs on the dusty American sedans of several Flats team members, and the Flats players retaliated by flinging bricks through the windows of the shiny, leased sports coupés of their rivals. Four years ago, a massive melee at a fast-food restaurant landed players from both teams in the hospital. Three years ago, the much-painted Seniors' Rock in front of Flats High was rolled into a nearby creek, and the brand-new Sciences Wing of Heights High was set on fire. Two years ago, each coach was kidnapped by still unidentified members of the opposing team and traded on Friendship Bridge at midnight of game day; and last year the Flats' beloved mascot, the Marauding Goat, was disembowelled before the war memorial in Peters Park, while not a mile away the starting quarterback for the Heights was partially paralysed in a hit-and-run incident outside a drive-up bank. The subsequent game was cancelled.

This year's game has also been cancelled, but for a different reason entirely. A steep drop in the population of our town has made the existence of both high schools fiscally untenable, and beginning with the fall semester the two will be combined into a single entity, to be called Area High. It remains unclear how the rivalry will play itself out, but many seem convinced that the solution lies in targeting a common enemy, such as the students of nearby Valley High, thought by all to be buck-toothed hicks, or those of faraway City Regional, who, everyone knows, are greasy-haired gang-bangers. Meanwhile the peace here in our town remains uneasy, and we await with trepidation the turning of the leaves.

Two

A local poet of considerable national fame completed a new collection of poems that had, due to a painful and scandalous series of personal problems, been delayed in editing and publication for some years. When the revisions were finally finished, the poet typed up a clean copy of the manuscript and got into his car to bring it to the copy shop for reproduction.

On the way, however, the poet was pulled over for running a red light and was subsequently found to be drunk. Due to a new and unforgiving drunk-driving law in our state, his car was taken from his possession and his licence revoked.

Upon regaining sobriety, the poet realized that his poetry manuscript was still in the car and asked the police to return it to him. The police, however, maintained that the contents of the car no longer belonged to him, and refused. Their refusal resulted in a protracted legal battle, during which our beloved poet died, leaving uncertain the fate of the manuscript.

But the poet's publisher, eager to issue a posthumous volume, struck a bargain with the police department: if someone at the station would read the finished poems over the phone, an editor could transcribe them and issue them in book form without the manuscript changing hands. After all, the publisher argued, even if the manuscript legally belonged to the city, its contents did not, as they were devised outside the poet's car. The police agreed to this scheme, the phone recitation took place, and the book was issued to great acclaim, assuring the poet a place in the literary canon that he had not enjoyed in life.

Eventually, however, the poet's estate won its legal battle against the city, and the original manuscript was recovered. All were shocked to learn that it bore little resemblance to the published book.

It was not long before a city policeman confessed to having improvised much of the manuscript during its telephone transcription. His only explanation was that he saw room for improvement and could not resist making a few changes here and there. Almost immediately, the policeman was asked to leave the force, and the acclaimed book was completely discredited. The true manuscript was published in its entirety, to tepid reviews.

The policeman has continued to write poetry. Most agree that it is excellent, but few will publish the work of someone known to be so dishonest.

Three

A farmer who lives on our road had lost three mailboxes in as many weeks to the drunken antics of some local youths, who had taken to driving past late at night and smashing the mailboxes with a baseball bat. Because the police had been uncooperative in apprehending the youths, the farmer devised a solution to the problem: he bought two mailboxes—a gigantic, industrial-strength one, and a small aluminium one—and arranged the boxes one inside the other, with a layer of cement between the two. He mounted this monstrous mega-box on a length of eight-inch steel pipe, which was set into a four-foot post hole and stabilized there with thirty additional gallons of cement.

The following weekend the youths sped past in their convertible, and T., the captain of the high school baseball team and a local slugger of some renown, swung at the box from a standing position in the back seat. With the bat moving at more than seventy-five miles per hour relative to the car, and the car itself travelling nearly as fast, the combined velocity of the impact was approximately 150 miles per hour. It was at this speed that the bat ricocheted and struck the head of J., a seventeen-year-old girl sitting in the car, killing her instantly.

A series of criminal charges and civil suits followed. T. was tried as an adult and convicted of involuntary manslaughter. The driver of the car was sentenced to community service on charges of vandalism and reckless endangerment. The farmer was also convicted of reckless endangerment and fined; in response he sued the police department for failing to address the problem beforehand. The parents of the dead girl lobbied to have all the car's living occupants, five in all, expelled from school; they also sued T., the driver and the farmer for several million dollars. They even tried, and failed, to sue the hardware store where the farmer had bought his cement-mailbox supplies, arguing that the store's employees ought to have figured out what the farmer was doing, and stopped him. In a peripheral case, T.'s parents sued the hospital where he was treated for a broken arm; apparently the doctors there had set the break improperly, resulting in a painful re-setting that was likely to ruin T.'s chances to play baseball in the major leagues. Their lawyers demanded a percentage of T.'s projected future salary.

In the end, all charges were reversed on appeal. It seemed that everyone involved was to blame, which the courts determined was no different from no one being to blame. All that remains, apart from the many legal debts incurred by the litigants and the accused, is the cement mailbox, which has proven too costly and cumbersome to remove.

Four

One night, while our cat was curled up on my lap, placidly purring, I noticed that his collar was somewhat crooked, and in the process of righting it I happened to catch a glimpse of the identification tag that hung from it. The tag, a worn, stamped-metal disc, told me that the cat's name was Fluffy.

Our cat, however, was named Horace. Reading further, I discovered that the tag bore an address on our old street in a faraway town we had lived in temporarily, and not our permanent address.

I gave the matter some thought, and concluded that there were two possible explanations. One was that, while we were living in the faraway town, our cat's collar was switched with another cat's, perhaps as some kind of prank. The other was that we had accidentally gotten hold of someone else's cat and abandoned our own.

Initially I dismissed the second possibility, as it had been five years since we lived in that town, and this cat had very much come to seem like ours, and the town we lived in permanently his rightful home. But as I reflected, I realized how very unlikely a prank the switching of collars was; and simultaneously I began to recall changes in our cat's personality around the time of our move which, quite naturally, we assumed to be consequences of the move itself, but which now suddenly seemed like the consequences of our having taken possession of an entirely different cat.

On impulse, I got up and called the phone number printed on the tag. A woman answered. I asked her if she had lost a cat named

Fluffy, and after a long pause she replied that yes, she had, many years ago, and did I have some information about him? I told her that I had found his collar, unconnected to any cat. Did she want me to send it to her? After a dramatic pause, the woman told me to go ahead and do so, and I did, the next day. I also ordered, through a pet-supply catalogue, a new tag with the name Horace printed on it.

Though I no longer consider this to have been a cowardly act, I went through several weeks of self-doubt at the time. As for now, I can only hope that the original Horace was taken in by a kind family.

Five

At a bend in a winding country road outside our town, there once lived a family whose only child, a girl, was born deaf. When the girl grew old enough to play outside on her own, the family had the county erect a yellow sign near the house, which read DEAF CHILD AREA. The idea was that motorists would drive more slowly, knowing that a nearby child could not hear their approach.

By the time I was a boy, the deaf child had become a teenager, and after a while left town for college. She returned occasionally to visit, but for the most part was no longer around. Eventually she married and settled in a faraway city. Her parents, aware of the sign's superfluity, wrote a letter asking the county to come and take it down; but though the county promised to see to the matter, no workmen ever arrived.

At about the time I myself married, the deaf child's parents retired and decided to move away to someplace warmer. They sold their house, and it was promptly bought by a local professor. The professor, however, was soon offered a position at another university, which he was obliged to occupy immediately. With no time to sell the house he had just bought, the professor hired a property management company to offer the house for rent. At this point it caught my attention. My wife was pregnant with our first child, and we had begun to worry that our small apartment would be unsuitable for raising a family. After a look at the house in the country, we decided to rent it, and soon moved in.

For several months we ignored the sign, which had grown old and battered, and at any rate had nothing to do with us. But as winter approached and my wife's due date drew near, I noticed that her eyes lingered on the sign whenever we pulled into the driveway, and more than once I caught her staring out at it from our future child's bedroom which we had furnished and filled with colourful toys. One night, as we lay awake in bed, my wife turned to me and asked if I might remove the sign somehow. She realized she was being irrational, but nonetheless feared the sign might bring some harm to our baby, and she didn't think she could sleep until the sign was gone.

This seemed perfectly reasonable. I got out of bed and dressed, then brought a box of tools out to the roadside, where I examined the sign. I saw that it had been bolted on to a metal post, and that I could simply remove the sign and leave the post where it stood in the ground. I did this quickly, and prepared to go inside.

But something compelled me to go out behind the house and find a shovel, which I used to dig the post out of the ground. The ground was cold, and the work slow going. When I finished, I took the sign and post and put them in the back of the car, and drove down to the lake, where I threw them out as far as I could into the water. They splashed on to the surface and sunk out of sight.

When I returned home, my wife didn't ask me where I'd driven. After that we slept comfortably, and did so every night until our child was born without illness or defect.

Six

There were six students in our school play: Jason, Heather, Kevin, Carol, Matt and me. But in the script, which our teachers had obtained from a catalogue, our characters were given other names: Scott, Jenny, Robert, Melissa, Bill and Larry. Since the oldest of us was seven, we had never before been in a play, and the difficulty of memorizing our lines was compounded by the necessity of learning new names for both ourselves and the others. For weeks we struggled through rehearsals, slowly gaining ground. Then, at the last minute, our teachers, fearing a debacle, told us to forget the stage names and simply use our own.

But our teachers had acted at the very height of our put-upon duality, and their command effected a desperate confusion, which manifested itself onstage that night as complete theatrical anarchy. We addressed one another by whatever names happened to pop into our heads, and forgot almost every scripted line, leaving our audience with only the vaguest notion of the drama's direction. The performance ended in chaos and tears, with our baffled parents applauding politely, and our teachers holding their shocked faces in their hands.

Sadly, the confusion didn't end there. For weeks, we were distracted during classes, failing to respond to our teachers' direct enquiries, and were moody and unresponsive at home. When we met in the halls or in the playground, we greeted each other with incorrect names or none at all.

Most of us recovered, but Jason has married seven times, and Heather, from whom no one has heard in twenty years, is rumoured to have gone mad. One lonely fall afternoon I called our local mental hospital in search of her, but was told that no patient by that name was in residence.

Seven

A local professor was honoured, and a national newspaper ran a photograph of him writing on a chalkboard before a classroom full of students. Not long afterwards, the professor was asked to speak at the annual meeting of a club for left-handed persons. In his letter, the club's president explained that he had seen the photo and noticed the professor's left-handedness; he believed the professor was a credit to 'lefties' and would make an inspiring and enlightening guest. Included with the letter was a booklet listing the accomplishments of left-handed people, photocopied articles asserting the creative and intellectual superiority of lefties, and a catalogue of whimsical products for the left-handed, including special coffee mugs, pens and eating utensils with pro-left-hand messages printed on them.

The professor agreed to speak to the club, and was given a large honorarium, free transportation, and a lavish hotel suite complete with mini-gym and sauna. When at last he stood before the assembled lefties, he thanked them for their invitation, then proceeded to berate them for their smugness and stupidity. He pointed out that he was, in fact, right-handed, and only appeared left-handed in the photo because the newspaper had reversed the negative; if they had looked a little more closely, he said, they would have noticed that the writing on the chalkboard was backwards. He told them that they should honour others for their achievements and not their genetic circumstances, and then, only minutes into his speech, stepped down from the dais and caught a cab to the airport.

When, years later, the professor lost his right arm in a highway crash, he was unsurprised to receive a flood of congratulatory letters, and the first in an endless stream of free 'lefty' gift items that have appeared almost daily on his doorstep ever since. Far from being angry, he views this unfortunate turn of events as a kind of poetic justice, and even tried to apologize to the lefties' club in a kind letter to its president. However, his speech had cut too deeply, and the lefties continue to bombard him with junk.

Meanwhile, the professor has learned to play a variety of left-hand pieces on the piano, and is said to be as dexterous with his left hand alone as he once was with both. He has also joined a national organization of people who have lost the use of one or more limbs, and is scheduled to speak at its next annual meeting.

Eight

A local novelist spent ten years writing a book about our region and its inhabitants, which, when completed, added up to more than 1,000 pages. Exhausted by her effort, she at last sent it off to a publisher, only to be told that it would have to be cut by nearly half. Though daunted by the work ahead of her, the novelist was encouraged by the publisher's interest, and spent more than a year excising material.

But by the time she reached the requested length, the novelist found it difficult to stop. In the early days of her editing, she would struggle for hours to remove words from a sentence, only to discover that its paragraph was better off without it. Soon she discovered that removing sentences from a paragraph was rarely as effective as cutting entire paragraphs, nor was selectively erasing paragraphs from a chapter as satisfying as eliminating chapters entirely. After another year, she had whittled the book down into a short story, which she sent to magazines.

Multiple rejections, however, drove her back to the chopping block, where she reduced her story to a vignette, the vignette to an anecdote, the anecdote to an aphorism, and the aphorism, at last, to this haiku:

Tiny Upstate town
Undergoes many changes
Nonetheless endures

Unfortunately, no magazine would publish the haiku. The novelist has printed it on note cards, which she can be found giving away to passers-by in our town park, where she is also known sometimes to sleep, except when the police, whose thuggish tactics she so neatly parodied in her original manuscript, bring her in on charges of vagrancy. I have a copy of the haiku pinned above my desk, its note card grimy and furred along the edges from multiple profferings, and I read it frequently, sometimes with pity but always with awe. □

THE LIVES OF BRIAN
Brian Cathcart

Two Brian Cathcarts, aged about 10. The author is on the right.

My name is Brian Cathcart. I grew up mainly in Northern Ireland. My father was headmaster of a secondary school and my mother taught English. I come from Protestant stock, though I have no religion myself. I studied history at university. I remember the Troubles starting, the war in Biafra, the Beatles.

His name was Brian Cathcart. He grew up in Northern Ireland. His father was headmaster of a secondary school and his mother taught English. He came from Protestant stock, though he had no religion himself. He studied history at university. He remembered the Troubles starting, the war in Biafra, the Beatles.

Two Brian Cathcarts, then: lucky boys, with their clever parents and their educations, both of them raised on what was the privileged side of Northern Ireland's communal divide. What is the difference between them? Chiefly, now, that the second one is dead. Do you ever look at a drunken man in the street, swaying and shabby, with no focus to his eyes and a can of lager in his hand, and think to yourself: why him, why me?

In 2002 I called up the Google search page on my computer and keyed in my name. I was looking for myself, wanting to see whether my latest book had been mentioned anywhere. Vanity has its consequences. As I tripped through the menu I came across this news item:

> A man has been jailed for nine years for the manslaughter of a Belfast street busker who died before Christmas 2000. Simon McCarey (25), from Rathcoole outside Belfast, was convicted of killing Brian Cathcart (51) by pouring flammable liquid over him and then setting him alight.

Mine is not a common name. There are Cathcarts in Northern Ireland and Scotland and some others scattered elsewhere, but I have never met another Brian Cathcart. I had known about one, though, for years, since the time I was a schoolboy in Belfast in the late 1960s and early 1970s. Then, a student at the local university got in trouble with the police a few times for demonstrating against (as I remembered it) the Vietnam War. Perfectly normal student behaviour elsewhere, in Belfast this was regarded as eccentric because everyone with a taste for protest was marching about Roman Catholic civil rights—the Troubles were beginning. This other Brian Cathcart occasionally made the newspapers and when he did I was teased about him at school. 'I see you've been causing trouble again, Cathcart,' teachers would say. I liked the association: this other Brian seemed an admirable, independent character. Those newspaper reports were my last sighting of him, but I never forgot the coincidence. Now, as I read the little item on the Internet, I suspected that he was the man who had died this appalling death; his age was right, and that he was a busker somehow seemed to fit. I wondered why he had been killed.

The officer at the police station in Belfast took my call in his stride—nothing could be more natural, it appeared, than a live Brian Cathcart in London enquiring about a dead one on his patch. The killing, he said, was not sectarian or political; it happened in the tough Rathcoole district after a long night's drinking. I enquired about the victim's background, mentioning the student protests and asking if this was the same person. 'That would fit the bill, yes,' said the officer. The dead man's father had been a headmaster in Larne, a town just north of Belfast, and his brother Matthew lived there now. When I contacted Matthew he said that yes, Brian had attended Queen's University in Belfast at the end of the 1960s and yes, he had been involved in protests, though they were not about Vietnam but Biafra, another cause of the time. Beyond doubt, this was the man I had heard about as a schoolboy.

I had never met Brian Cathcart, never so much as shaken his hand, and I knew nothing about his life bar one little passage thirty years before. And yet I felt a sense of loss. It was as though in some remote part of my mind one of the little props that support me, one of the many things that make me *me*, had been kicked away. For years I had assumed without realizing it that he was out there somewhere, being Brian Cathcart just like me, and I was happy to think he had once done something unusual, principled and brave. Now he had been burned to death.

So who had he been, this man who once worried about Biafra on the streets of Belfast?

From Matthew and another brother, James, I assembled a small biography. Brian Cathcart had never taken his degree, never married and never had a regular job. He got by largely on welfare payments and the proceeds of busking. He wandered, losing touch with his family for years at a time as he moved between squats and other makeshift homes around Britain. Matthew visited him a few times in England and he described spending one night in a squat in Archway, north London (a district I also lived in for several years). 'It was pitch dark and cold, with the wind coming in through the broken windows. The floor was bare boards, with broken glass everywhere.'

Brian chose this life. He did not simply lose his way. He despised comfort; he rejected it to the point that when he stayed occasionally at his parents' house he made his bed on the garage floor. He detested commerce; he could not bear to watch advertisements on television. He decided that he should not travel by car, and for years he never did. James said, 'He could make you ashamed to own a wallet.'

There were four Cathcart sons and Brian, the second oldest, had been his parents' favourite. He'd been bright in school, good at sports, art and music, with a lively, adventurous character and a charm and wit that he'd never lost. His father, the principal of Larne Technical College, was a disciplinarian in school and at home, a committed Presbyterian who took his family to church every Sunday, a social pillar of the town, a leading Rotarian, and also a gifted artist and teacher of art who spent some of his spare time with the town's amateur dramatics society. He adored Brian, but Brian repaid him with rebellion. One night he slipped secretly out of a window to go to a Roy Orbison concert. Another time he went into his parents' bedroom and took the savings book they kept for him there. These are the small transgressions of adolescence, but Brian was punished for them, and over time a crackling tension rose between father and son, which lasted until the father's death in 1972.

Brian's mother was an English teacher and (like my mother) a graduate of Trinity College, Dublin. She was musical and encouraged her boys to learn instruments—Brian and James played guitar. She too struggled to cope with Brian, but she never lost patience and always welcomed him home until her death in 1996. Brian failed to attend both his parents' funerals. Matthew said, 'He couldn't face a really bad time.'

Brian was so shy that a stranger might never have realized the depth of his passion and conviction. He needed fortification before he would express himself. 'If you met him normally you might not even notice he was there,' James said. 'Drink changed him. He could drink extraordinary amounts—six or seven pints and a whole bottle of spirits in one session. He became much more assertive and he was extremely quick-witted. He drank for courage.'

And he loved animals. He collected stray dogs; on the night of his death there was one waiting for him to come home.

The more I learned about Brian, the more I was left with an uncomfortable image of the two of us as a pair of well-matched laboratory rats in a sociological experiment ('Let's see how they turn out'). The similarities in our early lives were compelling. What did my half of the experiment produce? A middle-aged, middle class Londoner with a working wife, two sons, a preposterously valuable house, and work I enjoy. The other half of the experiment, the one involving the shy, passionate idealist who chose hardship over comfort, ended with the subject being burned to death in the company of strangers.

In October 2000, a little more than a month before he died, Brian turned up at his brother Matthew's house in Larne with his dog, his sleeping bag and his guitar, and after a couple of nights indoors moved his bed out to the garage. He had been back before, sometimes for long periods, and he followed a routine, signing on for welfare benefit and spending his days busking in Larne or a train ride away in Belfast (he always declared these earnings). He looked up old friends, among them Tommy Workman, who runs a picture-framing shop. 'I saw him on and off for ten years,' Workman told me. 'He would come into the shop for a cup of coffee and we would chat. Brian could paint and his father had been a good painter—he was very proud of his father. He used to call himself the black sheep of the family.'

On the morning of November 7, Workman told Brian that there was to be a meeting of the Larne Art Club that evening and invited him to come along. They arranged to meet at the shop at 7 p.m. At around three that afternoon, however, Brian began to drink. A barman would later testify that he appeared at the Cellars pub on Larne's main street at that time and that he remained until 6.45 p.m., drinking five or six neat whiskeys. He was dressed in a brown tweed jacket and cap, and the barman remembered that he was perfectly polite.

Brian left the Cellars in time for his rendezvous with Workman, but he never turned up. His next recorded appearance was again in the Cellars at about 9 p.m. This time the barman decided he was drunk—he had probably spent the previous two hours drinking elsewhere—and refused to serve him. Brian left without protest and made his way to Chekkers Wine Bar, a short distance away, where he bought a pint of lager and joined a conversation about Larne Football Club. Brian was talkative by now, and as he had played for Larne Reserves in his youth and even had one game with the senior team, he could talk knowledgeably. One former player he mentioned was Kenny Wilson and it happened that Kenny's son Tommy was one of those present. Tommy Wilson later described to police what passed between them.

Brian told him that, although he and Kenny trained at the club together in the late 1960s and used to go to the same pub afterwards, he was never part of Kenny's social group; in fact Kenny had nicknamed him 'Lonely Pint' because he tended to drink alone. Tommy recalled Brian's explanation:

> He told me he didn't join my father's company as he had a
> problem with his nerves and found it difficult to socialize. He told
> me he still had a problem talking to people unless he had a drink
> in him and then he would talk too much. He asked me if he was
> annoying me in any way and I told him definitely not... He
> grabbed my hand and held it to his heart and thanked me for
> listening and talking to him.

Brian's mood of apology and self-pity, however, did not last. Soon he became truculent and began to give the bar's customers his views on the leading Protestant paramilitary organizations, the Ulster Volunteer Force (UVF) and the Ulster Defence Association (UDA). At the time these two were effectively at war and Larne was one of their battlegrounds, so Brian's denunciations were dangerous not only for him but for the bar itself, and he was told to leave. It was late now and he had a half bottle of whiskey in his pocket, but instead of going home to drink it he went to a hotel for another whiskey and two pints of water. At around midnight the hotel bar also closed. There was nowhere left in Larne to buy a drink.

He was near Tower Road, where he had lived as a boy. It leads up from the town, crests a hill and then falls away towards the sea, and along one side of it are some fairly large houses, one of which had been the Cathcart home in Brian's boyhood. That November night, after nine hours' drinking and with a dozen whiskeys and a few lagers inside him, Brian wandered up Tower Road and rang doorbells. Someone answered the door at his old home and Brian asked for a cup of coffee, which was refused. He didn't make a fuss and, after fruitlessly ringing more doorbells, he headed off. As he crossed a small car park less than a hundred yards from the back gate of his brother Matthew's house, he bumped into Simon McCarey.

McCarey was only twenty-four, but already a drinker in a different league. He had a criminal record that stretched back nine years, embraced more than 120 offences and covered fifteen pages of police files. It included six convictions for theft, sixteen for burglary and four for 'going equipped' (to commit a crime). There were also eight for disorderly behaviour, five for assaulting police officers, and ten for criminal damage. Almost all these offences were committed either in the pursuit of alcohol or as a result of it. 'Time doesn't matter to me,' he would tell the police later. 'Because it's just the same, day in, day out, drinking.'

McCarey had also begun drinking at about 3 p.m. that day, in the company of a regular companion, Willie Watson, who was three years older and also had a criminal record, though a less serious one. They met at lunch-time and adjourned to McCarey's flat in Rathcoole, a housing estate on the road north out of Belfast, a road that leads the fifteen miles to Larne. McCarey, who had recently separated from his wife, had just moved into the flat, which was unfurnished, with bare boards and a rolled-up carpet in the living room. The two men sat on the floor and drank beer for a couple of hours. Then they took a bus into Belfast, where Watson had an appointment: he had been recruited to stand as a volunteer in a police identification parade. For this he was paid £10, which they promptly spent on more alcohol, settling in a McDonald's to drink it. By 7.30 p.m. that supply and their money was exhausted. They went into a small supermarket where, as Watson chatted to the assistant at the till, McCarey slipped down an aisle, got into the back office and picked up a cash box. Leaving the shop, McCarey led the way to a quiet back street and broke open the box, which contained £635.

They treated themselves to a taxi all the way to Larne, where they planned to call on a friend. At a Larne off-licence, they bought a bottle of Buckfast fortified wine and some cans of Harp lager and went off to look for their friend, first at his usual pub and then at his home. They never found him and spent the rest of the evening in The Kiln pub until it closed, when they moved on to a takeaway Chinese place. When that, too, closed, they asked the young woman behind the counter to call them a taxi and went outside to wait for it. They had with them two or three bags full of drink and another containing a mobile phone that McCarey had bought in the course of the evening. As they waited they sat on the wall of a car park. Eventually the taxi came, but it drove past before stopping and Watson ran to catch the driver's attention. When he turned back he found that McCarey had company. According to McCarey's later account, Brian simply appeared and asked: 'Are youse going for a drink?' When McCarey said they were, Brian pointed out that he had his own drink with him and asked: 'Do you mind if I tag along?' McCarey said he didn't. The three got in the taxi and set out for McCarey's flat in Rathcoole.

Northern Ireland is a place where people constantly tell you to be on your guard, to avoid that district, that street, that pub, that topic of conversation because it might bring you into contact with 'men of violence'. Brian himself had been warned, by Tommy Workman for one, of the dangers the paramilitary disputes posed for ordinary people in Larne. With their cropped hair, earrings and tattoos, McCarey and Watson could easily have been UVF or UDA foot soldiers and any sensible or sober person would have given them a wide berth. As it happens they were not, but they were dangerous company all the same.

No sooner was Brian in the taxi than he began airing his opinions about the paramilitaries, and McCarey took noisy issue with him. Watson, concerned about the reaction of the driver, had to shout at them to be quiet. It was about 1.30 a.m. when they reached the Rathcoole flat and settled down on the floor to drink and talk. Watson and McCarey would later say they remembered little of what was said but that the conversation was mainly friendly and if voices were raised it was from drunkenness rather than anger. Half an hour or maybe forty-five minutes passed in this way.

A kitchen led off the living room and the door to it was open. From where he sat, McCarey could see a bottle of white spirit in there among some decorating materials. This is the account he eventually gave police of what happened next:

> There was talk of actually drinking [the spirit]. I said to Brian to catch himself on [to get a grip on himself], that he wasn't drinking it, and out of pure stupidity and—[I] don't know what it was—or thickness, and with regret, I poured it on him. He never said one word back to me, never said nothing at all, and within the next four or five minutes he was on fire.

McCarey claimed that it was Watson who struck the light but Watson told a different story. By his account the trouble began when McCarey threw a beer can at Brian, hitting him on the forehead. The reason for this was not clear, but may have had something to do with the earlier exchange in the car. Although Brian did not react, Watson did:

> I started yapping on at Simon, 'What the fuck did you do that for? The fella hasn't done nothing on [to] you.' Simon went into the kitchen, came out with a bottle of flipping white spirit, poured it over him and he said to me, 'Watch this for a laugh,' and set him alight.... He just lit yer man.

Brian was engulfed in flames from the waist up. He did not cry out but rolled over on his side and twisted across the floor until he met the wall. There he lay, the flames still rising from his head and upper body. The other two men, after an instant of shock, made feeble attempts to extinguish the fire, opening beer cans and pouring the contents over him or rushing out to the kitchen and carrying back water in cupped hands. When the fire died down Brian lay still. A smoke alarm was going off. Pausing only to pick up the remaining beer, McCarey and Watson fled. The time was somewhere between 2 a.m. and 3 a.m.

Brian had suffered burns over thirty per cent of the surface area of his body and much of the damage was what is called 'full thickness', when the destruction is so complete there is no hope of natural healing. His scalp, face and neck were especially badly affected and his nose and ears had largely burned or melted away. It is likely that he was unconscious when McCarey and Watson left, and remained so for a couple of hours. Then he must have woken up and stumbled around the flat—bloodstains and other traces were discovered in various rooms—until he found a way out. It is impossible to say for how long he wandered about in the open, but it was around 5.15 a.m. and he was 500 yards from the flat when he finally encountered a milkman doing his rounds. This was the morning of November 8; he would live another twenty-three days.

Even as Brian was being taken to hospital, McCarey and Watson were giving themselves away. They took a taxi into town, buying more drink along the way, and then settled down again in McDonald's. When that closed at 5 a.m., McCarey decided to go to have an old infection on his hand examined, so with beer and bottles in hand they adjourned to the warmth of another hospital's waiting room, where Watson struck up a conversation with a family sitting close by. 'See that guy I'm with?' he said, indicating McCarey, who was asleep. 'Wait till I tell you what he done...' And he described how his companion had set fire to a man. 'You watch the news tomorrow. We'll be on the news tomorrow,' he said. The family did not believe him and it took the news reports later that day to convince them that they should ring the police. McCarey spent a further day adrift in an alcoholic haze before giving himself up, while Watson fled the one hundred miles across the border, to Dublin.

At first McCarey claimed to police that when he left the flat Brian was alive and well. He and Watson had seen hooded men approaching the front door, he said, and had fled through the back, so what happened must have been the work of the hooded men. The police never believed this and before long McCarey was admitting that he had poured the white spirit over Brian, though he insisted he had not been the one to light it. Next Watson reappeared in Belfast and was arrested, and he insisted just as strongly that it was McCarey who lit the flames. Both were charged with attempted murder and, when Brian died, with murder. Prosecutors later came to the view, however, that they had no concrete evidence against Watson. He was charged only with failing to report what had happened, and even that charge was dismissed. As for McCarey, the charge of murder against him was reduced to manslaughter on grounds of diminished responsibility: not only had he drunk so much that, in the words of his counsel, 'he did not appreciate the gravity of what he was doing', but he was also suffering from brain damage caused by sustained alcohol abuse. The jury found him guilty and he was sentenced to nine years in jail.

Back in 1995, Brian had the idea of getting some songs he had written performed by a professional band and singer. He aimed high, recruiting two former players with Them, the band in which Van Morrison had made his name, as well as the former lead guitarist with Paul McCartney's Wings and a well-known pianist. It would have been difficult to put together a group in Northern Ireland with a better pedigree. They recorded half a dozen songs over two nights but these were never released. 'They were a bit like early Them,' one member, Jim Armstrong, told me. 'The guy was mad keen but very nervy. He had difficulty communicating.' Brian then had the idea of a public performance and went so far as to book one of Belfast's big venues. 'He had a date and the gig was supposed to go ahead, but it never happened,' said Armstrong. 'I heard he had cracked up.' Brian had recruited a young singer to perform at the concert, but when she pulled out he lost his nerve, dropped the project and simply disappeared. A year or so later it took the Salvation Army to track him down to let him know that his mother was dying.

When she died, Brian inherited some money with which he bought a cottage in North Wales, a tumbledown affair in the village of Bethesda with no gas or electricity. While there he renewed an acquaintance with Ifor Hughes, whom he'd first come across while busking in nearby Bangor, in 1988. In a letter, Hughes told me something of Brian's life in the 1990s. He had three dogs, called Ups, Tups and Midge. Midge was lame 'but Brian carried a vet's letter in his pocket to prove the dog had the vet's attention'. Besides playing the guitar and singing, Brian could do tricks to entertain children such as playing a tin whistle while he balanced a football on his head, or playing a banjo and mouth organ and twirling on one toe all at once. He had also been teaching himself to tap dance and owned a pair of tap shoes. Hughes described an incident:

> The last song I heard Brian sing was 'Hey Joe' of Jimi Hendrix fame outside the NatWest bank in Bangor High Street. I asked Brian to record that song for me but his radio cassette was in need of repairs. I regret now that I did not get batteries for my own cassette and take it outside NatWest bank and record him singing it. When I asked Brian several times to do it he said: 'You can get the record in a shop. It's by Jimi Hendrix.' It was one of those answers that made you feel feeble. You say to yourself: 'But I don't want any of them, I want you singing it. You're my friend.'

Hughes knew about the death, and his verdict was simple: 'Brian was a bit too trusting and vulnerable to the wrong sort of people.' He also described Brian's departure from Wales a few weeks before he was killed.

> I was the last person to see him when he left Bangor. I met him by the panda crossing on the A5. Ups and Midge had died recently [but] Tups was with him and [he had] his trolley and a black sleeping bag after a week of bad weather in Oct 2000. Brian was walking up to Bangor railway station to see if he could get a train and boat to Ireland.

The inquest into Brian's death took place in May 2003, and I caught a flight from London to Belfast to attend it. A modest redbrick building, Belfast's Coroner's Court had been the city's main courthouse in the days before big, high-security premises were required. Inside, the courtroom was small; the coroner was a mildmannered woman and the proceedings were low-key, almost homely in tone. Even at this stage, after months of gathering information, I had not become accustomed to hearing the name Brian Cathcart when it did not refer to me. When I read documents about the case, I caught my breath at almost every mention. 'Did you know Brian Cathcart?' McCarey and Watson were asked. 'Why did you go with Brian Cathcart to the flat?' 'Did you pour white spirit on Brian Cathcart?' The pathologist described Brian's injuries in detail. There were no marks, he said, to suggest that Brian had been struck or knocked unconscious (nor, incidentally, was there any damage to his liver of the kind associated with sustained heavy drinking). So badly was Brian burned, it seemed, that even if he had been admitted to hospital within minutes it was very unlikely that he could have been saved.

The milkman explained how he discovered Brian that morning. He was on his regular round in Rathcoole and had reached Carnmore Drive when he spotted a man who had obviously been badly burned—his clothes were smouldering, his head was blackened and bits of skin were falling away from his face. 'Help me,' said the man. The milkman knew some first aid: seeing wet grass around him and thinking the cool water would do Brian good, he persuaded him to sit on the ground while he summoned help. Then, fearing Brian would lose consciousness and die before the ambulance arrived, he kept him talking. Brian gave his name and his Larne address and the milkman also heard some muttered words, something like, 'Keep me out of the game.'

The milkman had been in the security forces in the past, he said, and had seen some terrible things on duty, but nothing to match this. 'He was in that much pain he wasn't even squealing,' he said. I could see in my mind a figure so brutalized he scarcely appeared human, muttering while smoke rose from his body, and at his side the stranger, jerked from his daily routine and struggling to give comfort and keep him alive. It was like an image from a devotional painting on a theme of suffering and charity.

There was evidence from police officers, a paramedic, the taxi driver who took them to Rathcoole and members of the family at the hospital who heard Watson describe the killing. Finally Simon McCarey's mother spoke. Tiny and thin and terrified, Audrey McCarey was like a trapped bird in the witness box, but it was soon clear she had no illusions about her son. She knew from long experience that he was a drunk, and a violent one at that. On the day after the killing he turned up at her home in a state of panic and confessed to the attack. She told him to give himself up but instead he changed his clothes, burned the outfit he had been wearing, and left. In response to a question from James Cathcart, she said her son was the sort who would agree to seek help for his drink problem but would never turn up for appointments. She was obviously uncomfortable addressing the brother of her son's victim and did not know where to look. James asked whether Simon had expressed remorse. She didn't visit him in prison but he rang occasionally, she said, and he'd told her that he thought all the time about the events of that night. 'He says he doesn't remember what happened but whether that's true I don't know.' And then, just as James was telling the coroner he had no more questions, she turned at last and looked him directly in the face. In a voice from the depth of despair she said simply: 'I'm awfully sorry.' Sitting there listening, I found that tears were running down my face. I had written about violent death before, but it had never affected me in this way.

Brian was not without attachments. For a time in the 1980s he lived with a Dutch woman in Rotherhithe, south London, and they had a daughter. After the relationship ended mother and daughter moved to New Zealand. He had older attachments too. Anna Doran lives on the Welsh borders now and has a family, but after his brothers she is probably the person who knew Brian best. They met, she told me, in 1969, by which time Brian had given up study but still haunted the Students' Union at Queen's, where he was known for disrupting political debates with drunken shouts of 'What about Biafra?' Anna was attracted to him at first sight. 'He had beautiful brown eyes, wavy, curly hair and great legs, and he had a way with people. He was also very, very clever.'

Biafra was one of the first television famines—certainly the first time I saw pictures of infants with big bellies and flies all over their faces. Millions were affected and it was reported at one stage that 1,000 children were dying there every day. 'What about Biafra?' therefore was a good question to ask in the Students' Union, even at a time when local politics in Northern Ireland were so dramatic and pressing. Brian was very emotional about it, Anna said, and believed that disruption was justified if it made people pay attention. 'And he was too shy to do it sober.'

Malachy Scullion, another student of that time who is a university teacher in Austria now, confirmed this picture. Brian eventually forced the Students' Union to stage a meeting about Biafra, which he addressed. Scullion described the event in his diary: 'I heard Brian Cathcart making a speech about Biafra at the Union Debating

Society. Indescribable. I have never heard a Christian sermon that I would even compare with it.' More than thirty years later, in a letter to me, Scullion elaborated:

> I don't remember any of the specifics of what Brian said that evening. What I still remember was the force of it. He was one of those rare speakers who talk very directly from their gut with absolute feeling and absolute conviction—no sense of the mind contributing logistical support in terms of conscious logic, audience awareness, or rhetorical stratagems of any kind—just a powerful message direct from the centre of feeling. The feeling was outrage that what was going on in Biafra could happen, and could be allowed to continue happening. The outrage was the message, and it really hit people.

Thus inspired, Scullion attached himself to the cause. The Biafra campaign included various fasts and demonstrations, some of which attracted publicity, and it reached its climax in January 1970, when Brian called for a march on the BP–Shell depot in Belfast docks. He held the oil companies partly responsible for the disaster. Scullion described what happened:

> [Brian] decided to try to gather up a crowd in the Students' Union snack bar where a lot of people went for lunch. He had a very strong fear of speaking in public, and that morning bought half a bottle of vodka. We went to my bedsit where he drank the lot. It had no obvious effect on him. We went to the snack bar, and he got up on a table and started to talk—or to harangue. He was very successful. Many students followed him down to the front of the Union, and eventually we headed off with a substantial procession to Shell—a touch of the Pied Piper.

About eighty students staged a short sit-in at the dock gates and Brian addressed them through a megaphone. They dispersed peacefully, but the matter did not end there. Because of the political crisis in Northern Ireland the government had banned all demonstrations and so the Biafra march, modest as it was, broke the law. Brian was charged with organizing an illegal demonstration and, after several court appearances, he was given a six-month suspended sentence.

This had consequences. Brian and Anna Doran left Northern Ireland to try a life of simplicity, which meant living in a tent on the Mull of Kintyre in western Scotland. 'We would come back regularly—there was a boat—to sign on [for unemployment benefit] in Belfast, and we would do some shoplifting,' Doran told me. 'Then one day we were caught, or rather I was caught and Brian insisted on taking responsibility.' When it emerged that, if convicted, he would have to serve the suspended sentence in jail, however, he changed his mind and they fled to Dublin. It was the start of several years of wandering together. After Dublin came Stoke, then Sutherland in Scotland (where they tried to live off the land), the west of Ireland and Cardiff. At one stage they went to London to join a group aiming to send people to Bangladesh to help with famine relief there, but the scheme didn't work out. They had dreams, too, of settling on St Kilda, a remote and unpopulated Scottish island, but these also came to nothing. For a short time they had some money, from summer work packing tomatoes in Guernsey, but Brian blew it at the dog track. 'He thought he had a system,' Doran said. 'Life was basically a series of disasters as idea after idea fell apart. Brian was a dreamer; he couldn't handle hard business.'

In 1974 he became an apostle of the tepee, convinced that the traditional tents of nomadic Native Americans were the key to a new alternative life. With a group of friends he toured pop festivals providing free food from a thirty-foot-tall tepee, cooking up whatever fruit and vegetables they could scrounge. At the same time he took up busking. He was a sort of leader, Doran recalled. 'There were about thirty of us. It was very, very intense. He could gather people around him and inspire them. He had real charisma.' Brian had schemes to run a food kitchen in London, to send tepees to Turkey, where there had been an earthquake, to deliver Land-Rovers to another earthquake zone in Italy, to raise horses in Wales. But nothing ever came of anything. 'People got fed up with him,' Doran said. 'The energy was going and they were turning against him. He had appeared to be a Messiah.' She witnessed his response when people criticized him. 'He would smile at the time but when you found him on his own he would be in tears. He couldn't understand why they would be like that. He would castigate himself if he thought he had done something wrong. He had a beautiful soft spot in him.' Doran, too, eventually went her own way: they split up in Bristol and after that he slowly 'went out of my ken'. This was the middle of the 1970s. Malachy Scullion lost track of him at about the same time.

Brian Cathcart was conscious on admission to hospital but was sedated to spare him pain. Eventually the doctors had to reduce his sedation to raise his body activity enough to allow skin grafts to be accepted. When the drug levels were reduced, however, Brian's brain activity ceased altogether—his system crashed, as it were—and soon the brothers were asked to authorize turning off the machinery. 'It was like you see on the television,' James said. 'The line just went flat.' That was on December 1, 2000.

Three years later I visited his grave. He is buried alongside his parents in a hill-top cemetery outside Larne, close to an impressive if incongruous avenue of palm trees. IN OUR HEARTS ALWAYS are the words on the stone. I thought—I still think—two things. He chose the difficult life and, for what it's worth, I admire that. But his death was no part of that choice. Lots of people get drunk in Belfast, no doubt many of them in dubious company; they don't burn to death. Brian should be out there today with a dog at his feet, playing guitar on some street corner, being Brian. ☐

YOU GO WHEN YOU CAN NO LONGER STAY
Jackie Kay

Jackie Kay

It is not so much that we are splitting up that is really worrying me, it is the fact that she keeps quoting Martin Amis. The other day we were in our bedroom having a silly argument about where things hang in the wardrobe when she said to me, 'Like Martin Amis says, you go when you can no longer stay.' It seemed odd to me. I looked outside the window into our street and saw Mr Davies post a letter. I saw three-down's white cat walk daintily along our wall, and then jump off. I often say nothing at all when she says something that is perturbing. It seemed odd to me, because here we are two very long-term lesbians, who have been in it so long we look as if we could have knitted each other up, been in it so long we have grown to look the same, wear similar clothes and have almost identical expressions on our plain faces, that Martin Amis should be coming into our lives in this way.

I hadn't even realized she was so keen on him until she made that remark; the one thing we don't share is books. It is the only area of our lives where we are both truly different. I read thrillers and human interest books, about somebody who has done something that I am not likely to do, or somebody who is interested in something that I know nothing about. She reads novels and then she rereads the novels she has read. And sometimes she reads slim volumes of poetry which always look a little sinister and have very peculiar titles. We are not the kind of couple that share a book, one after the other, which is maybe a shame, and maybe if we had been that kind of couple we wouldn't be splitting up now. It seems to me from the amount that she has started quoting Martin Amis that she's had a secret passion for him all along.

We were in the kitchen the other day arguing again about sex. It is a sore point between us. A kind of Achilles heel. 'All marriage turns into a sibling relationship,' she said terrifically confidently.

'Who said that?' I asked with a sickening, sinking heart. She paused, stirring her coffee.

'Do you want a coffee?' she said.

'No thank you,' I said. 'Don't tell me it was Martin Amis.'

'Yes,' she said defensively. 'He's quite right. You just don't fancy each other after a while.'

'I fancy you,' I said, then instantly regretted it.

'No you don't, you think you do,' she said, adding a big splash of milk into the coffee mug. 'Sure you don't want a cup?' she said.

'All right then,' I said. And she quite gleefully got another mug out of the kitchen cupboard. I think I bought the mug but I can't be sure. She smiled at me. When she smiles at me, I remember who she is.

Then she said, 'You become far too similar, especially two women. It's like looking in the mirror. You need a bit of difference to feel real passion.'

'Oh,' I said and sipped at my coffee anxiously.

'Life is too short not to feel passion,' she said. I knew where it was all going, but I didn't want her to tell me. I wanted to hide. I wanted to run up the stairs and hide in the airing cupboard. I couldn't stop thinking about my eighty-two-year-old mother who was even fonder of Hilary than she was of me, who had taken years to accept our relationship and then had finally totally embraced it. My old mother would be devastated. I felt edgy just thinking about it.

'Do you want a Jaffa with your coffee?' she asked me, as if a Jaffa could be the answer to all my troubles, as if a Jaffa could truly console.

'Yes please,' I said. I'd got into the habit of saying yes to as many things as possible, thinking that if I said yes enough she might stop saying no. She put three Jaffas on my plate but I noticed she took none for herself.

'Aren't you having any?' I asked her, a bit alarmed.

'No,' she said.

'Why not?' I said.

'Oh for goodness' sake, Ruth, stop trying to control me. After a while all relationships turn into power struggles,' she said. 'Would you ask that same question of a friend?'

'I'm just wondering why you put three on a plate for me if you're not having any yourself,' I said suspiciously. I was becoming very suspicious of her because she had started to change all of her habits and it was very worrying to me.

'Do you know something?' she said, very nastily. 'I think you are going mad.'

'Does Martin Amis say that?' I said furiously. 'Does he say one person in a couple during a break up will always accuse the other of going mad?'

She sighed and shook her head. She was actually looking quite beautiful these days. The person I didn't want to hear about was clearly making her feel good about herself. 'I'm just trying to have a cup of coffee with you, that's all. If I can't have a cup of coffee with you without fighting, we will have to put the house on the market even sooner than we said. As Martin Amis says, you go when you can no longer stay,' she said, standing up in the kitchen and drinking her coffee. She wouldn't sit down these days. There it was again, that bloody awful quote. It was deliberate then. She knew it was agitating me; she'd started to repeat it at random in whatever corner of our house we found ourselves in. I could even hear it in my sleep.

She left the room, coffee in hand, and I heard her playing music up the stairs. She'd taken to playing music a lot recently, another big change for her. This was a thin voice I didn't much like, one of those new English jazz singers with a very insipid style. I preferred the Dinah Washingtons of this world. I got up from the table and put two of the Jaffa Cakes in the bin. I gave the third to our dog. I saw what she was up to. She was trying to fatten me up as she lost weight. Well, we were both a little on the generous side. I was about three stone overweight and Hilary was at least two. Whenever we went out to a big lesbian do, I noticed that we weren't the only long-term couple that was overweight. I used to think that was happiness, being fat together, rolling about from one side of the big double bed to the other. Most of our old relationship revolved around food. Our idea of a super day used to be a day when we were both off work. (Now I notice her days off don't coincide with mine any more.) Hilary didn't have to go into the Council which was depressing her and I didn't have to go into the Tax Office which was depressing me. We'd get into our big bed with lots of treats—a couple of Chow Mein Pot Noodles, a big plate of chocolate biscuits, a big tub of cookies and cream Häagen-Dazs. Bliss. And we'd watch *The Maltese Falcon* for the umpteenth time or *Now Voyager* or *All About Eve*. Heaven. A day like that was even nicer if it was raining outside. At the end of *Now Voyager*, we'd both say that line together, 'Oh Jerry, don't let's ask for the moon. We have the stars,' and clutch at each other as if we were frightened of losing everything.

A lot of the people who know us often get us mixed up as though we were identical twins. Some people call me Hilary and Hilary

Ruth. It's a bit silly because we don't really look all that alike. Admittedly we do both buy similar looking clothes in Marks & Spencer. Our casual clothes days and smart clothes days are always the same. But recently Hilary has started to shop in Harvey Nichols. I went in there one day on my own and took a look at some of the prices. They actually made me feel quite ill and I felt terribly worried. That night I said to Hilary, 'I don't think shopping at Harvey Nichols on your salary is very sensible.'

She was reading the new Martin Amis at the time, *Yellow Dog*. 'This is about a man who suddenly becomes very violent,' she said quite menacingly.

I said, 'I feel as if I'm living with a gambler. You have run up massive bills on our joint Visa.'

'I told you we should never have had a joint account,' Hilary said and got up and opened a bottle of red wine which was another curious thing, because we only usually have a nice bottle of white, a Chardonnay, at the weekend. Now Hilary has taken to red wines, big heavy reds like Cabernet Sauvignons and Riojas, and she's taken to drinking them during the week. She slurped her wine. I suddenly noticed that she'd lost quite a bit of weight.

'Anyway, I think you should be a bit more careful,' I said, trying to sound calm.

'I think you should stop being a control freak,' she said. Then she got up and left the room again, taking her glass and the bottle with her. I heard the music go on up the stairs. She was playing it really quite loud. This time it was Otis Redding. We haven't played Otis Redding for years. She came running back down the stairs. I thought she was going to apologize, but she just picked up *Yellow Dog* without a word and went back upstairs. I could hear Otis singing 'Sitting on the Dock of the Bay'.

I was annoyed at myself. I started clearing away the remains of our meal. I noticed that Hilary had left all of her rice. She'd eaten her salad though. I didn't know quite what to do with myself because we usually watched *Frost* on the TV together or *Miss Marple* or *Midsomer Murders*. But lately Hilary had said, 'That isn't me, watching *Frost*. That's you.' She'd started saying this a lot recently. 'I'm not the kind of person who does such and such or who says such and such or who watches such and such.' I wondered furiously if Martin Amis had put her up to that too. Perhaps there was something in one of his books that advised people in long-term relationships to stop doing everything that they used to enjoy doing. Perhaps he, being so resolutely heterosexual, so smug with his roll-ups, was trying to destroy the lesbian relationship. I suddenly had a brainwave. If she was reading him, the only thing I could do to read her was read him too. I rushed into Waterstone's in town and bought everything they had by him. I hid the books under the spare room bed, the spare room which I have now been consigned to. Hilary needs space to think about what we should do, she has said. She needs space and calm. For my part I have stopped reading my murder mysteries for the moment. Hilary always looked down upon them. Of course she thinks she is much cleverer than me. 'It's always the woman that gets it,' she'd say whenever I picked up another thriller.

I've started to feel very odd within my own life. It's most peculiar to feel lonely inside your own life. It's a secret of course, because nobody would know and all of our friends still think everything is fine between us, though I must say they have all taken to admiring Hilary recently and saying things like, 'You're looking great.' This morning we had breakfast together which was a nice change. Sunday breakfast. Hilary had bacon and egg but no toast and no newspapers. She has even given up the Sunday papers; I'm not sure why. When I asked her about it, she said, 'Do I have to explain everything to you?' Then when she saw my slightly hurt face, she said, 'I'm engrossed in *Yellow Dog* and newspapers are a huge waste of time.'

I suggested we go out for a Sunday walk or a run in the car in the afternoon. Hilary said yes, good idea. I felt very pleased about this because it seemed to me that if we could go out for a walk in some beautiful countryside normal life might return, encouraged by the light on the hills or a gushing waterfall. 'Shall we go to Coniston Water or Derwent Water and then go for Sunday lunch in a pub somewhere?' I said excitedly.

'No, I don't want to make a big production out of it,' Hilary said. 'Let's just go to the park with Orlando. I've got other things I want to do today.' The dog was wagging her tail as Hilary fetched the lead, wagging her tail frantically.

It was a freezing cold day. I had my scarf tied firmly around my neck. Hilary looked a bit bare but I daren't suggest she put a scarf on. I rather like the winter cold if I am well wrapped up. We were walking side by side, with our golden retriever Orlando running on happily in front of us when Hilary suddenly said to me, 'I thought it best that we talk about this outside of the house rather than in. You know I have not been happy for some time.'

'I didn't know that,' I said, hurt.

'Oh come on. You did, darling,' Hilary said, quite gently. I shook my head and put my hands in my pockets. Our dog ran back towards us. I picked up her stick and threw it again really quite far. It was truly an astonishingly beautiful winter day; even the clouds were lit up from behind as if they had highlights in their hair. 'Isn't it lovely light today?' I said. 'Isn't it absolutely gorgeous?'

'Why won't you let me talk about this?' Hilary said.

'Don't spoil our walk, darling,' I said, picking up the stick again and throwing it. It was the coldest it has been yet. Freezing bitter cold, but still very beautiful, beautiful in an icy, frosty way. The ducks and the geese were sitting on top of the ice on the pond as if they were on holiday. Hilary sighed beside me. I could tell she was about to try again.

'I know that you are finding this hard, that's only natural. I know that we thought we'd be together forever. But stuff happens; life changes. We have to move on.'

I walked beside her. At least she hadn't quoted again from Martin Amis, nor had she told me her name. I presumed it was a she anyway. I didn't want to know her name; I didn't want to know what she looked like; I didn't want to know anything about her. 'Could you at least do me one favour?' I asked Hilary. 'Could you tell me nothing about her, nothing at all?'

'That's silly,' Hilary said. 'I'm not buying into that. I've done nothing to be ashamed of.'

'You've stopped loving me,' I said, quietly.

'We weren't good for each other any more,' she said. I looked at her and suddenly noticed that she'd lost at least three stone. 'How have you lost all this weight?' I asked her. 'I don't want to tell you,' she said. 'I don't want you copying that too. You copy everything. If you hadn't copied everything, we might still have been lovers.'

'What do I copy?' I said, feeling extremely alarmed.

'Nothing,' she said. 'Never mind.' We walked round the pond in silence. I noted a few things I think about the geese but I can't remember what they were.

I noticed that Hilary was sweating quite profusely even though the temperature was sub-zero. I sneaked a look at her. She had that mad look on her face, eyebrows knitted together, quite unappealing if I am honest. It occurred to me that she might be having her menopause and that all of these changes of behaviour were actually the change of life. She had after all been behaving very erratically recently, flying off the handle at the slightest thing. 'Are you having a hot flush?' I asked her.

'No I certainly am not!' she said.

But it was out and now I knew. Hilary was having her menopause and keeping it secret from me. That explained everything: it explained why she no longer wanted to share the double bed. The sheets were probably soaking in the middle of the night! It explained the temper tantrums and the outbursts. 'Why didn't you just tell me? For goodness' sake we are both lesbians,' I said.

'You might describe yourself like that. You know I don't,' she said.

'Well, whatever, why didn't you tell me you were having hot flushes?' Hilary is three years younger than I am and I could tell she was fuming, absolutely fuming about getting her change of life first.

'It can happen at any age,' I said. 'I've just been lucky I haven't had mine yet. I was a late starter with my periods. When you start late, you apparently have your menopause later. Did you start yours early?'

'Don't do this,' Hilary said, beside herself now. 'I am not having my menopause. I don't know how many times I have to say this,' she said, tired. 'This is typical of you. You are in denial. I am in love. This is a love story of all the strange things happening to me so late in the goddamned day.'

She wasn't going to get me this time with that Martin Amis. I said, 'When I come in the door I go tee hee hee. The place kills me.'

She said, 'Have you been reading him?'

'Yes,' I said, quite pleased.

'See, I told you you always had to copy me,' she said, apoplectic with rage now. 'And now you've gone out and got him. Nothing's sacred.'

I smiled. I shouted *Or-lan-do*, my voice going up and down merrily. 'Who is going to have the dog?' I said.

'I am,' Hilary said. 'I'm much fonder of Orlando than you are. Orlando is my dog.'

'She is not,' I said indignantly.

'I don't think I want to do this,' Hilary said.

'Do what?' I said, still like a fool feeling a little hopeful.

'Have these silly fights. We are two grown-ups. We have to be able to sort this out amicably. It's not like we have kids.'

'Having a dog is like having a kid,' I said.

'It is not. Don't be stupid.'

We walked in silence then round the pond for the third time. I couldn't count the amount of times we have walked round and round and round that pond. I thought of all the walks over our twenty-five years together. Our walking books are the only books we truly share, tiny leaflet-sized books that tell us of lengths and grades of difficulty in Strathglass and surrounding Glens. I thought of our favourite walk from just below Beinn Mhor, and the lovely waterfall in the woods up the hill from the old sheep fanks. And the odd little cemetery you come across as you reach the end of the walk. Rumour has it that once a burial party arrived there from Tomich village minus the coffin. I thought of all the walks over all the years—off the beaten track and out of breath. Parts of the country, we used to believe, truly belonged to us: the Lakes, the Highlands, the Peak District. I couldn't bear to think of Hilary anywhere, in any of these places with some other love, her dark fleece zipped up, her walking boots thick with mud, and a map in her hand. I looked at Hilary. I couldn't imagine her even wearing a fleece in the future. She looked so slim now; she looked like somebody else, oddly focused and deliberate looking as if the resolve to do this had made her quite certain of herself. I couldn't quite believe it. Hilary had slimmed her way out of my hands. If only I'd followed her example I could have squeezed myself through to where she had gone. When we got inside our cream kitchen, I thought she might have a cup of tea and a scone and jam for old times' sake. 'Scones are a thing of the past,' Hilary said and I had the impression that she wasn't quoting from Martin Amis this time.

It seemed to me that Hilary wanted to consign our whole life to the past. The other day I arrived home, very excited, with a classic copy of the *Dandy*—December 30, 1972. Hilary and I have collected

comics for over ten years and have spent many a happy hour
laughing over the antics of Dennis the Menace or Desperate Dan or
Beryl the Peril. I said triumphantly, 'Look what I've just found!'
thinking that Hilary would remember our love through Beryl the
Peril's impersonation of an Abominable Snowman. But Hilary just
stared at it a little disdainfully and said, 'You can have the comic
collection, that was always more your thing. I'll have the CDs.'

I put the kettle on and got out a fresh jar of rhubarb-and-ginger
jam. I pulled the little bit of tracing paper off the top. I opened our
cake tin and took out one of yesterday's home-made scones, a nice
batch that had risen properly. I buttered my scone quite thickly and
spread the nippy jam over it. I made a fresh pot of tea and put the
cosy on. I sat down alone at the table. I poured us both a mug of
tea. Hilary watched me eat my scone with some satisfaction, sipping
at her mug of tea, standing, leaning against the fridge. She said
nothing. She eyed me eating my scone. I wasn't the least bit
bothered. I thought ahead to night-time in the spare room. I said to
myself secretly another Martin Amis line: 'Jesus Christ if I could
make it into bed and get my eyes shut without seeing a mirror.' She
smiled at me and I smiled back at her and both of our faces looked
the same. We both had his tight, cool grin.   □

THE SURGERY
OF LAST RESORT

Daniel Smith

Early one morning in the fall of 1999, Steven R., a forty-seven-year-old man with fair skin and grey hair, was in the front yard of his home in suburban Nebraska, picking up leaves. Overnight the maples bordering his property had shed some of their foliage and he was making sure, as he did each day, that the lawn was free of debris. But here his resemblance to a typical property owner ended. Steven was on his hands and knees, and he was clearing the grass one leaf at a time. If even a single errant leaf were to escape his attention, he felt, it would cause a catastrophe: his wife would slip and fall, or she would pop the back tyre of the car as she backed out of the garage, and have a fatal accident. A lone leaf could even have grave spiritual consequences: his parents, now in heaven, could be demoted to hell if he did not eradicate the leaves from the lawn. And so Steven patrolled the property for the next four hours even though he knew that what he was doing was irrational.

Steven R. was diagnosed with obsessive-compulsive disorder in 1976. Since then he had checked himself into hospital three times. He had tried behavioural therapy, psychotherapy, biofeedback therapy and group therapy, a score of medications—and eleven electric shock treatments—but nothing had worked. After suffering from this condition for twenty-three years, Steven was now deeply depressed. He had been unable to work for over a year. He seldom saw anyone but his wife (his third) and even she was losing her patience with him. He had two sons and four brothers but for the most part they were strangers to him. It was beginning to seem as if there were nothing left for him but suicide.

Then, that evening, he watched a television programme about obsessive-compulsive disorder in which a doctor spoke about an operation that could be used to treat the most severe cases. The following week he went to his own psychiatrist, in Omaha, and asked to undergo the same surgery. His psychiatrist, who knew about this option but had not yet considered it, looked at Steven's case and agreed that yes, at this point perhaps this was something that should be tried.

The surgery that Steven saw mentioned on television is called cingulotomy. It is one of only four psychiatric neurosurgical procedures still in existence. It is performed by drilling two burr holes into the skull and, with an electrically heated probe, burning a lesion or series of lesions into the cingulate cortex of the brain's limbic system—the seat of emotions. The operation is primarily used to treat obsessive-compulsive disorder, or OCD, but it can also be used to treat major depression, bipolar disorder and intractable pain.

I first heard of cingulotomy in summer 2001, in the course of some research I was doing on mental illness. I had already written a fair amount about psychiatric treatments, but had only a dim idea that psychosurgery—as psychiatric neurosurgery is also (and often derogatorily) called—was still being carried out. In fact, psychiatrists have never stopped offering brain surgery for mental illness, but for two reasons they now rarely advertise its existence. The first reason is fairly obvious: psychosurgery has a sordid past, characterized by coercion and abuse. This is especially true in America where, in the late 1940s, the infamous Washington neurologist Walter Freeman became in effect a travelling salesman for transorbital lobotomy whereby a thin tool—often an ordinary ice pick—was poked through a patient's eye socket and swished back and forth, severing the white matter that connects the prefrontal lobes with the rest of the brain. Freeman's lectures and demonstrations, which he delivered at dozens of hospitals across the country, were wildly successful. By 1951, close to 20,000 patients in the United States had been lobotomized, usually relieving their distress but also leaving them, in Freeman's own words, with 'little capacity for any emotional experience'.

Like lobotomy, cingulotomy removes brain tissue, but it produces none of lobotomy's negative effects; unlike the frontal lobes, the cingulate cortex plays a complex role in personality or cognition and the results—like the procedure itself—are not nearly as dramatic. When cingulotomy works, patients must wait several weeks for their symptoms to improve, and even then they improve slowly. Despite these differences, the sinister associations of lobotomy compel doctors who wish to preserve surgical options for their patients to adopt a low profile.

The second and more important reason for the reticence of psychiatrists about cingulotomy is that it is performed with great discrimination. There are only two sites in the world where the operation is regularly performed today: the Karolinska Institute, in Sweden, which awards the Nobel Prize in Medicine, and the

Massachusetts General Hospital, in Boston. Mass General usually performs fewer than ten cingulotomies a year—approximately one third of all the psychosurgical operations performed annually worldwide.

In the summer of 2001, I asked Bruce Price, a neurologist at Mass General, if I could meet a patient who was undergoing the procedure. Price was apprehensive—the last time they had granted a writer access to the procedure, he said, the *Boston Herald* had run an article with the headline MGH STILL DOES 'LOBOTOMIES'—but, after consulting his colleagues, he eventually agreed.

Mass General has a laborious screening process for psychosurgery. Patients referred to the hospital are reviewed by a body known as the Psychiatric Neurosurgery Committee, a five-member team comprised of a neurosurgeon, three psychiatrists and a neurologist—Bruce Price. The committee meets once a month and will only consider patients who have tried and failed all other available treatments. Even when they accept a patient for cingulotomy he must travel to Boston and submit himself to a week-long battery of evaluations, testing, examinations and neuro-imaging, at the end of which, if these tests show no reason to stop and he still wishes to proceed, he is admitted for surgery.

In July 2002 I got a phone call from Price to say that they had a patient I could follow. For five days I spent nearly every waking hour with Steven R., attending his appointments with psychologists, neurologists and psychiatrists and watching as he had his brain imaged and took tests. Finally, I watched as he had the surgery itself.

Steven R.'s illness began in 1974 as a crisis of faith in himself. He was twenty-one years old, married to his high-school girlfriend, the father of a young son, and working for a computer manufacturer in Omaha. Steven was a good, even impressive, employee but 'overnight', he says, he began to be overwhelmed by doubts. How could he be sure he had entered the memory on that hard drive a half-hour ago? Even if he had, how could he be certain he had done it correctly? Each of these questions came with twin 'what if I hadn't?' questions, and these had terrible answers: his failure would harm himself and his family.

The terror of these doubts and the swiftness of their arrival was too much for Steven to bear, and in 1976 he admitted himself to the hospital for the first time. His wife, who was pregnant with their second child, filed for divorce soon after he was diagnosed with obsessive-compulsive disorder. Steven went on disability benefit, returning to work for only brief periods. He got married again, but to a woman he hardly knew; they were soon divorced. He went golfing with his brother Bill, who saw Steven pulling away from his own friends, but these outings became another source of torture for him. On the golf course he could not trust the number of swings he had taken, and every divot swept out from the ground was a command to replace the grass he had knocked away ('It got to the point where I should have been working for the golf course,' he said.) He spent most of these years living with his parents and when his father died, in 1987, his depression and despair deepened.

In 1993 Steven got married for a third time, to a devout Catholic twelve years older than him. His wife suffered from fibromyalgia, a condition of unknown cause similar to chronic fatigue disorder, and so seemed well equipped to understand Steven's own suffering. Steven, who had been raised as a Catholic, now became devoted to the church, attending Mass every morning at 7.30. But soon his faith became entwined with his illness. He couldn't kneel without being paralysed by fears that he was kneeling incorrectly; when he prayed, which he did in great repetitive torrents, he agonized over the placement of his fingers. Steven's priests—in whom he confided his illness and, later on, his hope for some relief in surgery—were by turns cruel and comforting. One told him that he would burn in hell if he went through with the surgery; a kinder priest wished him luck, reminded him that God is loving, and told him that, as far as his prayers go, it is the 'quality and not the quantity' that God responds to.

Steven applied for cingulotomy in 1999 through his psychiatrist in Omaha. The doctors at Mass General denied his referral on the grounds that he had not yet made an earnest attempt at behavioural therapy, one of the most effective treatments for OCD. They suggested that he undergo a three-month course of 'exposure therapy' at the Obsessive-Compulsive Disorder Institute at McLean Hospital, in Belmont, Massachusetts, and in 2001 Steven made his first trip to Massachusetts. The therapy failed. Steven's most debilitating obsession still centred on foliage but despite the copious supply of leaves at McLean, they didn't cause him any anxiety—

'They weren't my leaves,' he explained. At his doctor's suggestion, Steven had his wife videotape the leaves strewn over his front lawn in Nebraska—a sight that would have caused his anxiety to spike to an unbearable level had he seen it in person; but the tape caused him only a slight tug of discomfort. And so, after only one month, Steven left McLean without any success. He soon reapplied to Mass General, which reassessed his case and, more than a year after they first considered his history, approved his application.

Soon afterwards, in June 2002, Steven's wife left him. He moved out of the house they shared and into an apartment, where he still lives alone.

On the afternoon of Monday, July 8, I sat with Steven in the office of Rees Cosgrove, the neurosurgeon on Mass General's psychiatric neurosurgery committee, and an associate professor of surgery at Harvard Medical School. It was Steven's first appointment of the week, and he was wearing starched blue jeans with sharp creases down the legs and a white, short-sleeved Nebraska football shirt. Sitting on his right was his older brother Tom—a father of three and a maintenance worker at a Catholic church. His brother Bill, who is an executive at a medical-supply company, was scheduled to arrive on Wednesday, the day before the surgery.

Steven had told me on the phone a week earlier that he preferred to come to Boston alone; he was worried he would not feel comfortable explaining the details of his illness in the company of his brothers. But he had little choice in the matter. The cingulotomy assessment committee insists that patients be accompanied to Boston by a 'supportive family member', a rule intended to lessen the considerable strain of the process and to ensure that all patients make an informed decision on whether to proceed. However, since his divorce Steven did not, strictly speaking, have a 'supportive family member'. To his surprise, his brothers arranged to take time off work and accompany him to Boston.

Rees Cosgrove is an imposing man with a light brown moustache and bright, unblinking eyes. His speech is crisp and his manner is confident, exacting and—unusually for a surgeon—compassionate. Unsurprisingly, Cosgrove has been criticized—by colleagues as well as laymen—when they find out he performs cingulotomies. These critics typically invoke ice picks and zombies and Cosgrove typically responds with a measured explanation of what exactly cingulotomy is (not a lobotomy) and a reproach that anyone should be so cruel and ignorant as to deny any medical option whatsoever to people suffering so acutely.

'We begin,' Cosgrove said, 'by making a small incision in the scalp, here.' He pointed to a spot on the crown of his head, near the hairline. 'We then retract the skin and drill two small holes through the skull, about an inch apart. Then we take a thin probe about the width of—' (he scanned his desk, picked up a Bic pen and removed the ink tube) '—this, insert it through the top layer of tissue and into the cingulate cortex and heat up the tip.' With the pen, Cosgrove mimed the insertion of the probe, making a motion like an oil drill. 'We do this three times on each side. It's a very simple operation. Ultimately you create a lesion about a cubic centimetre on each side.'

Steven sat silently throughout Cosgrove's description. It was hard to tell whether his quiet demeanour was due to a naturally quiet personality, his depression, or the unfamiliar surroundings but, as Cosgrove was to point out, Steven is the sort of person who almost never complains, even if in physical or emotional distress.

'The operation is not a cure for illness,' Cosgrove told Steven. Nothing would ever cure an illness as persistent and acute as his. The operation aimed only to reduce the severity of his symptoms to a degree that might make other treatments, such as medication and behavioural therapy, more effective. Nor could he guarantee even this limited sucess. Mass General has seen a wide and, Cosgrove admitted, somewhat lacklustre spectrum of results: 'Anywhere from thirty-five to sixty-five per cent of patients who undergo cingulotomy experience a reduction in their symptoms. This isn't a silver bullet. People tend not to see improvement for eight to twelve weeks, or longer. And improvements occur so gradually that patients rarely notice them in the short term.' The hope was that, like a dark bruise healing slowly, the effects would accumulate to such a point that one day Steven would wake up and notice that the bruise had faded to yellow.

The good news was that the risks were minimal. Mass General has been the site of more than 1,000 cingulotomies since 1962 and in all that time there have been only four cases of haemorrhage and two cases of infection, and no deaths. No one has experienced a stroke since modern imaging technology replaced the old imaging protocol, whereby air was pumped into the brain's ventricles prior to X-ray. Most important: removing a part of the cingulate cortex would have a minimal risk of affecting Steven's personality, or his intellect, in any way. In the week or two after surgery internal swelling would probably cause some minor but temporary side effects—headaches, confusion and disorientation, some swelling around the eyes, possibly urinary incontinence—but Steven could be certain of leaving surgery the same person he was when he went in.

After the meeting, I walked with Steven and Tom back to their hotel on Beacon Hill. I asked Steven if he had been surprised by anything Cosgrove had told him. Steven then revealed that, prior to the meeting, he had known next to nothing about what cingulotomy really involved. He had been under the impression that he would be more or less assured of results, and that those results would be immediate. They would be cutting out a part of his brain, after all, and it was difficult for him to imagine that they wouldn't also be cutting out his illness.

This misconception is common among cingulotomy patients, and the doctors at Mass General do their best to counter it. As Cosgrove and other doctors would tell Steven throughout the week, no one knows for certain why cutting away a part of the cingulate cortex helps to alleviate the symptoms of mental illness. The theory, supported by imaging studies, is that the cingulate cortex makes up part of the circuitry of obsessions and compulsions, and that by severing the cingulate you induce the brain to produce new, less damaging connections. But like many psychiatric treatments—and like many 'physical' treatments for that matter—cingulotomy is performed not because doctors are sure of why it works, but simply because it sometimes does.

Steven was troubled by the lack of certainty that the surgery would help him, but it was not what frightened him most. When I asked him what did, he thought for a moment before answering: 'That they won't let me go through with it,' he said.

On Wednesday afternoon, Steven took a long series of intelligence and psychological tests in an administrative building across the street from the hospital, in a small office decorated with a table, two chairs, a glass vase with six plastic flowers in it, and a framed three-by-five photograph on which was printed a single word: GOALS.

An extensive series of tests is given to each patient who comes for cingulotomy for three reasons. The first is to provide the doctors at Mass General with statistics with which they can document their activities. The second is to provide a 'baseline' for the particular patient being tested (the hospital then contacts them every six months to follow their progress). The third is to make certain that any cognitive deficits that the patient may have are not serious enough to preclude the surgery.

At first, I considered the testing administered to Steven throughout the week a dry, clinical interlude. But then on Tuesday, a single test had revealed the profundity of Steven's suffering more starkly than anything else that had come before. This test was the Yale-Brown Obsessive Compulsive Scale (Y-BOCS). It attempts to measure the severity of a patient's symptoms with ten questions—five about obsessions and five about compulsions. For example: 'How much distress do your obsessive thoughts cause you?' Each question is scored on a scale of zero to four, four denoting the highest level of distress.

0 None
1 Not too disturbing
2 Disturbing, but still manageable
3 Very disturbing
4 Near constant and disabling distress

Out of curiosity I took the Y-BOCS after Steven. I scored a two on the above question, and an eight on the entire test. When I asked Darin Dougherty, the junior psychiatrist on the assessment committee, to explain what this meant, he told me an eight was somewhat high, but still within the range considered normal. What did Steven get? I asked. He rifled through the papers on his desk, and held the sheet he was looking for up to the light. 'Steven scored a thirty-eight.'

The implications of that number became clear during his Wednesday testing session. The tests were administered by a psychologist named Cary Savage. Upon reading this surname off Steven's schedule, his brother Tom commented, 'That isn't a good sign.' In fact, it was not the administrator of the tests that caused

Steven discomfort—Savage was nothing of the sort—but what the tests showed.

The tests with which the session began were basic—'What's missing from this picture?' 'What is the meaning of the word "winter"?'—but Steven quickly began to sweat and fidget. He gave fewer and fewer accurate answers. Soon, he was responding to almost none of the questions at all, and asking anxious questions of a sort that he had not asked all week. 'Are you finding this data helpful?' he said to Savage. 'Do you give every patient the same tests?'

While some of the questions Savage asked Steven were tough enough to give anyone pause ('What is the main theme of the Book of Genesis?' is one I still can't answer), Steven's difficulty with most of them stemmed from a different cause than ignorance. Most patients who come to Mass General for cingulotomy reveal significant deficits in their intellectual and cognitive abilities: abstract thinking, memory, strategy-making, visualization etc. Steven's depression—a condition associated with decreased activity in the frontal lobe—probably broadened the scope of those deficits.

The testing went on from 11.30 in the morning to 5.00 in the evening. I had begun by taking careful notes—writing down the specifics of each of the tests—but by the seventeenth test I could no longer bear to watch, and I put down my pen and quietly left the room. As I did I heard Steven say, 'This is going to make the surgery a breeze.'

On Thursday afternoon at 1 p.m., Steven lay on a gurney in Induction Room 27, on the verge of tears. To his side were a series of shelves containing a cornucopia of medical supplies: tourniquets, syringes, catheters, electrocardiogram pads, needles, adaptors, urinals, bedpans, transfusion filters, alcohol swabs, purple examination gloves. A sign read CAUTION: SHELVES NOT STABLE. Through a bank of double doors another brain surgery was in session; Steven was next in line.

Cosgrove came by, in scrubs and a surgical cap, and greeted Steven. How did he feel? 'Okay,' Steven said. Cosgrove explained that, with the help of an anaesthetist, he was about to fix a 'halo'— a circular metal frame with four metal arms similar to the frames used to stabilize the heads and necks of trauma patients—on to

Steven's head. Steven, eyes wide, nodded his assent and Cosgrove removed the clunky brass-coloured frame from a sterile bag; it looked like a round coffee table with the glass top removed. He placed it over Steven's head, arms side up—two in front and two at the back—and injected lidocaine, a common local anaesthetic, into each of the spots where the frame's arms met Steven's head. There is little flesh between the scalp and the skull, so as the lidocaine was injected it raised tall, white bumps on Steven's head. These bumps pushed against the arms of the frame and held them in place, freeing up Cosgrove to take out four plastic screws that he would use to secure the frame against the surface of Steven's skull. As Cosgrove inserted the front right screw a stream of blood dripped into Steven's eye. Cosgrove wiped away the blood with a square of gauze. He tightened the screws. 'This frame is held in place really well,' he said. He took hold of the part of the frame that circled around Steven's mouth and moved it up and down, to the left and to the right. Steven's head went with it.

Cosgrove then placed a strange-looking piece of plastic scaffolding over Steven's head and on the metal frame. It was composed of a series of clear plastic posts filled with petroleum oil. Unlike the frame itself, which is 'non-ferromagnetic', the fluid in these posts would show up on the pre-operative magnetic resonance image (MRI) scan which would provide Cosgrove with a geometric guide to pinpoint lesion coordinates in Steven's brain. This method is called stereotaxy. 'The stereotactic system was introduced in 1947 for just these purposes,' Cosgrove said, slipping into professorial mode. 'The system allows us to remove the human error in finding lesion targets. The MRI takes pictures of Steven's brain in slices, and slices of the posts show up in each picture. It's like a 3-D map. Guided by the frames we're unlikely to make any mistakes in inserting the electrodes.'

After taking the MRI—the third period of time Steven would spend in a neuro-imaging machine that week—Cosgrove rolled Steven into the operating room. The room was crowded with more equipment than people. Besides Cosgrove and me, there were only a neurosurgical resident named Ramin Amirnovin, two nurses, and a technician whose job it was to work the various monitors. Cosgrove transferred Steven to the operating table. He locked the halo into a hitch towards the bottom of the table, securing Steven's head, which was held up only by the metal frame, firmly in place. He then shaved a small patch of hair from the top of Steven's head, creating a clean runway of scalp, and Amirnovin cleaned the incision spot, switching back and forth between rubbing alcohol and soap until he had gone over the spot exactly twenty times, as surgical tradition dictates. Amirnovin then stretched a thin plastic sheath over the sterilized area and Cosgrove began injecting it with lidocaine, again raising a large white lump on Steven's scalp. At one point the scalp became so engorged with fluid that some anaesthetic squirted out through a pin hole, splashing Cosgrove's scrubs. Steven was still conscious; since the brain has no pain receptors, neurosurgeons prefer to forgo the use of general anaesthesic which is the main culprit in surgical complications. 'Can you feel anything any more?' Cosgrove asked Steven, whose face and body were now obscured behind the operating room's blue drapes. 'It hurts a little,' was the reply. Cosgrove injected more lidocaine.

Amirnovin made the incision, a clean straight line through flesh now spongy with liquid. As he did so Cosgrove leaned in and inserted retractors to separate the flesh, and there it was: Steven's skull—ivory-white and blotched with blood. Cosgrove drilled the first burr hole. The drill itself looked like an industrial-strength electric toothbrush. As he drilled he swivelled his arm in a circular motion, as though he were stirring oatmeal. Small pieces of wet bone sprayed on to the blue drapes. Amirnovin drilled the second burr hole, but he had trouble breaking through the skull. With a miming motion, Cosgrove reminded him to stir.

Setting aside the drill, the doctors used forceps to pick out stray pieces of bone from the holes and then a scalpel to cut through the dura mater, a thin fibrous membrane that serves as the second layer of defence for the brain. Steven began to snore. Cerebrospinal fluid, tinged red by blood, filled the wells in his skull, and with each heartbeat the fluid pulsed, rising and foaming with each systole and falling and calming with each diastole.

Cosgrove attached a second brass halo to Steven's head, securing it to the first in a mirror image and completing the imaginary x, y and z axes that compose the stereotactic system. He then showed me what the electrodes looked like. They were thin metal rods with copper-coloured tips—each indeed the approximate width of a Bic pen tube—and they were attached to a boxy electronic device. This device would heat up the tips of the electrodes to exactly eighty-five degrees Celsius for exactly ninety seconds, the uniform heat and timing creating uniform lesions within Steven's brain. 'Eighty-five degrees is just the right heat,' Cosgrove said. 'It doesn't bubble. It just gently cooks.' This metaphor is accurate—the electrodes would not so much burn the identified tissue as coagulate it, the way a frying pan coagulates the protein in egg whites.

The actual lesion-making part of the operation was comparatively mundane. Cosgrove fixed a barrel for the electrode to the elaborate apparatus attached to Steven's head, adjusted the coordinates on the frames, double-checked his work with a 'ghost frame' set up on a table behind him, inserted the electrode through the burr hole, and pressed a button. We waited while the tip of the electrode heated up. 'It's really quite simple,' Cosgrove said, in a sincerely casual manner popular among successful brain surgeons. 'Unchallenging, even. The people who protest against this sort of thing do so out of complete ignorance. They don't understand the gravity of mental illness. The pain is horrific—much worse than physical pain. I see a lot of death and suffering in my practice: injuries, trauma, tumours, seizures, intractable pain, Parkinson's. But nothing comes close to the suffering of my mentally ill patients. Nothing.'

Cosgrove produced three lesions on each side and then left Amirnovin to fill in the burr holes with packing material and sew up the wound. The stitching was by far the longest phase of the operation. 'The skull will actually heal over,' Cosgrove explained.

It was a textbook procedure.

I walked into Steven's room a little after eleven o'clock the following morning. He was standing beside his bed, holding an electric razor and looking a bit dazed. They'd given him morphine the night before and it had kept him up. 'My head is swollen,' he said and touched the points on his forehead where the screws had been inserted. He was about to shave, and seemed eager to do so. Shaving was one of Steven's most persistent rituals. It often took him longer than an hour to run the razor over his face until he was satisfied that he had removed every hair.

It was a bright June day, and the window in Steven's room presented an expansive view of Boston—of the Charles River and the Longfellow Bridge, which carries the Red Line between Boston and Cambridge. I pointed out the view and Steven walked over. I pointed out the duck tours—amphibious vehicles that the city bought surplus from the military—and the neon Citgo sign on Commonwealth Avenue, saved from demolition in the 1980s by industrial-art conservationists. On a playing field on the bank of the Charles there was a frisbee competition going on. Little college-aged figures performed elaborate tricks: throwing discs into the air and spinning around like baton twirlers, tossing them between their legs, rolling them up and down the crooks of their arms. Steven and I watched them tumble and catch and throw for a long while in silence. 'Are you feeling down this morning?' I asked him. He was taken aback. 'You can hear it in my voice?' I nodded. 'Yep,' he said. 'I don't know why.' For twenty minutes or more we stood like that, not saying anything.

A nurse walked in to check up on Steven and told me that he had been doing fine. She assumed I was a relative: 'We took his blood pressure and temperature this morning and everything is normal. If you want to go down to the cafeteria or go outside to get some air, that's fine.' After she left, Steven sighed quietly and headed to the bathroom to shave. Since I knew he didn't like people to watch him indulge his compulsions, I headed downstairs for a cup of coffee.

The next day, less than forty-eight hours after his surgery, Steven was released.

The most dangerous time for a patient undergoing cingulotomy are the days and weeks immediately following surgery. There is a simple psychological reason for this. It is that no matter how often and how forcefully the doctors issue the requisite disclaimers—that cingulotomy is not a cure for obsessive-compulsive disorder but part of its treatment, that it has a modest success rate, that it can take months if not years to notice any results—patients tend to persist in their hope that a radical treatment will yield a radical result. Many therefore experience a bout of depression when they return home and conclude that they feel just as terrible as they did before the surgery. A few patients, Cosgrove told me, had committed suicide shortly after surgery.

I called Steven as soon as he got back to Nebraska and it was clear that he had already begun to fall into this post-operative depression. However, it seemed to grow less out of false expectations than from an unforeseen complication. The doctors had warned Steven he might have trouble controlling his bladder after the surgery, but Steven had trouble controlling his bowels as well—a near catastrophic development for an obsessive-compulsive. On the way home he had two accidents—once during a stopover at a Chicago airport, and once in the car on the way home; the experiences had nearly paralysed him with shame. When I called again at the end of the week, he had not yet left his house.

The incontinence lingered for two months but even when it dissipated, the depression remained. And in the cruel, circular nature of mental illness, the depression nourished his obsessions and compulsions. The time it took him each day to clean, to shave and to shower lengthened by hours. Soon even the merest hint of a command became enough to goad Steven's mind into vigorous action. When I called him on November 2—the Catholic holiday of All Souls' Day—he told me that he had been to church, and that the priest had mentioned that it was customary on that day to visit the graves of loved ones. It was a casual remark, but for Steven it could not have felt more insistent if it had been received at gunpoint. Horrified by how strong his illness had become, he found himself behind the wheel of his car on the road to the cemetery. Standing above the graves of his parents, Steven began seriously to consider suicide for the first time in years.

Alarmed, and not knowing what to do from so far away, I called Steven's brother Bill. He drove over to visit Steven whose suicidal thoughts seemed to abate for a time. But the approach of Christmas, which he was to spend single for the first time in years, only made matters worse again. When I spoke to Steven in late January 2003—more than six months after the surgery—he told me he was more symptomatic and more depressed than he had ever before been in his life.

I spoke to Steven once a month during 2003. Slowly his depression settled to a manageable level and his suicidal thoughts receded. But a disappointment remained. As I write, in January 2004, he has still not benefited from his surgery. The question, of course, is, why? There are three possibilities.

The first is that Steven did not pursue follow-up behavioural treatments—a crucial partner in the efficacy of psychosurgery. In the wake of his divorce he was forced to drop his private health-insurance policy. He is now on public assistance and so cannot afford the cost of therapy. That no one predicted this over the many months that Steven was evaluated for surgery, both locally and in Boston, is frustrating, but it is hard to find a culprit. Procedures like cingulotomy are available only at certain medical centres and those centres effectively act as outside contractors. Though the doctors at Mass General work hard to follow the progress of the patients who come in for cingulotomy, their efforts are thwarted by distance and by the fact that once a patient leaves he is no longer in their care.

The second possible reason for the failure of Steven's operation is simply that the treatment itself was inadequate—too weak or too unsophisticated to combat a condition as severe as Steven's. In an article in the journal *CNS Spectrums* in 2000, Cosgrove wrote: 'One valid criticism of psychosurgery is that the theoretical basis of surgical intervention for the treatment of psychiatric illness is not well-established. Even though the scientific evidence implicates the limbic system and its interconnections in the pathophysiology of major psychiatric disorders, the neuroanatomical and neurochemical basis of emotion in health and disease remains undefined.'

Then there is the third possibility: that Steven is simply one of those unlucky people for whom nothing will work. This possibility is, after all, implicit in the conditions of patients who travel halfway across the country at great financial and emotional cost to seek out a treatment that, to most people, belongs to a more barbaric era. They suffer from a disease about which relatively little is known and for which there is no known cure.

Steven R.'s current apartment has no front yard, and so the problem of leaf-clearing has been solved. But equally troubling compulsions remain. Today Steven typically gets up before dawn, sometimes as early as 2 a.m., so that he will have enough time for the hours it takes him to shower and shave and clean. He then goes outside to the apartment building's parking lot and scours the asphalt for nails and screws that might pop a tyre ('Why are you doing that?' one tenant asked him. 'That's why we have a super.')

In the early afternoon, Steven eats lunch and then searches the floor on his hands and knees for crumbs. The remainder of the day is spent on more cleaning: dusting, vacuuming, soaping, scrubbing, disinfecting. He is in bed by seven, exhausted by the day's work, anticipating the next.

Lately, Steven has seemed more hopeful, more defiant of his fate. In lieu of formal treatment, he has devised his own cognitive therapy: he uses his obsessions against himself. For example, he decides, 'If I clean that table one more time, my parents will go to hell.' It is a dangerous gambit, one that in the past has backfired on him, for in giving in he is left more distraught than he was before. Recently, I asked Steven if the technique has been working. 'It's hard to tell,' he said. 'I have to work at it. I have to work for little improvements. I just hope it will help.' □

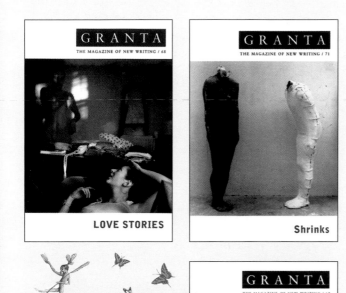

SAVE OVER 40%!

Each quarterly issue of *Granta* features a rich variety of stories, in fiction, memoir, reportage and photography—often collected under a theme, like those shown overleaf. Each issue is produced as a high-quality paperback book, because writing this good, deserves nothing less. Subscribers get *Granta* delivered to them at home, at a substantial discount. Why not join them. Or give a subscription to a friend, relative or colleague? (Or, given these low prices, do both!)

GRANTA 'ESSENTIAL READING.'

OBSERVER

ORDER FORM

I'D LIKE TO SUBSCRIBE FOR MYSELF FOR:
- ◯ 1 year (4 issues) at just £26.95
- ◯ 2 years (8 issues) at just £50
- ◯ 3 years (12 issues) at just £70

START SUBSCRIPTION WITH ◯ this issue ◯ next issue

I'D LIKE TO GIVE A SUBSCRIPTION FOR:
- ◯ 1 year (4 issues) at just £26.95
- ◯ 2 years (8 issues) at just £50
- ◯ 3 years (12 issues) at just £70

START SUBSCRIPTION WITH ◯ this issue ◯ next issue

MY DETAILS (please supply even if ordering a gift): Mr/Ms/Mrs/Miss _____

_____

Country _____ Postcode _____

GIFT RECIPIENT'S DETAILS (if applicable): Mr/Ms/Mrs/Miss _____

_____

Country _____ Postcode _____

04CBG85

TOTAL* £_____ paid by ◯ £ cheque enclosed (to 'Granta') ◯ Visa/Mastercard/AmEx:

card no: __ __ __ __ __ __ __ __ __ __ __ __ __ __ __ __

expires: __ __ / __ __ signature: _____

* POSTAGE. The prices stated include UK postage. For the rest of Europe, please add £8 (per year). For the rest of the world, please add £15 (per year). DATA PROTECTION. Please tick here if you do not want to receive occasional mailings from compatible publishers. ◯

➡ POST ('Freepost' in the UK) to: Granta, 'Freepost', 2/3 Hanover Yard, Noel Road, London N1 8BR. PHONE/FAX: In the UK: FreeCall 0500 004 033 (phone & fax); outside the UK: tel 44 (0)20 7704 9776, fax 44 (0)20 7704 0474 EMAIL: subs@granta.com

GOOD FATHER
David J. Spear

David J. Spear

My father was up early. Everything was in place: his books in their bag; each prayer and reading marked; his shoes shined, his shirt and collar, his cassock and cope pressed. He sat calmly on the couch. He was always very confident but also very humble and caring before leaving for church. When it was time he would go to the car and sit inside and in his silence, alone, he would heed the call to serve. Occasionally, when I had forgotten his pre-church routine and would ask my mother, 'Where's dad?', she would reply, 'Your father's in the car, which means it's time to go.'

For most of his adult life, my father John Spear was an Episcopalian priest. He was ordained in 1948 in Hartford, Connecticut and his life in the church took him first to Manhattan and Brooklyn, then to missions in Panama, Wisconsin and Texas.

I am the oldest of his five children and I realized very early that, for me, the church resembled a stage. As his son, I saw what went on behind the scenes, but I could also watch the liturgical drama taking place before the altar. I got used to the figure of my father—his biretta, white robes and bright-coloured cope—bringing up the rear of the procession behind the cross and the feeling of tension that the beginning of a church service brings. As he passed, people would steal glimpses of him, and it was as if a piece of God in some quiet way touched them. He would approach the sanctuary, the altar bathed in light, the brightest place in the church. He would read the lessons, preach the sermon, consecrate and serve bread and wine and proclaim God's will. Lastly he would bless his flock and send them into the world. He did this in churches, in prisons and in hospital rooms. He did it for large groups of people and for a few. He did it for himself and, more importantly in his mind, 'for the greater glory of God'. After the service my father would change from black into a T-shirt and shorts. This is when I began to feel the father side of my father emerge. Often exhausted and drained, having given his energy to God and to the people, he started the journey back to us, his family.

One day in 1981 I asked my father if I could make pictures of him. He had shared his work with me and now I wanted to involve him in mine. He looked at me and winked, tilted his head and with a half smile in his soft raspy voice he said, 'Yes'. I photographed him until his life ended early on a Sunday morning in 1995. With his death, my journey with him in these pictures was done. □

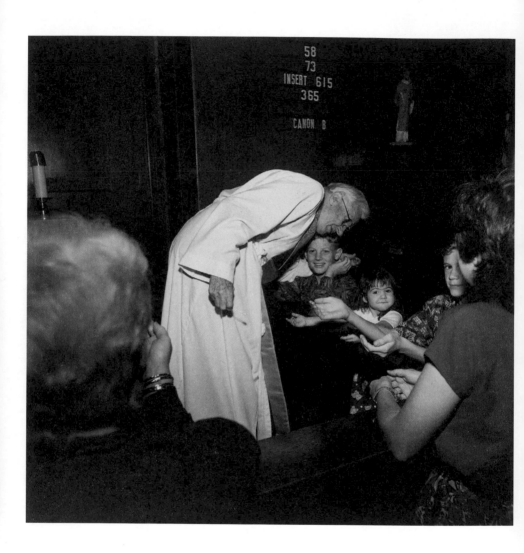

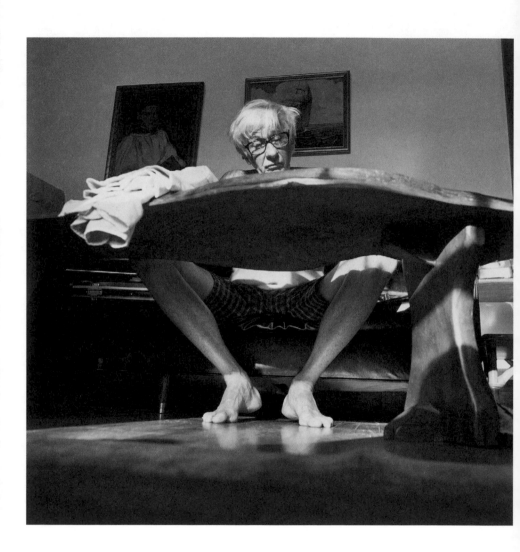

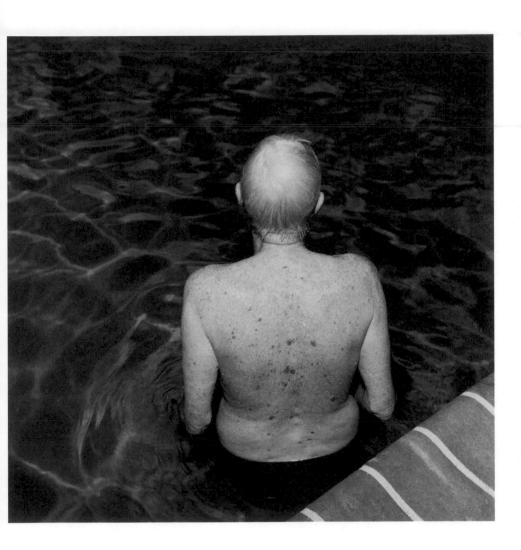

HUNTING
MIDNIGHT

Richard Zimler

AUTHOR OF *The Last Kabbalist of Lisbon*

A work of visionary scope and beauty taking the reader on an epic
adventure from 19th-century Europe to pre-Civil War America.

'I defy anyone to put
this book down. It's
a wonderful novel:
a big, bold-hearted
love story that will
sweep you up and take
you, uncomplaining,
on a journey full of
heartbreak and light.'
Nicholas Shakespeare, author
of *Bruce Chatwin* and
The Dancer Upstairs

'An American
Umberto Eco'
Francis King on Richard Zimler

£8.99 paperback

CONSTABLE
an imprint of Constable & Robinson Ltd
www.constablerobinson.com

TIGER'S GHOST
Jennie Erdal

For nearly fifteen years I wrote hundreds of letters that weren't from me. They ranged from perfunctory thank-you notes and expressions of condolence, to extensive correspondence with the great and the good: politicians, newspaper editors, bishops, members of the House of Lords. The procedure I followed with a more intimate letter was to type it up, double-spaced in large font, and print it out. My employer—the sender of the letter—would then copy it painstakingly on to embossed notepaper using a Mont Blanc pen and blotting paper, signing it with a flourish at the bottom.

Aside from the correspondence, I wrote a great many newspaper articles, speeches, the occasional poem, and several books. The books generated many reviews and profiles of the man whose name appeared on the cover. A number of literati entered into correspondence with the 'author', unaware that the replies also came from a hired hand. We make a great team, the author often said. And we did. When he was pleased, I too was pleased. We worked well together, and on the whole I was a willing partner, interested in the job and fascinated by the psychological processes involved on both sides. Over the years I learned a great deal about vanity, the desire to belong, the lengths a man will go to in pretending to be something other than he is. And the lengths a woman will go to in colluding with the pretence.

How I met my employer is a long story, and here I need to shorten it. Briefly, then, we met through my interest in Russian, and my work as a translator. It happened in 1981. I'd travelled down from St Andrews in Scotland to help him in his efforts to buy a series of paintings of Palestine by Leonid Pasternak, whose memoirs I had recently translated. I explained that Pasternak's daughters, Josephine and Lydia, had vowed never to sell their father's paintings. But he took no notice.

'You don't understand,' he said. 'I have to have them. It's imperative. They remind me of my childhood, my homeland. It's all gone now, all destroyed. *I have to have those pictures.*'

I had never met anyone so strange and flamboyant—like a rare and tropical bird. His plumage was a wonder to behold; when he flapped his wings the lining of his jacket dazzled and glinted like a prism. He wore a large sapphire in his lapel, a vivid silk tie, one pink sock, one green. There were two gold watches on his right wrist and a platinum one on his left, and on his fingers a collection of jewels—rubies, emeralds, diamonds.

We went to Oxford to see Josephine Pasternak. She was an erudite and determined woman, not easily impressed, but in the presence of this exotic creature she became girlish and coquettish. To my amazement, she sold him the paintings.

Afterwards he took me to London in his chauffeur-driven Rolls-Royce. During the journey I said very little but as we neared London he asked about my life and what had led to my interest in Pasternak. He listened intently and then surprised me by saying that he had always wanted to publish foreign language books and that I must come to work in his publishing company and manage the Russian list. There had to be a catch. If you have three children under five it is possible to believe that you will never work again, that you will never read anything other than bedtime stories. And yet here I was being offered an interesting, brain-alive job, working from home in my own time, as much as I could manage to fit in with the children. There was no catch, at least none I could see. The salary would be £5,000 plus expenses—'All my girls start on five thousand a year, isn't it?'—and I was to begin straight away. I was to travel from Scotland to attend editorial meetings, work for a day or two a month in the London offices, and the rest of the time I could be at home and keep in touch by telephone. It seemed too good to be true. We shook hands on it in the back of his Roller.

He then told the chauffeur to take a detour to his offices where he would show me round. 'You are going to enjoy working for me. I have a good feeling about it. My motto is when we work, we work, and when we play, we play. That way everybody is happy, isn't it?' There are terrible complications in the English language when it comes to inviting someone to agree with you. Most languages make do with a one-size-fits-all solution but in English there is no single phrase that can be used on all occasions to mean 'isn't that so?' And so the unsuspecting are ensnared by opting for a simple *isn't it?* when actually what is needed is an *aren't they?* or *didn't she?* or *can you?*

We arrived in a spacious penthouse overlooking the heart of Soho. The first thing I noticed were the pictures on the walls—not the gentle landscapes of the Holy Land I might have expected, but an assortment of naked or semi-naked women and several large cats clawing their way out of gilt-edged frames. But the centrepiece, mounted on the wall behind the leather-topped desk, was not a painting at all: it was a huge tiger skin complete with head. Apart from the fact that it was dead, it seemed very alive, its bold orange and black stripes setting the wall ablaze.

'You like it?' he asked, motioning me to sit down opposite him at the desk. 'I call him Kaiser. You know what is Kaiser?' And then, as if it explained everything, he added, 'My father fought on the side of the Germans in the First World War.

'I identify with the tiger,' he said, without a hint of abashment. 'The tiger eats everything, but *nothing* eats him. He will even eat a crocodile if he wants to! He is King of the Mountain, King of the Forest, King of the World.'

He drew himself up, regally, in his chair. The tiger's head was just above the talking head, its eyes shining brightly, curiously round and manlike. For just a second, in that little corner where fantasy and reality collide, the two heads merged and became one.

'What would you like me to call you?' I asked as we shook hands on parting.

'You can call me what you like,' he said. 'I shall call you Beloved—all the girls who work for me are Beloved—but you can call me whatever you want.'

'In that case,' I said, 'I shall call you Tiger.'

'I like it,' he said, and kissed my hand.

Arriving in Tiger's publishing house for the first time was like turning up in someone else's dream. It seemed a very long way down the rabbit hole. There were no familiar points of reference, no compass bearings. It felt high-voltage and slightly dangerous. The first thing to notice was that there were abnormally high levels of emotion—lots of spirited laughter, shrieking and embracing. The atmosphere seemed to teeter on the edge of hysteria, and it was hard to work out the sounds. Were they angry, or were they just loud? None of it made sense to begin with. It did not seem to accord with any place of work, real or imagined. I suppose I had the mistaken idea that only clever serious people worked with books, and that they probably operated in a quiet, meticulous and, well, bookish manner.

I had pictured earnest men of letters, old-fashioned gentlemen, slightly tweedy and with pale skin that was seldom exposed to natural light.

In fact the building sizzled with youthful vigour, in the shape of stunning, sophisticated young women. They had patrician accents, exceptional poise and uncommonly long legs. Their skin was not pale but healthy and bronzed. And there wasn't a man in sight. Indeed the mythical Martian, if he had happened to drop in, could not have imagined that women had ever been oppressed, or that their role had once been secondary and passive. Here in this office, in 1981, women ruled. Yet there were no bluestockings, only silk stockings.

The premises were in a run-down part of Soho and extended in a ramshackle way over two buildings, separated by an Italian restaurant and a hairdresser's salon. A faint odour, a mixture of garlic and hair lotion, hung in the air. The offices covered four floors, with staircases slightly aslant and walls off-centre. The furnishings were quite shabby and a layer of black London dust rested on the surfaces. Everywhere there were piles of books and high-rise manuscripts. And, curiously for a publishing house, there were clothes suspended in doorways and draped from light fittings, as if the premises might actually be shared with a dressmaker. Boas and belts hung on the backs of chairs, and on several doors there were coat-hangers bearing evening gowns and stylish jackets. In the loo I found underwear, tights and nail varnish.

Tiger had a conglomerate of companies connected with publishing, fashion, films and theatre. He had been dubbed 'a cultural tycoon' by *The Times* newspaper and he lived up to this dubbing assiduously. The ethos in the empire was not one of profit and loss, but of name and fame. Like its proprietor, the publishing house was *sui generis*, and it had a reputation quite disproportionate to its size. It was known to be radical and risk-taking. Tiger took chances with books and seemed to act mostly on impulse. He would meet people at parties and sign them on the spot. Sudden ideas were converted into improbable publishing ventures, and books were invented that ought never to have existed. He acted speedily and never flinched from taking a decision. He loved controversy, courted it indeed, and any whiff of scandal merely strengthened his resolve to publish. 'Let them sue! Let them sue!' he would say, rubbing his hands together. 'But I am a fighter, and I fight to win!' Tiger basked in this image, and we basked in it too. By association, we felt as if we were also fighters, that we too would win, and although at editorial meetings there was hardly ever a discernible rational plan, the atmosphere was highly charged and there was a lot of heady talk about noble ideals. There was, too, a good deal of frivolity, but the frivolity was curiously serious, and much of the time we behaved as if we might be engaged in decisions of supreme importance.

'Do you like my girls?' Tiger asked not long after I had started my new job. He was wearing crocodile-skin shoes and odd socks in purple and yellow. 'They are amazing, isn't it?' His girls were scarcely ever out of the gossip columns and they always knew somebody who knew somebody. Their most important work, as Tiger himself affirmed, was done out of office hours—at dinner parties, first nights, charity events, gallery openings, fashion shoots and hunt balls—for they ensured that news of his latest exploits was trawled through London's most fashionable hotspots. The smart outfits hanging from the office doors began to make sense.

I was introduced to Cosima, Selina, Lucinda, Davina, Samantha and two Sophias. There seemed to be a conspicuous homogeneity of Christian names. Surely there ought to be a collective noun for this phenomenon, I thought, this concentration of cognates. An assonance perhaps? An artillery? I then met Andrea (a Baroness) and Sabrina (an heiress), and in due course, Alethea, Nigella, Eliza, Candida, Mariella, Zelfa, Georgia, Henrietta and Arabella. It was a lot to take in, the sort of list I would have been made to learn by rote at school, like books of the Bible or irregular Latin verbs. When walking around London, I sometimes recited the names to myself, trying to fix them in my head, marvelling at the sound patterns they made. After a while I found it was possible to turn them into the wonderful metrical patterns of English poetry—for example, you could get a perfect trochaic tetrameter if you started with:

Arabella, Henrietta
Cosima, Lucinda, Georgia

as in *The Song of Hiawatha*:

By the shores of Gitche Gumee
By the shining Big-Sea-Water.

It was clear that I did not belong in this world. I was looked upon, with some justification, as one of Tiger's whims; I lived in Scotland after all, and I turned up only for editorial meetings, staying for just a few days at any one time. Even then it was clear that I was just passing through this foreign land—I was in it, but not of it. Besides, I didn't know anyone. Not even anyone who knew anyone. It was a strange place for me to dip into and out of, and its sheer otherness never lost its impact. At home in Scotland, there were two small children and a baby, the centre of my universe. But in the London office I never mentioned the fact that I was a mother. I was at pains to fit in, and I sensed that talk about children would not be wise. I therefore pretended to be someone else, someone I was not.

My work as a translator fed into this pretence. To be any good as a translator you have to do a kind of disappearing act. I liked being invisible, absorbing the text and living with it a little, then turning it into something new—unique but not original, creative but not inventive. As the years passed, I moved sideways and took another sort of invisible presence, one that also tried to catch the voice of the author and be a conduit for his creation. I became Tiger's ghost.

Our partnership produced lots of newspaper articles, interviews with well-known figures and several non-fiction books. But although they brought Tiger a sense of fulfilment, there was no lasting contentment. Eventually he became convinced that the way ahead for us lay in a different sort of publication. Interviews, journalism, book reviews were all very well, but *the real test* was the novel.

'We need to evolve,' he said.

I did not demur.

It is 1994 and we are in Tiger's house in France. Tiger believes that France is the best place in the world to create a work of art. 'We will have everything we need—the best food, the finest wine, a high-tech music system, a studio to work in, the fresh Dordogne air.'

How to write a novel? How to write someone else's novel? These two questions seem absolutely central. I wonder how I have arrived at this point without actually meaning to.

'What sort of novel are we thinking about?' I ask.

'We are thinking about a beautiful novel, very beautiful,' he says, and he looks somewhere into the middle distance, smiling rapturously, already transported by the sheer imagined beauty of it. 'And it will have a beautiful cover. We will make sure of that.' He taps out the last six words on the table.

'But what genre are we talking about? Are we thinking of a romantic novel? A thriller?' (These conversations are always conducted in the first person plural. The idiosyncratic use of pronouns is part of the charade and has become second nature.)

'It will be thrilling, oh yes. And also romantic. *Very* romantic. Oh, yes.'

'So, a love story then?'

'But of course! It *has* to be a love story. People associate me with love. I am *famous* for love.'

'What sort of love story do we have in mind?' I ask, as if we are discussing wallpaper or home furnishings and he has to pick one from a limited range. 'Is the love requited or unrequited?'

'Definitely requited. Oh yes, very requited.'

'And who are the characters?'

Even by our standards this is becoming an odd exchange.

'Sweetie,' he says, his tone long-suffering as if humouring an imbecile. He takes hold of my hand in a kindness-to-dumb-animals sort of way. 'It *has* to be the love between a man and a woman. Do you think I could write about *poofters*? No, it has to be a man and a woman—a beautiful woman and very sexy. There will be lots of sex, but very distinguished. We will do the sex beautifully. Isn't it?'

'Long? Short?' I'm feeling desperate now.

He strokes his chin, weighing up the possibilities. 'Not too long, not too short.'

'And do we have a storyline? Do we have any idea of what it is *about*?'

'Of course, Beloved! I have thought of *everything*.' He squeals the last word in a spasm of exuberance. 'Let me tell you the idea. It is very simple. There is a man...he is like me somewhat...he is married...he falls in love with a woman...there is a huge passion...and then...well, we will see what happens after that, isn't it?'

There is another pause while I weigh things up. Then: 'Does he tell his wife? About the huge passion, I mean.'

'Darling, are you *mad*?' Tiger points a finger to his temple and screws it from side to side. 'Why would he tell her? Why would he hurt her?'

How to proceed? Write what you know, they always say. But what did I know? Suddenly I knew nothing. In a bid to avert panic I decided to make a list of things in my favour. The list was not long but it was a start:

1. I have written a lot already (just not a novel).
2. I have read lots of novels.

For the first of these to count as an advantage you have to believe that all writing comes from the same place. I'm not sure that I do believe that. Writing prose is not writing fiction. The most I could hope for was that the experience of writing journalism, literary pieces, book reviews, and so on would act as some sort of training ground for writing a novel.

As for reading a lot, there is, sadly, no causal connection between the fact of having read fiction and the ability to write fiction. I know this at an instinctive level, and I think perhaps I have always known it, but this did not prevent me gathering together dozens of novels and taking them to France in my suitcase. It was an eclectic heap, selected from my shelves of paperbacks at home. I did this partly in the hope of discovering how to write a novel, and partly because I thought the systematic approach might compensate for lack of inspiration. The next two days were spent dipping into books by Penelope Fitzgerald, Anne Tyler, Carol Shields, Beryl Bainbridge, Alison Lurie, Anne Fine, Jennifer Johnston. At the end of the second day I realized that I had been reading only women writers, surely a foolish exercise if I was to learn to write like a man. For the next two days, fighting off a slight feeling of frenzy, I read William Trevor, John Updike, Ian McEwan, Tim Parks, John Banville.

What I discovered was that when time changes are handled well, you scarcely notice them; as a reader, you are perfectly happy to move through days and weeks and years, in either direction, provided your author has a safe pair of hands. The devices are subtle—the judicious use of a pluperfect tense, for instance, or the foreshortening of a character's history. The same applies to point of view: the narrator—even when the story is told in the first person—has various tricks up his sleeve to allow the reader to know what the other characters are thinking and feeling. And the handling of dialogue was a revelation. Critics are fond of saying, 'The dialogue doesn't work,' but when it works well it is, paradoxically, a kind of dialogue that people *believe* is spoken, or feel comfortable with, not what actually is spoken, which would not work at all. Often the very best dialogue is not in the least authentic.

I needed a beginning, a middle and an end. I needed them badly. I also needed at least two characters in order for the story to function at even a basic level—the main character, who was to be 'our hero', and the woman with whom he was to fall in love. The man, according to Tiger, was married, so perhaps his wife would also play a part in the story? Which made a total of three. Three characters don't sound terribly daunting—not as daunting as, say, four—but three characters can be quite daunting enough, especially when none has yet taken shape.

From one or two remarks Tiger had made I had a hunch that he already identified with the main character in the book. Confirmation came from an unexpected source, an interview with Tiger that appeared in the *Scotsman* newspaper around that time.

> … His whole demeanour suggests passion constrained. He cannot sit still for long. He talks quickly, almost imploringly, and the words tumble over each other… From now on he is going to be a novelist. This is what is fresh. This is what is *now*. 'It is not going to be a *beeg* novel… It will be more a philosophical and a literary book. It's about my love of women and what would happen—what the consequences would be of such a love if…well, anyway, it's about a man who loves two women.'

'*My* love of women.' There, I knew it. A dead giveaway. If it was a slip, it was surely a telling slip. There was now little doubt in my mind that Tiger saw himself as the protagonist. In some ways this simplified things—at least there was an abundance of source material to work on. But I soon realized that the fictional version of Tiger would have to be based on his own self-image. He could not be, like the most interesting characters in fiction, seriously flawed. No, our hero would have to be sensitive, compassionate, successful in business, of strong moral fibre, devout, impassioned and wise. He would probably also be something of a self-styled philosopher and he would have to have a great capacity for love.

And so, to work. I sketched out a plan in which the main character would be a wealthy businessman whose ordered life would be turned upside down by an extramarital affair. This would arrive like a bolt from the blue and would coincide with a crisis in his life—the death of his beloved mother. I tried this out on Tiger. He pulled a face. Something wasn't right. It wasn't immediately clear what it was.

'Darleeng, PLEEEase, do we have to have the death?' He spoke imploringly, drawing out each word.

'You don't like the death?'

'I don't like the death.'

'Well,' I said, caught a little off-guard, 'I do think we need to have some sort of crisis, and a funeral is always quite a good focal point in a novel.' Then, gaining in confidence, 'Also, the emotional upheaval associated with bereavement would be a neat way of allowing the affair to take place. It would make it more understandable in a way.' Now the *coup de grâce*: 'I mean, we don't want to make him an uncaring bastard who cheats on his wife, do we?'

The mention of an uncaring bastard would surely be enough to win him round, but instead he pulled another face. I wasn't sure what was bothering him. He stroked his lower jaw and made a prolonged moaning noise, the sort you might make when someone is sticking a needle in your arm. Eventually he said, 'It's no good. We have to find another crisis. You see, my mother is still alive and, well, I don't want to upset her.'

This was endearing in its way, but not endearing enough to jettison the planned death. By now I had convinced myself I needed this death. We seemed to be nearing the edge of the unsayable, but I decided to say it anyway. Gently but firmly, I suggested that it was important that the life of the main character was not matched in every single aspect with his own, indeed, it was essential that it wasn't; that the proposed book should be, in essence, a work of imagination; that it would be a pity if the critics dismissed it simply as a replica of his own life rather than a serious literary endeavour;

and that it could quite properly reflect his own concerns whilst at the same time retaining its own artistic integrity. After which, he agreed—albeit somewhat ungraciously—to the death of his mother.

For the next week or so, I tried to free up the flow by telling myself that it was just another job that had to be done, that none of this mattered, that I was free to write anything that came into my head. But the fact that I was writing with a mask on bedevilled the whole process.

I decided to call the main character Carlo—I had once known an Italian student named Carlo—and make him a successful advertising executive living in London. The novel would begin with Carlo's return to his native Italy to attend his mother's funeral. The reason for giving him dual nationality was twofold: it fitted very generally with Tiger's own background, and it would act as a metaphor for further conflict and dichotomy. The trip to Italy was surely a stroke of genius: it would allow for our hero's journey in all senses—physical, mental, spiritual and emotional. It would also enable the affair to take place in the hot and steamy Mediterranean climate and, finally, it would conveniently provide the backdrop of Catholicism—Tiger's professed faith—which would in turn introduce the familiar tensions between faith and reason and passion. I warmed to my theme. So far, so good.

Predictably, I agonized about the opening line. Again, it is a matter of confidence and belief. When you are searching your mind for that first sentence it is difficult not to be assailed by truths universally acknowledged and the similarity between all happy families. And easy to think that anything less brilliantly epigrammatic is small potatoes. The opening line also marks you. It can imprison you in a style and tone that are not easily shaken off. I pondered the possibilities, weighed and considered, wavered and faltered to the point of paralysis. Eventually, desperately, I wrote the first sentence: *'Carlo surveys the land of his birth and contemplates death.'*

It would do. I tried to think myself into what I imagined Tiger's style might be, but the more I searched for his voice, the more I caught my own breaking through; the more I tried to realize his literary aspirations, the more my own seemed to intrude. The novel did not grow organically; it was force-fed and boosted with steroids. Set pieces and ruminations on the human condition were thrown about like salt. It became a stilted, studied thing. I was consumed by doubt. The characters were not 'real'; they were mouthpieces for various ideas, which shoved them around and kicked them to the ground. André Gide said something to the effect that the true novelist listens to his characters and watches how they behave, whereas the bad novelist simply constructs them and controls them. Without a doubt, I was constructing and controlling.

Almost the one thing I didn't mind was that it was to be a love story. After all, what else is there? It's only half a life without love. And a novel would be surely nothing without it. The prospect of writing about love was even faintly appealing. It is one of those eternal themes that can be endlessly reworked. But every silver lining has a cloud; as I had feared it might, love was coming perilously close to denoting sex.

Tiger was obsessively concerned with its place in the novel. Each day when I returned from the studio he would ask, 'Have we done the fucky-fucky yet?' I counselled against it, as anyone in my place would have done, suggesting that discretion was the better part of ardour. But he pooh-poohed and said that a novel by him would be *unimaginable* without sex.

'Beloved, we *need* the jig-jig! Don't you *see*?'

He laughed and clapped his hands, willing me to share his enthusiasm. But I didn't see.

I held out for a long time, pointing out that countless authors had believed they could 'do' sex in a novel and had ended up falling into a terrible black hole. I reminded him of the *Literary Review*'s Bad Sex Prize, awarded annually by Auberon Waugh, a friend of Tiger's and a man who had made it his mission to discourage the tasteless and perfunctory use of sexual description in the modern novel. Surely he agreed with Bron? I argued that sex in the novel was nearly always bad sex, and that it was best avoided. I said that not even fine writers could manage it without sounding ridiculous or absurd or embarrassing.

'You are talking like a *nun*!' he said. 'What's got into you? Trust me, beloved, we will do the sex beautifully! It will be very distinguished.'

The literary treatment of sex is beset with vexed questions. First there is the problem of getting the characters to take their clothes off—

buttons and zips and hooks can be so awkward, and you couldn't ever allow a man to keep his socks on. Then there are the body parts which either have to be named (very unwise) or else replaced with dubious symbolism. And what about the verbs, the doing words? How can you choose to make people *enter, writhe, thrash, smoulder, grind, merge, thrust*—and still hope to salvage a smidgen of self-respect? Not easily. If you doubt me, try it. The sound effects are even worse—*squealing, screaming, the shriek of coitus*. No, the English language does not lend itself to realistic descriptions of sex. We are too used to irony. The alternative is to use metaphors, but metaphors are just asking for more trouble—all that edge of volcano and burning fire stuff.

What to do? What to *do*? Then, a sudden flash of brilliance, and I *knew* what to do. Tiger had an abhorrence of bodily fluids. His hatred of people who coughed or sniffed or spluttered was legendary. Provided that the sex scenes could be made sufficiently liquid, he might decide to abandon them altogether. *Nil desperandum*. Bodily fluids would be my deliverance. I set about my purpose with a devil-may-care recklessness.

> Strong and gentle as the waves, he swells and moves towards her
> like the sea to the shore. He dips and dives, eagerly but hesitantly,
> still fearing rebuff, until that moment of absolute clarification,
> when her ardour too is confirmed beyond doubt. Her lissom limbs
> quiver and enfold him into the sticky deliciousness of her sex.

Of course, one thing led to another, and it was hard not to get carried away. Tiger, far from feeling squeamish, seemed relieved that at last the lovers had got down to the business. I pressed on, telling myself it was a means to an end. He would soon change his mind. Every new splash or splosh was a fresh hell. But still Tiger held out. There was no capitulation. In fact he was exultant. He opened a bottle of Château Margaux and we drank to sex. 'Bravo!' he said—his highest accolade. This wasn't working out as planned. I would try one more act of sabotage. I had to make certain this time. Go for broke:

> They play with each other like wet seal pups, their bodies making
> succulent, slipping sounds. With his tongue he caresses her and
> spins a silver spider's web from the threads of her wetness. The

pathway to heaven pouts like the calyx of a flower turned to the sun, the inner petals drenched in nectar. Her beautiful mound rises and falls as she rubs herself against his chin.

As she trembles and gasps and comes, he feels a surge of happiness and an infusion of supreme power. Her juices trickle down like a cluster of stars from the firmament. He can do anything now. He is God in one of his incarnations, spreading love and joy. Her amber thighs rear on either side like the waters parted for Moses. He rises and enters her.

At least four things happened as a result of all this incontinence. Tiger was overjoyed; he raised my salary; the *Sunday Times* described the novel as 'a strong contender' for the *Literary Review*'s Bad Sex Prize; and my teenaged children were mortified.

The novel was launched in the spring of 1995. It was a glittering occasion with all the usual suspects, beautiful creatures plucked from London's fashionable set. Tiger had a well-deserved reputation for throwing the best parties in town. Lots of glamour and glitz and permanent tans. People asked if I knew Tiger and if I had read his novel. Afterwards I returned to Scotland and waited for the patter of tiny reviews. On the whole, the critics were kind; there was scarcely any venom, and derision was reserved for the sex scenes. According to the *TLS* reviewer, 'It is only in these scenes that the author comes close to losing control of his spare, precise prose.' The *Sunday Telegraph* reviewer wrote, 'I prefer to forget those brief, explicit embarrassments,' while another review was entitled simply: 'LESS SEX PLEASE.'

In the summer of 1995, just a few months after the publication of Tiger's first novel, we were back in France. We were there to begin another novel. It was difficult to feel cheerful about the prospect. Indeed I could scarcely bear the idea of going through the whole process again. But Tiger had other ideas. We had had one of those 'repetitive strain' conversations in which Tiger did a lot of repetition and I took the strain.

'If we do just one, nobody will bloody believe us,' he said.

'What do you mean exactly?' (I often asked this.)

'What do I *mean*?'

'Well, what is it that nobody will believe?'

'What *is* it that nobody will believe?'

'Yes, what *is* it?'

'What *is* it? I'll tell you *exactly* what it is. I'll tell you *exactly* what nobody will believe. Nobody will ever believe we can *do* another one. Isn't it?'

'Well, *is* that really so important?'

'Is it important? Is it *important*? Darling, what's the matter with you? What's got into you?'

'Well, is it important? What people think, I mean.'

'I don't believe I'm hearing this! Of course it's important. They won't take us seriously! Don't you see? They will think the first one was a fluke!'

I set about the second novel with a joyless heart. This only made things worse because Tiger loathed low spirits in others. It was *joie de vivre* he loved—he often said so—and he could not bear even the slightest lack of enthusiasm for something he favoured. Whenever he detected reluctance on my part he would put on his evangelist hat and set about converting me. Before too long it would usually strike me that the idea I was rejecting was preferable to the process of indoctrination, so I would cave in.

With this new novel he had explained that I could have *carte blanche*—'You can do *whatever* you like,' he had said, and he clapped his hands together like a pair of cymbals, sealing his lavishness. He then sat back in his chair and smiled benignly. His expression was one of utter benefaction. It was not possible for a man to be more reasonable.

But it wasn't true. It turned out there was a requirement, though to hear him, you might easily have imagined it was nothing at all. He was talking it down so much—'It's just a small idea, that's all, it's not anything *big*'—and as he continued it got so very small that I imagined it as a tiny dot on an old television screen, disappearing into the void. Alas, this scarcely-a-requirement-at-all, this small thinglet, this little idealet, slowly began to take on monstrous dimensions. As before, there were to be two women and a man. The man, so Tiger explained, was to be the lover of both women, and each woman would be aware of the other and quite relaxed about the sharing arrangement. The women were to be cousins who had been born on the same day—'Under the same star sign, so they're more like sisters,' said Tiger. Sounds quite manageable so far, I thought. There followed a lot of eager talk about how very close sisters can be, how twins can feel each other's pain, how they seem almost to inhabit each other's bodies. 'It's like they're one person, not two,' he said.

'Yes…' I said, beginning to wonder where all this leading, looking out for the catch. I was not prepared for what came next.

'So,' he said, clasping and unclasping his large soft hands, working up to the *pièce de résistance*, 'when the one girl gets *orgamsi* the other gets *orgamsi* also!'

'How do you mean exactly?' I asked. I felt sure I had missed something. I took a few moments to consider the possibilities before venturing, 'Are we talking about simultaneous orgasm?'

'Precisely!' he purred in a go-to-the-top-of-the-class way. 'Simultaneous *orgamsi*. You've got it! Bravo!'

But I knew I hadn't got it. Not really anyway. As far as I was aware, simultaneous orgasm happened—if it happened at all—between the two principal players, as it were. It was not something that could be dispensed at will to a third party, not even a close cousin.

'And how do you see that working exactly?' I asked, matter-of-factly. We might have been discussing a new business plan or profit-sharing scheme. 'Is the man stimulating both of them in such a way that they climax at the same time?'

Wrong question. Tiger smote his brow with the palm of his hand. It was his God-protect-me-from-imbeciles gesture. '*Daaarleeeng*, you don't understand!' He was right. I didn't. I had led a sheltered life. 'The women are not *together*! They are *miles* apart!' He was shouting now. He always shouted when stupid people failed to grasp the essential point.

'I'm afraid,' I said—and for once perhaps I was a little afraid—'you're going to have to spell it out. I don't quite get it.'

He rose from his desk and started pacing up and down, his body language a narrative in itself. He enfolded himself in his own arms and rocked slightly from side to side, the way a man might move about a padded cell, trying to control the violent turmoil within. He fixed me with a look that said, how can you be so dim? The explanation when it came was bad-tempered and delivered *de haut en bas*. The gist of it was that the two women would be so closely harmonized, so much in tune with one another that, even if they were separated physically, even by oceans and by continents, they would be capable of experiencing the heights of pleasure at the same time. As he spoke he became more and more animated, his tiger eyes shining brightly in his head, his whole body in motion, semaphoric, balletic. And since I had been so obtuse, he did not mince matters. The speaking got plainer. To remove any lingering doubt he spelled it out: 'Look, it's simple! If one woman is in London, say, and the other is in New York, when he is fucking the one in London, the one in New York feels it in her fanny also!

'Now do you understand?' he said, regaining his composure.

'I understand,' I said.

I sat alone in the studio wondering what to do, how to begin. It was a blow to be required to write another novel, especially so soon after the first. I felt curiously depleted, emptied of the will to repeat the exercise. If I was to commit to another novel, I would have to move away from what I saw as the flat, two-dimensional, soulless canvas. It had to be something layered and fully imagined, something more from the heart.

Then again, whose heart? Can one write from another person's heart? I am not sure it can be done. You can get all kitted out, only there's nowhere to go. Personal experience, which includes the imagination and what feeds it, is essentially the base people write from. And personal experience is highly specific, each take on the world unique. You cannot write another's experience, only your own. Of course you can try, but it will always be in some sense attenuated. Without a doubt there is something intrinsically contradictory about ghosting a novel. It is *possible* to fake fiction, but it is difficult to see how it can be meaningful or eloquent. You have to write from inside your own skin, otherwise there is too much of a psychological struggle. It's like trying to fake sincerity.

Being intent on getting the job done makes you concentrate on the technical problems, but it leaves no room for the spirit of the thing. You report for duty each day and you hope that the target number of words will be written. You consider the architecture of the book, the dramatic structure, the characters, the voice. The trouble is that you don't believe the voice, and you don't quite trust the characters, and you certainly don't suffer with them. This time I wanted to change all that. I wanted the writing to be alive at the centre, not just a technical exercise. I wanted it to be something that sprang from my own energy. I had to write about something that moved me.

In 1987 I read Ian McEwan's *The Child in Time*, a chilling piece of fiction that starts with the disappearance of a young child, Kate, while on an ordinary shopping expedition to the supermarket with her father. The assumption is that the child has been snatched, but there are no clues, no leads, no ransom demand. No body is ever found. When I was reading *The Child in Time*, my own daughter Kate was just seven years old and this no doubt led me to identify even more closely with the story. The book addresses larger political and social themes, but over time I forgot them. What held me, and continued to hold me, was the personal story of grief and anguish. I was struck by the way in which happy lives can be turned by a single moment in time into the bleakest of landscapes. Ian McEwan's spare prose is perfectly honed to capture the essence of despair and the concomitant disintegration of ordinary lives. It is a consummate execution of sorrow, perhaps the cruellest sorrow of all. It seemed to me the grief was almost too sharp to be borne. I was tormented by the book, and it went on haunting me for years.

The snatching of a child—how could one bear it? How could one go on? How might one go about surviving a loss of that order? At that point, in 1987, during the immediate aftermath of my marriage breakdown, I felt stripped bare by events and had the instincts of a nervous animal protecting its young. It was difficult to dislodge a vague sense of calamities to come. I could drive myself mad with imagined tragedies. They arrived in my mind in no particular sequence, and no effort of will seemed strong enough to keep them at bay. It felt like continuing to throw up long after you believed you'd finished.

Eight years on I sat in the cool blue light of the studio on a hillside in the Dordogne, and as I looked beyond the trees and back in time, the scent of that fear came wafting back. It had lost its sharpness, but I knew it was still fetid in the memory trenches. I would start Tiger's second novel with the disappearance of a child and see where it led. I opened the laptop on the desk and typed the first paragraph:

The summer's afternoon when it happened was to be etched, as if by a splinter of glass, in the hearts of all those who were there. The memory was validated by pain and the sharp sounds that broke a perfect Sunday in two. It was like a pencil snapping, and its jagged edges stuck out, waiting to snag anyone who came near.

A week or two later, the nuts and bolts were in place. The setting, the main characters and the voice had all been decided, though there was a whiff of compromise about all three. I had started out in the first person, hoping to achieve the immediacy and conviction that can come with a first-person perspective. But it felt too personal, too intimate, and I soon abandoned it for the third person. I had also thought of setting the story in Scotland, but that too would have been too subjective, and besides, Tiger would have hated it. Although he claimed to love Scotland, it was purely an abstract love, for he regarded it as a curious foreign land, quite inscrutable, and much more 'abroad' than further-flung places. So instead I chose a sleepy Oxfordshire village in middle-class England. This is not my territory at all, but it allowed me to make one of the characters an academic at Oxford University (my daughter was there at that time and I had come to know it a little), and also to set a dramatic scene in the Ashmolean Museum (where I had first seen paintings by Pasternak). I drew up a list of main characters: the two married couples, their remaining two children, the vicar next door and his long-suffering wife.

One of the more pressing difficulties with the book was that I did not feel confident about being able to fulfil Tiger's orgasmic stipulation. I had hinted to him that there might be complications in the literary execution, but he continued to regard it as a *sine qua non* of the action. I had been proceeding on the assumption that Tiger's idea was a male sexual fantasy. Men love the idea of having a third person in on the act—or so women think. A little elementary research, however, led me to believe that it was not an absolutely standard male fantasy, yet I still thought it would be best to treat it as fantasy in the novel. I broached this line of reasoning as delicately as possible, but Tiger was having none of it.

'What nonsense!' he said.

'But surely, it's the only way,' I said. 'Otherwise it won't be plausible.'

'How can it be plausible if he doesn't do it? It can only be plausible if he *does* do it. Why don't you see that? We have to make him do it.'

There was a lot at stake here. I had to hold my ground.

'If he just thinks about it,' I said, 'if it stays in his head, then it will be more convincing. People have all sorts of strange fantasies. The imagination is a weird place. I think we can make it work at that level.'

'But who are we going to convince if it's all in his head? It will only convince him! And what's the good in that? He has to do it! It has to happen! For people to believe it, it *has* to happen! Isn't it? What's the matter with you? What is this nonsense?'

His heart was clearly set on it. The book would be a travesty without it—Hamlet without the Prince. Much of his eagerness, I believed, could be put down to his identification with the protagonist. As had happened first time round, he was projecting himself into the principal role.

Each day after I had finished in the studio he would ask for a progress report. 'Have we reached the *orgamsi* yet?' he would enquire with dispiriting regularity, although it is only fair to say that the question never seemed salacious or even coarse. It was more like a child asking that familiar question from the back seat of the car: 'Are we nearly there?' If I even hinted at possible difficulties, he became downcast for a moment or two before firing questions in rapid succession, all of them beginning with 'but'—his way of seeking reassurance.

'But they're not serious, these difficulties?'

'But we can solve them, no?'

'But we don't have to abandon the plan?'

'But we will finish soon, isn't it?'

Tiger was obviously keen to break new ground, in the sense that our hero, and he alone, would be capable of producing this amazing synchronous effect on two women in different parts of the globe. Of course, illusions have to be rendered, but how do you stop yourself from pricking them? As I understood it, the joint cousinly climax was contingent upon the exceptional closeness of the women in question, so, unless they were both virgins, not to mention unlucky in their experience of lovemaking, they must surely have climaxed concurrently before. With someone else. Someone other than our hero. And if not, why not? Thus the armature of contrivance kept breaking through, and I was continually hampered, not by a failure of nerve exactly, rather by humility before ordinary reality. An inbuilt crap detector is an awkward piece of equipment for any woman trying to carry out this kind of mandate for a man. Yet it had to be done, so I pressed on. The hero in John Banville's *Shroud* says, 'I cannot believe a word out of my own mouth,' and I suppose I had arrived at a similar position.

In the circumstances it was not an easy matter to deliver quality orgasms to those taking part in the story. And so, a compromise was reached, though it had all the drawbacks of a trade-off and no obvious benefits, at least not for Tiger, whose high hopes were cruelly thwarted. The idea of the two families remained, but I simply could not effect the needful with grown-up, sexually mature, sane adults. So instead, and in a spirit of greater realism, the cousins—together with their fanciful frolics—were switched to the younger generation.

This is how the ground was prepared: establishing the bond early on allowed it to be infinitely strengthened by the disappearance of the young boy—the brother of one of the cousins. Ordinary life is suspended after the tragedy and the days seem to merge one into another. The adults are so busy coping with their own grief that the girls—by now fifteen years of age—are left to get on with life and their own feelings largely by themselves. They befriend the boy next door, only son of the vicar who is helping the bereaved parents, and gradually they retreat together into their own world, all three bound by a common neglect.

Tiger did not conceal his disappointment. It was absolute and comprehensive.

'But they're children!' he scoffed. 'Why are we writing a children's book?'

'It's not remotely a children's book,' I said, slightly horrified. 'It's an adult book with children—young adults—in it.'

'They are *children*!' he insisted. 'They haven't even done it before!'

'That's the beauty of it,' I said, glimpsing a straw that might be clutched, 'they're not yet set in their ways.'

'And they're doing it all together! They are not apart at all. We agreed they would be miles apart! We've made it into an *orgy!*'

So sudden, this prudery. So unexpected.

'Well, it's hardly an orgy,' I said, trying to placate. 'They are just feeling their way. It's a kind of innocence in fact. And anyway they love each other.'

This was desperate stuff.

Tiger was not to be appeased. He scowled as he read the passage again. Then came another objection, overlooked the first time.

'We don't even say that the girls have *orgamsi together*. At the same time. Why don't we *say* it? How can people understand if we don't say it? We have to *say* it.'

And so we said it, but it was a terrible let-down for Tiger. It was not at all what he had dreamed of. The pinnacles reached were not transatlantic, and our hero, far from being a representation of the author, was a sixteen-year-old spotty youth.

I finished the book at home in Scotland. I travelled to London and handed it over, glad to be free of it. When I arrived back in St Andrews a few days later, a large package was waiting for me. The covering letter informed me that the author had delivered his typescript and it was now ready for editing. Could I kindly turn it round as quickly as possible?

The party to launch the book was a bizarre event for me. People asked if I'd read the new novel, and what did I think of it. Sometimes I said, yes, and that it was very good, and sometimes I said, no, but I was looking forward to it. What I said didn't matter, I told myself. But later that same evening it did matter, because Tiger took me by the arm and introduced me to one of the guests, a well-known (but not to me) literary agent.

'This is my editor,' said Tiger to well-known agent.

'But she told me five minutes ago she hadn't read your book!' said well-known agent to author.

'Bloody hell, if she hasn't read it, I'm in trouble!' said Tiger. Awkward laughter all round. Our alliance was a curious compound and we were held together by its strange elements.

The reviews of the new novel were mostly kind; by far the most interesting and favourable review came from the novelist Alice Thomas Ellis. In the *Literary Review* she wrote:

[The author] has an uncanny awareness of the atmosphere of loss, how it affects the bereaved and those on the periphery...he knows how people gather 'in small groups, like vultures sensing the presence of death. They discussed and told what they knew and what they did not know, and felt the particular dismay reserved for other people's misfortunes.' He knows that Kate moves in a 'sort of sepia fog' and he knows about the 'huge surge of happiness' that overwhelms her when she sees a child in a party of schoolchildren and mistakes him for her son. 'For the rest of her life that feeling did not come again, neither in its intensity nor in its immediacy.' This is heartbreaking.

Tiger was thrilled with this review and read it out to me on the telephone. I too was pleased, but I also felt something else—something akin to shame and compunction. For I knew from a newspaper article that some twenty years before Alice Thomas Ellis had lost her son, aged nineteen, in a freak accident. Suddenly, this fictional account of loss struck me as a trivial counterfeit. I had believed all my adult life that writing was important, that the novel mattered, that the reader should be able to trust the author.

Now I had sullied that belief. ☐

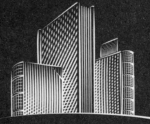

WHITE MEN'S BOATS
Giles Foden

Members of the Naval Africa Expedition on Lake Tanganyika, 1915
A skirted Commander Spicer-Simson at the bow, perhaps

Deo Gratias stood on the deck of the *Liemba* with his prisoners at his feet. I leaned on the rail, studiously casual. Nobody spoke. I was trying to ignore the cuffed men beside us, trying to remain unaffected by the way they were kneeling and shivering. We were in the tropics, it was hot, but they were huddling into each other. It was the action of fear, this permanent trembling motion, and the deep furrows in their brows—they were marks of dread. I had fallen silent wondering why these heavily scored lines in the men's foreheads were more disturbing to me than the most noticeable thing about the pitiful pair. That was a knife-gash across the throat of one with tufty hair and up-staring eyes. The edges of his wound had been sewn together with spiky stitches—recently and roughly, too, by the look of it.

The engine churned as the slow grey flanks of Lake Tanganyika passed by beneath us. We could still see the Tanzanian shore, but the Congolese side to the west was lost in a haze of mist. Finally I asked Deo Gratias what crimes were most commonly committed on the ship. Mainly stealing, he told me, lisping like a schoolgirl.

'And *lape*,' he added, grinning now, spittle flying excitedly from his lips. 'You know *lape*? It is when you go inside.'

He made a sign with his hand, sighing gleefully.

His full name was Deo Gratias Webiro. He was twenty-seven years of age. Wearing a linen suit and a red baseball cap, and carrying a leather satchel, he was employed by the Tanzanian Ministry of the Interior. He was to be distinguished from the khaki-clad *askaris* on board. They were just ordinary policemen. Uneducated men, as he described them to me. *Uneducated men*, I wrote down in my notebook.

Deo Gratias's two charges were crouched with their backs against a capstan. One was grizzled; he had a stricken expression that reminded me of sinners in Renaissance paintings. The other, the one with the stitches across his throat—he was wild-haired, trampish, like a reggae star fallen on hard times.

Deo Gratias pointed at this man with the nappy hair and ragged gash. 'This one, he keeps trying to cut his own throat.' He pointed at the grizzled sinner: 'He murdered a friend, beating him with sticks. This one will be hanged, I think.'

Nearby, a man in a skullcap had unrolled his mat and begun to pray. Above him I spotted a piece of graffiti, written in black felt-tip on the ship's white paintwork. The Swahili words read WAPI MAMA SHAKIRA? 'Where's Mama Shakira?' It was apparently a reference to the *Liemba*'s most famous prostitute, now dead. Also written on the wall were the words GOOD LUCKY KAJEMBE and, in a different hand, AL QAEDA.

A woman in a print dress, her breasts heaving, rushed up to tell us that someone had started brawling in the hold. Deo Gratias went off to investigate, his satchel bobbing on his thigh. I slipped the murderer a bottle of mineral water, putting it down on the steel deck next to his uncuffed hand. Brand name: *Maji Poa*. Good water, pure water. He did not acknowledge me, simply kept staring out across the forbidding grey waves of the lake.

Throughout the nineteenth century, control of the great lake and the area around it was in doubt. A Congolese tribe, the warlike Holo-Holo, had been settling on the shore for most of it, ousting other African tribes that had been here since ancient times. The Holo-Holo were superstitious as well as fierce. Their supreme god was Kabedya Mpungu ('remote in the sky'), to whom appeals were made through witch doctors, secret societies and intermediary spirits. Until the arrival of the Arabs, the crossing of the lake by the Holo-Holo was the biggest political change the region had seen. The Holo-Holo were themselves reacting to Luba expansionism in Congo. They brought with them the practice of ordeal by poison and of drowning newborn babies whose top teeth happened to grow first. Arab slave parties began arriving on the lake shore from 1820; they employed the Holo-Holo to guard the slaves and shipments of gold and ivory.

And then the whites came. It was the British explorers Burton and Speke who reached Lake Tanganyika first, among European travellers. Starting from Zanzibar and following the caravan route, they reached the lake in January 1858. On his last great journey Livingstone also landed up here, arriving sick and tired in the lake-shore town of Ujiji in 1869; the story of his meeting there with Stanley in 1871 is these days sometimes the only thing people know about him.

At 420 miles long, with an average width of thirty-one miles, Lake Tanganyika is the world's longest freshwater lake. It is also the world's second deepest lake, and the lowest point in Africa below sea level. It has evolved utterly separately even from the other great African lakes of the Rift, and its depths contain innumerable unique forms of life. Burton wrote on first seeing it:

> It filled us with admiration, wonder, and delight. Beyond a short foreground of rugged and precipitous hill-fold, down which the footpath painfully zigzags, a narrow plot of emerald green shelves gently towards a ribbon of glistening yellow sand, here bordered by sedgy rushes, there clear and cleanly cut by the breaking wavelets. Farther in front stretches an expanse of lightest, softest blue, from thirty to thirty-five miles in breadth, and sprinkled by the east wind with crescents of snowy foam.

If you were an explorer who has come all the way across from Zanzibar, rather than a prisoner on his way to the gallows, it might indeed seem a very beautiful stretch of water.

In the 'scramble for Africa' that took place in the last two decades of the nineteenth century, it was Germany that won Tanganyika and its lake. Britain took neighbouring Kenya and Uganda. Through a series of sham treaties, the Belgians had already taken the Congo in the 1870s. Many of the treaties were arranged by Stanley, whose activities on behalf of the Belgian King Leopold had spurred on the other powers, Germany in particular. Covering roughly the present area of Tanzania, Rwanda and Burundi, German East Africa was established in 1885. It would be administered by the *Deutsche Ostafrikanische Gesellschaft*, or German East African Company, until 1890, and thereafter by the Imperial Government. On the far western side of the territory lay the inland sea of Lake Tanganyika.

'*Tanganjikasee*' was well stocked with fish, hippopotamus and crocodile, but its main appeal was strategic. During the early 1900s, as the colony developed, the Kaiser was keen to extend his empire further into Central and East Africa. He saw clearly how modern transport could bring remote regions as yet unconquered into his orbit. In 1904, he began building a railway through the centre of German East Africa. The *Mittellandbahn*, as it was known, would link the capital Dar-es-Salaam with the port of Kigoma on Lake Tanganyika—effectively connecting the Indian Ocean in the east to the Congolese border in the west.

It was at Kigoma that I boarded the *Liemba*, a ferry that every week makes its way up and down the lake. The loading of the boat was a chaotic business that lasted the best part of three hours. But eventually, once the interminable sacks of dried fish and the pinch-beaked chickens, the cobs of maize in their bright green sheaths and the heavy pineapples had all been stowed away, once the foghorn had sounded and the ripcord-muscled stevedores cleared the gangplank—and the gangplank itself been lifted on board by the ship's own crane—we got under way.

My principal purpose in making the journey was to investigate the bizarre naval episode that had wrested the lake from German control, and to find out what legacy—if any—those tumultuous events at the far edges of the Great War had in the memory of local people. One of those memories I knew about, because it took physical form. The *Liemba* itself in a previous incarnation had been a German warship. Then known as the *Graf von Götzen*, it had been transported in pieces from Hamburg in 1913 and sent down the *Mittellandbahn* to Kigoma. Reassembled on the lake shore, by the summer of 1915 it had potentially put the whole of Central Africa—perhaps much more—in the Kaiser's reach. It was the half-crazed genius of one man, a quixotic Royal Navy officer called Geoffrey Spicer-Simson, that would set history on another course. The expedition he led would help put an end to the German quest for power in East Africa. But when he set out, in June 1915, Spicer-Simson had no idea at all that the *Graf von Götzen* existed.

Born in 1876, Spicer (as he was known to friends) entered the Royal Navy as a teenager, embarking on what for a considerable time would be a disastrous career. This was partly due to the peculiarities of his character and person. Boastful and vainglorious, he took every opportunity to show off his arms and upper torso, which were heavily tattooed with depictions of snakes, birds, flowers and butterflies. He liked to brag, too, about his individual bravery in the many dangerous situations he had encountered. Most of these tales were lies. An expert on every subject, even in the presence of genuine experts, Spicer also liked to tell jokes (no one laughed at them) and to sing (he was invariably off-key). It is not surprising that by his fellow officers he was thought of as at best peculiar, at worst downright dangerous.

Spicer had always wanted to be a hero. After joining the training ship *Britannia* in 1890 as a cadet, he advanced some way through the ranks, serving in the Gambia and on the China Station. But a series of bumbling errors and catastrophic misjudgements had left him stuck in the naval hierarchy, snickeringly known as the oldest lieutenant commander in the Navy.

There was, for example, that time during the Channel manoeuvres of 1905 when he suggested it would be a good idea for two destroyers to drag a line strung from one to the other in a periscope-hunting exercise. He nearly sank a submarine. Or there was that other time, in an exercise intended to test the defences of Portsmouth Harbour, when he drove his ship right up on to a beach nearby. He was court-martialled for that.

He was also court-martialled for sinking a Liberty Boat in a collision, smashing his destroyer into it. Someone was killed. The incident was reported in the local papers. Lieutenant Commander Spicer-Simson had a reputation.

In August 1914, at the start of the war, Spicer was put in charge of a coastal flotilla consisting of two gunboats and six boarding tugs, operating out of Ramsgate. He felt confident enough of the anchorage of his gunboats to come onshore and entertain his wife and some lady friends in a hotel. He could see HMS *Niger*, one of the ships in question, well enough from the window, could he not?

Fate answered this question with a resounding yes. Yes, from the window of the hotel bar Spicer could see *Niger* as the Germans torpedoed her. He could watch her sink, too, in just twenty minutes. And going down with her, he could see his hopes of advancement to the highest echelon of the Navy disappear beneath the waves.

Such was the state of Spicer's fortunes on April 21, 1915, when a big-game hunter called John Lee arrived at the Admiralty with an appointment to see the First Sea Lord, Sir Henry Jackson. Lee had great experience of Lake Tanganyika, and he had a plan to bring it under British control. Even though the Navy was in the throes of the Dardanelles crisis—Winston Churchill had been sacked not long before—Sir Henry was happy to listen to Lee's plan. Britain had no ships on Lake Tanganyika, and it was not an area he knew about.

First of all, the big-game hunter outlined the German naval contingent on the lake as he saw it. They had two steamers under military orders—the 570-ton steel *Hedwig von Wissman* and the twenty-ton wooden *Kingani*. There was a petrol motor boat, the *Peter*, donated to the German forces by the *Gesellschaft fur Schlaftkrankheitsbekampfung*, the Society for the Fight against Sleeping Sickness. The Germans also had a number of 'Boston whalers'—wooden boats based on an American design that were originally brought to East Africa in the early 1900s—and a fleet of dhows. Lee had heard vague talk of another ship coming, but he made no particular mention of the 1,200-ton *Götzen*, and nor did the Belgian army intelligence report that Jackson commissioned as a follow-up. The fact was, the *Götzen* was at the lakeside in Kigoma in April, but not launched until June 8. About two thirds the length of a football pitch, it could carry 1,800 troops.

Lee's scheme to attack the other German steamers was simple in concept, but difficult to execute. If two British motor boats could be sent to South Africa, up the railway to the Belgian Congo, and dragged through mountains and bush to the lake, they could then sink or disable the *Hedwig* and the *Kingani*. Taking control of the lake this way would allow Belgian forces from the Congo and British forces from Kenya and Northern Rhodesia to drive the Germans back to the eastern seaboard. That was the argument, anyway.

Sir Henry ratified the plan, for philosophical reasons as much as any others. 'It is both the duty and the tradition of the Royal Navy to engage the enemy wherever there is water to float a ship,' he wrote in a memo. The only question was: who would command the 'Naval Africa Expedition', as it was to be called? Sir Henry sought out candidates, but the service was short of officers on account of the Dardanelles fiasco. When Spicer heard the job being offered to someone else, who turned it down, he volunteered. Despite his chequered record, he was given the post. Perhaps Sir Henry saw something of the incipient hero in Spicer; perhaps the quality only needed to be drawn out by the right situation. Or maybe there was simply no one else to fill the slot.

In any case, it must have seemed to Spicer that the First World War would be his last chance to make good. His brother, the sculptor Theodore Spicer-Simson, had become famous for his portrait medallions of celebrities such as Toscanini and the philanthropist Andrew Carnegie. Why shouldn't he be famous too? Why was he now stuck in a desk job at Navy headquarters in Whitehall, not out seeing action on the high seas?

By the time I emerged from my cabin, night had fallen. Having an appointment with the captain, I followed the maze of pipework and narrow corridors that made up the *Liemba*'s double deck structure. The whole place stank. People were lying about everywhere on mattresses, amid piles of fruit and the long white sacks of *dagaa* (dried fish) which were the ship's main cargo. Many of the passengers had yellow plastic jerrycans of water and thin steel messtins. A large proportion of the travellers were refugees from wars in Congo and Burundi, hoping for a better life in Zambia, the ship's destination at the south end of the lake.

The gangway was tight. One woman, sad-faced and cuddling her ten-year-old daughter, asked me in French for money as I squeezed by. '*Voudriez-vous, monsieur, nous faire un contribution matériel?*'

I gave her five US dollars.

'*C'est rien,*' she said. Then, to my amazement, she handed it straight back.

The bridge, as I entered it—after asking permission of the bearded crewman on guard outside—was revealed as a place of almost total darkness. A radar screen showed the ship's course as a straight green line; its glow was more or less the only light in the room. A mass of fleshly curves on his stool, the moon-faced captain did not want to talk about the past. He was looking into the night—watching out for whalers, watching out for canoes.

'It is all written down in the books,' he told me, with some irritation.

As he spoke, one hand gripped and ungripped the polished wood of the wheel. The wheel itself seemed rigid, fixed. It must be on autopilot, I thought, imagining a kind of clamp down below.

'This is the ship of history,' the captain said. 'It is well known.'

He glanced down at the radar.

'No,' I insisted. 'Only the white man's side of the *Liemba* story is written down. Not your side.'

He looked at me, perplexed. I tried to explain what the difference between African and European history might be—if such a difference exists—and of course, it came out like an impertinence. The captain shook his head. I felt as though we were talking a different language.

Giles Foden

Not the difference of black and white, but the difference between a technocrat and...whatever I thought I was, right then.

I peered through the gloom at the other instruments, oddly illuminated by the radar's spectral light. The captain moved his hand slightly, the wheel moved accordingly. No autopilot.

Tanzania's national museum is a poor place, down at heel and badly lit. I visited it before leaving for the lake. Walking through the section 'Africa', I found myself looking at a display of amulets. One was a small piece of lion skin (about the size of an envelope), upon which were written protective Arab verses. Near to this was a statue, of the type anthropologists call a fetish object. A rough, red-clay model of a human figure holding outsize goggles to its eyes, it stood about two feet high. The goggles were binoculars. With a start I realized that the statue was probably made by the Holo-Holo, the tribe I had come to Tanzania in search of. They once dominated the shores of Lake Tanganyika; now they are almost extinct. I studied the finger marks in the clay. Beneath the exhibit was some writing on a card in Swahili. *Wazungu wanaweza kuona mbali kuliko watu wengire.* 'The European can see beyond the range of other people.' The *fundisho*, or moral, was also explained: 'Beware of Europeans, they put glasses in their eyes and can see a person on the hill opposite.'

The only hill opposite right then was a plaster of Paris model of Tanzania's geological strata, stretching down through time. I experienced a bizarre feeling of tumbling as I recalled a similar native fetish made by the Holo-Holo in 1915. Like this one, it had a large head and bandy legs. Like this one, the figure grasped a pair of binoculars in its tiny hands. It also had small incisions on its chest and forearms. They marked the tattoos on the body of the man in whose tracks I had come: Commander Geoffrey Basil Spicer-Simson, RN.

Navyman God, as his servants called him. Lord Bellycloth, as his followers among the Holo-Holo called him. A very remarkable person, in spite of his failings. The story of his pursuit of and by German warships on the lake would be very loosely fictionalized in C. S. Forester's novel *The African Queen*, and the movie with Katharine Hepburn and Humphrey Bogart that followed. The true history was much more unbelievable than the film, which is fanciful

164

enough. Finding it, I was beginning to realize, was like reaching into the dark. It wasn't African or European; it was just strange, at one remove from all of us.

Another of the attractions at the museum was 'The Hall of Man'—an echoey tunnel in which were displayed model skulls from different eras of human antiquity. These included the seminal discoveries made by Louis and Mary Leakey in Tanzania's Olduvai Gorge in the 1960s and 70s. I was pleased to see these pointers to my own evolutionary history, though they did not help with a problem I had. At some point, however many times I read about it or heard it explained, I always got lost between the Neanderthals and the archaic hominids. Some ape-like creature (those *Australopithecus* whose heads do grow beneath their shoulders), *Homo habilis* (the tool-user), *Homo sapiens*: was that the order? With the Neanderthals off the main drag and subject to demise, possibly genocide by our ancestors? Was that today's thinking? I couldn't remember.

There were also cabinets of minerals and metals in 'The Hall of Man', which seemed like a category mistake, and then again not. In lumps of rock, gold pyrites glittered. Precious motes were sprinkled on the surfaces—the jagged edges, the smooth faces—like expensive pepper. Yet the lumps also seemed to shine from deep within. A geologist could tell the story of these fragments. I stared at them in the semi-darkness.

The method of the section 'Europe in Africa' was denigration and statistics. Railways and time-management were not the civilizing benisons they were once thought to have been. Among cabinets of curios and curling photographs of imperial soldiers of one sort and another, an evil connection to the genocide of Neanderthals was illuminated: Germany's extermination of the Herero tribe in South West Africa in 1904, and its equally ruthless suppression of the Maji-Maji rebellion here in Tanzania over the following three years.

The same Swahili word on the plastic bottle I'd given to that prisoner—*maji*, water—gave its name to the rebellion. From 1905 to 1907, the Africans of this region revolted against German rule: against hut taxes, against forced labour, against a stated policy that made them economically dependent on the white invader and his cash crop, cotton. Foreign seed was imported and planted under duress, usually at the end of a whip—most Germans in the colony carried these as a matter of course.

The word *maji* in this context refers to a political movement whereby a secret communication about driving out the invaders was passed from one individual to another. The secret was that a powerful medicine (water) had been found that would make the white men vulnerable. The special water was carried about the person in small containers made from maize or millet cobs. Before battle a little would be drunk and sprinkled about the body in order to ward off bullets. The weapons of the opposition were endowed with the characteristics of the medicine: rifles were supposed to spurt only water, and bullets to trickle like water from the body of the target.

It didn't work. Anyone suspected of involvement in the rebellion or who displayed the slightest resistance to agricultural schemes was hanged by the neck. Close to 120,000 Africans died as a result of the executions and the famine that followed. It wasn't just a case of black and white. While Indian traders—of whom by 1905 there were nearly 7,000 in Tanganyika—were accused by the Germans of fomenting the rebellion, a number of Papuan and Melanesian troops were drafted from German possessions in the Pacific to help put it down.

The man responsible for the 'mild administrative pressure' (as he called it) that caused the revolution, and the bloody counter-measures that suppressed it, was Count von Götzen, military governor of German East Africa from 1901 to 1906. The ship I would travel in was named in the Count's honour, before it was called the *Liemba*.

I stared at the wall in the museum. There was a large imperial German flag, the 'Iron Cross' type, and a ship's wheel. It was the original wheel of the *Götzen*. The explainer mentioned that the ship had been salvaged from the bottom of the lake by Belgians after the war. It said nothing about what had happened to her before or since.

In London during May 1915, Spicer threw himself into the Tanganyika project with gusto. He first of all concerned himself with fitting out the two motor boats that had been chosen for the operation. They were forty-foot motor launches, made of mahogany, each about eight feet wide. They had two propellers each, driven by 100 h.p. petrol engines. Originally designed as tenders for the Greek seaplane service, they had been made by the famous boat-builders Thorneycroft, who kept a yard at Twickenham on the Thames.

At this stage the boats only had numbers, and it fell to Spicer to name them. He suggested—they were really very small, after all— that they be christened 'Cat' and 'Dog'. The Navy was not amused. Spicer went back to the drawing board. The boats did have to have names: they would be HMSs, the smallest ever to hold the title. But what would follow the HMS? It was the kind of topic to which Spicer liked applying his febrile imagination: the same imagination which had so far blighted his career with madcap schemes that ended in disaster. Was the Naval Africa Expedition to be yet another?

There was also the question of staffing to consider. One by one, over a period of weeks, prospective members of the team came to see Spicer at the Admiralty to be signed up. Here was fifty-ish Sub Lieutenant Tyrer with his dyed canary-yellow hair, who'd previously been in the Royal Naval Air Service. One of the earliest British aviators, he was addicted to Worcester sauce (as an aperitif). Tyrer was a handsome man, but he spoiled the effect by wearing a monocle and generally addressing people with the prefix 'Dear Boy'—even if they were older than him.

A second member of the team was Engineer Lieutenant Cross. A former racing driver—he'd twice won the Grand Prix—he didn't actually know much about internal combustion engines. He took offence easily and would become the butt of jokes on the expedition.

Another of the twenty-eight was Lieutenant Wainwright. He would be Transport Officer. A Belfast man originally, he had worked on the railway that came from Beira in Portuguese East Africa (now Mozambique) inland to Rhodesia, where he had a cattle farm. He knew about locomotives. It would be his job to drive the traction engines that would pull the boats part of the way.

Wainwright would become great friends with the expedition's medic, Doctor Hanschell, himself an old acquaintance of Spicer's. Prior to his appointment to the team, the Doctor had spent some time in West Africa's Gold Coast researching the causes of yellow fever. While there, he had contracted amoebic dysentery which had never quite gone away.

Other men included the Chief Gunlayer, James Waterhouse. He would take charge of the three-pounder guns and Maxim machine guns that would be mounted on the launches: really far too much weight for such small craft, but there was no point in going all that way and not having enough firepower to do the job.

Also on the team was Frank Magee, a 'scallywag journalist' according to Doctor Hanschell. He was commissioned Petty Officer Writer and would take charge of clerical and photographic duties on the expedition. He would later write it up for the October 1922 issue of the *National Geographic* magazine (the other main source for the expedition is the naval historian Peter Shankland's marvellous book *The Phantom Flotilla*, based on interviews with Doctor Hanschell and published in 1968). Of the same rank as Magee was PO Flynn, a fisherman from Donegal whose flaming red hair would distinguish him among the crew—as would his habit, when speaking of his wife, of calling her 'mother'.

These men were mostly recommended by friends and colleagues of Spicer or Lee. One or two, however, heard about the expedition through more unorthodox routes. These included Tait and Mollison, two hulking Scotsmen. They learned of the mission in a bar in the West End and came to the Admiralty to volunteer. Both were lance corporals of the London Scottish Regiment and had played for its rugby team. Tait had lost a finger at Ypres. They generally wore their kilts.

The Admiralty accepted Spicer's second set of names for the launches, HMS *Mimi* and HMS *Tou-Tou*. As he explained to the crew later, those words meant 'Miaow' and 'Bow-wow' in French. No one found this quite as amusing as the Commander, who professed himself delighted with the names. In the meantime he had also had the motor boats altered for the job in hand, cutting their height so they could go faster. The Maxim machine guns had been mounted in the bows and the three-pounder guns fixed aft. He had the petrol tanks lined with extra steel sheeting to deflect bullets: if they were ignited the wooden boats would go up in a flash. To Spicer's design, the Thorneycroft yard made some special cradle-trailers on which *Mimi* and *Tou-Tou* could be carried overland.

On June 8, it was agreed, the boats and guns would be tested on the Thames at Chiswick. They looked rather forbidding now, *Mimi* and *Tou-Tou*, with their forecastles removed and the big guns up front. Various members of the team, including Engineer Cross and the dour Chief Petty Officer Waterhouse, joined in the tests. There is a photograph. Amy—Mrs Spicer-Simson—comes along for the ride, sitting in the bows of *Mimi* as the spray flies upon either side. *Tou-Tou* follows close behind. They make their way downriver.

Spicer had obtained a licence to fire a practice shell from the three-pounder into an old dockside. What happened, when the moment came, would in some way set the tone for the whole expedition: success, but success in an atmosphere of high farce. *Mimi* was at full throttle as they went past the dock (it was actually the old yard of Messrs Thorneycroft, the boat's manufacturers). Waterhouse took aim and fired. The round hit its target. Unfortunately, at the moment of firing both Waterhouse and the gun flew off the side of *Mimi* and fell into the river. It turned out that the gun had not been properly locked to the deck. The next day, *Mimi* and *Tou-Tou* were driven to Tilbury, where they would be loaded on board the liner *Llanstephan Castle*, bound for Cape Town on June 15. The main party would join the ship on the day it sailed.

The week prior to their departure saw the various members of the expedition collecting the kit and personal items they would take with them. Doctor Hanschell had ordered his medical stores from an Admiralty stocklist. He was not very happy with the proposed material, as most of it came from a pamphlet entitled 'Medical Stores as supplied to Gunboats West Africa Station', dated 1898. Each member of the expedition was issued with a camp bed and a woollen Jaeger sleeping bag, adjustable to single or double tog. Only Spicer would have a tent; everyone else would sleep under the stars. Tarpaulins were ordered with which to protect petrol and ammunition from the heat of the sun. For their own protection, each man had a sun helmet.

A Union Jack was ordered for ceremonial purposes, and spare swords in case any officer should lose his own. Meals were to be eaten off folding tables and chairs. The main source of protein was to be canned beef. Doctor Hanschell, worried about nutrition, had taken precautions against beriberi by bringing plenty of tinned tomatoes. A large number of razor blades were also brought—as much for trading with the natives as to enable the men to shave each day.

Spicer took a pair of binoculars—the item that would be associated with him later, when Holo-Holo tribesmen began to make his effigy in clay. He forgot to order food stores for Lukuga, their destination on the lake, which he should have logged with the Director of Naval Victualling. But he did pick up a supply of personally monogrammed cigarettes from the Army and Navy Stores (he liked to keep them in his revolver holster). He also had a personal supply of sherry and vermouth. Tyrer had his cases of Worcester sauce, and a liqueur glass from which to drink it. The Doctor had a pair of long leather mosquito boots, a set of Jane Austen and the *Oxford Book of English Verse*. PO Flynn had pens and paper with which to write to his 'mother'.

Much to the bemusement of onlooking Londoners, the expedition paraded at St Pancras railway station before taking the train to Tilbury. Spicer had designed them a special uniform for such ceremonial occasions, consisting of army khaki tunics, grey flannel shirts and navy-blue ties. Each officer, even Doctor Hanschell, was to carry a sword. Spicer was very insistent upon this, tearing a strip off the doctor when he questioned the point of wearing the accoutrement. It was in this gear that most of the officers lined up under the Victorian Gothic portals of St Pancras. The sight cannot have had quite the effect Spicer intended, given that the ratings were in bell-bottomed sailor's trousers and Tait and Mollison in their kilts. He marched up and down the line all the same, carefully inspecting each man.

The performance was repeated on the quay at Tilbury, whereupon Spicer marched his men up the gangplank of the *Llanstephan Castle*—to the only slightly suppressed laughter of the liner's Merchant Navy officers. Some of the passengers were not so amused, complaining to the *Llanstephan Castle*'s captain about the ship's use for military purposes. They argued that this made them more liable to be torpedoed by German U-boats, as had happened to the *Lusitania* the previous month.

On the *Liemba*, after a few beers in the bar and a plastic dish of beef and rice, I had gone to sleep with stories of Hutu bandits in my head. There had been threats of their attacking the ship recently, though I hadn't given them much credence. So when the screams awoke me, I thought that was it. Finally years of travel in Africa had caught up with me; this time I was for the chop, in a place where the machete was the weapon of choice.

Out of the night came a ritualized screaming, a caterwauling woman's voice. *'Pata rowe! Pata rowe! Pata rowe kwa samaki!'*

I stirred uneasily on the leather couchette which, when I'd come in, had been slick with the sweat of others. Now it was wet with mine.

Someone banged on the door. *'Katlesi ya samaki!'*

They were Swahili words, but I couldn't catch what they meant. *'Pata rowe! Pata rowe!'* Then, tailing off, *'Katlesi...'*

There wasn't just one woman, I realized. They seemed to be shouting all over the ship, in a number of voices. The noise was drowning out even the thud of the engines as it reverberated through the rivets near my head. I looked at my watch. It was about one in the morning. Slowly I became aware that the ship had stopped, and the engines were just idling. There were more shouts. I went to the window to see what was happening, but all I could see were dark shapes and the occasional flicker of light. I would have to go out. I unlocked the door and turned the handle. It wouldn't move; there was someone outside. I had to push the door hard—into a flowing mass of people—to get out onto the walkway. I really had to put my shoulder into it, like a prop forward.

Tumbling out of the cabin, finally, I saw that the flowing mass of humanity covered the decks and extended down the side of the ship. Some sixty-seven metres long, ten metres down, more or less the whole side of the *Liemba* was covered with climbing figures. Some were climbing down, some up. There was fighting on the way: punching, pulling, kicking, stamping. It wasn't entirely the habitation of cruelty, what was happening on the side of the boat—there was some altruism, some handing me up and handing me down—but the atmosphere was mostly Darwinian, there was no getting away from it.

There were boys as well as women, and they were shouting too. *'Pata rowe! Samaki-samaki-samaki.'*

Someone fell, cracking a rib on the side of a boat down below. Others ate their dinner. Groggily, I began to understand what was happening. We were at a fast-food station, that was all, even though it was the middle of the night, in the middle of the lake. I asked someone what the words meant. *'Pata rowe kwa samaki.'* Fish with cassava-flour puddings. *'Katlesi ya samaki.'* Fish cutlets.

Because of the threat of ambush, and a lack of natural landing places, the *Liemba* does not stop close to the shore during its 800-

mile round trip every week. Instead, it halts at 'stations' in the middle of the lake. Boats come out from the villages on the shore to sell food, trade with passengers on board, and enable others to embark or disembark. This is what was happening; chop was in order, but not the kind I had imagined.

Having sold their fish, the boys in the boats were up for fun. They sped round and round the *Liemba*, gunning the outboards on their whalers, calling out at girls on board. Plumes of exhaust hung in the air. It was half like a big party in the night now, half still like a kind of fight as people jumped from craft to craft, clambered up and down, stuffed fish cutlets into their mouths, or tried to catch bananas thrown up from the boats below and throw coins back.

Perhaps thirty boats were caught in the spotlights the *Liemba* threw out on to the turbulent black water. Most were dug out canoes; some were wooden rowing boats. There were also five or six Boston whalers carrying between twenty and thirty people each. Powered by roaring outboards, they kept ramming the dug outs out of the way to get a better position alongside the *Liemba*. Furious arguments were taking place.

A man in a red loincloth had his rowing boat knocked over; perhaps not quite over—I struggled through the crowd on deck to get a better view. Water was pitching in… The man was standing up and howling, just on the edge of the pool of light. I watched as he slowly sank. At the last he started bailing frantically, but it was no use. The boat started to slip beneath the waves. The man jumped out. I caught a glimpse of his arms waving above the side of the boat: two wet black sticks in the spotlights.

Young men began to jump out of the other boats and swim towards the sinking one. They grabbed it and started to shove it from side to side. Eventually enough water was slooshed out over the gunwale for the man in the red loincloth to climb back in. With more bailing, buoyancy returned. His boat had been saved. It was a small victory for civilization, but the scene did not come to order. The noise and mayhem continued for a good hour—all at a banshee scale, echoing out across the waves. The *Liemba*'s spotlights shone out over it all, casting out pearl-grey sheets over the chaos.

On arriving in Cape Town, after a two-and-a-half-week sea voyage of more than 6,000 miles, *Mimi* and *Tou-Tou* were unloaded. The Naval Africa Expedition went into digs in Adderley Street; Spicer himself stayed in the salubrious Mount Nelson hotel. Six years before, Churchill had stayed in this pink-pillared palace during the Boer War while working as a journalist. After some days of further preparation—Doctor Hanschell was right: the team did not have the correct medical supplies—the expedition boarded a train for Elizabethville in the Belgian Congo. *Mimi* and *Tou-Tou* were fixed to wagons and covered in tarpaulins; a seaman was posted next to each to make sure sparks from the train did not set the wooden boats alight.

It was another long journey, of about 2,500 miles. During it Spicer pondered reports that Lee, the big-game hunter whose idea the whole thing had been, was a drunk and had been 'blabbing' about their top-secret mission. In fact, many people knew about the expedition and Lee was innocent. He had worked hard blazing the trail. But on arrival in Elizabethville on July 26, Spicer sacked him and wrote a damning report to the Admiralty. The truth seems to be that he could not abide his men talking about 'Lee's expedition'.

As they would soon be entering a region where sleeping sickness was endemic, Doctor Hanschell ordered that fly whisks should be purchased in Elizabethville market. Spicer picked out a special one for himself made of lion skin.

The next part of the journey involved further travel by train, to the end of the line at Fungurume, which they reached on August 5. Now came the hard part, a 146-mile passage through the bush and over the Mitumba mountain range. The expedition's labourers levelled a track through the jungle, stocking up firewood along the way to fuel the traction engines that would drag *Mimi* and *Tou-Tou*. A team of 150 women brought water for the engines constantly, carrying pots on their heads. Food was shot en route: antelope; elephant; fowl of one type or another. There were many difficulties. The traction engines kept tumbling over on their sides. They bogged down in streams. Sand silted up their boilers. Bridges were built, rivers were forded, trees were uprooted with dynamite. The oxen that helped the engines when they stuck began to die. From tsetse fever, from tick fever, from exhaustion. There was nothing the Boer driver or his Zulu assistant could do.

The bridges kept collapsing, as did the trailers on which *Mimi* and

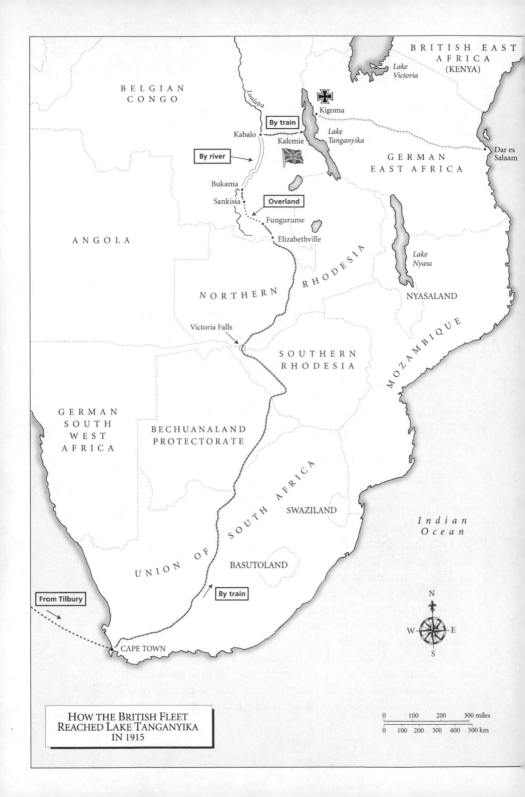

BRITISH EAST
AFRICA
(KENYA)

BELGIAN
CONGO

Lualaba

*Lake
Victoria*

Kigoma

By train

Kabalo

Kalemie

*Lake
Tanganyika*

GERMAN
EAST AFRICA

Dar es
Salaam

By river

Bukama

Sankisia

Overland

Fungurume

ANGOLA

Elizabethville

*Lake
Nyasa*

NYASALAND

NORTHERN

RHODESIA

MOZAMBIQUE

Victoria Falls

SOUTHERN
RHODESIA

GERMAN
SOUTH
WEST
AFRICA

BECHUANALAND
PROTECTORATE

UNION   OF   SOUTH   AFRICA

SWAZILAND

*Indian
Ocean*

BASUTOLAND

From Tilbury

By train

N
W   E
S

CAPE TOWN

HOW THE BRITISH FLEET
REACHED LAKE TANGANYIKA
IN 1915

0   100   200   300 miles

0   100   200   300   400   500 km

Tou-Tou were carried. But through all the accidents Spicer stayed relaxed, constantly smoking his special cigarettes.

Eventually they crossed the Mitumba Mountains and came down to a plain and the village of Sankisia. Here the railway started again, linking them up to a place called Bukama. From there they embarked on a dangerous, 350-mile passage along the Lualaba, or upper Congo river. Where the river was shallow, *Mimi* and *Tou-Tou* were towed by barge. At other points they used their own engines or were loaded aboard river steamers. The Lualaba was fickle in the disposition of its banks and bottom, and the gunboats often had to be hauled over sandbanks. (Thirty-six years later, this was also a problem for the crew of *The African Queen*, much of which was filmed on a tributary of the Lualaba.)

Finally the expedition reached Kabalo, a dismal village on the river whose only virtue was that it connected to the Belgians' new rail network in the Eastern Congo. From Kabalo it was another rail journey (200 miles) through mountain gorges, followed by a further journey through the bush to the lake: the railway had not quite been completed.

Through heavy rain, Spicer saw Lake Tanganyika for the first time on October 27, over four months since he had set out from St Pancras. He stood on a high cliff, with his binoculars round his neck. On his side was a Belgian camp next to the Lukuga river. On the other, German side of the lake, even through the storm that was lashing down, could be seen the great peak of Mount Kungwe. For Africans the mountain is still notorious for its resident intermediary spirit, or *nzimu*. His name is Mkungwe, and he demands great sacrifices of his followers.

Soon after his arrival on the lake, Spicer fell into dispute with the Belgians, Britain's allies against Germany. They controlled the western part of the lake and did not take kindly to this pompous Englishman who announced that he was now in charge of all military operations in the area. He must have cut a strange figure, anyway, as he threw his weight about. To be more comfortable in the heat, he had taken to wearing a skirt instead of trousers. 'I designed it myself,' he told another member of the expedition. 'My wife makes 'em for me.' The Belgians began referring to him as *'le commandant à la jupe'*.

The skirt was part of Spicer's mystique among the Holo-Holo tribesmen who congregated round the expedition and became its labour force. To them he was known as Bwana Chifunga-Tumbo, or Lord Bellycloth. They took greatest pleasure in the ritual of Spicer's four o'clock bath, during which he would emerge from his hut with a towel round his waist and his tattoos on full show. As a canvas tub was filled, he would smoke a cigarette in a holder, as the Holo-Holo clapped in admiration. Then, after flexing his muscles to display his tattoos all the better, he would step into the tub and lather himself with perfumed soap. Once he was finished, he would stand up and a servant would rinse him with buckets of water. Wrapped in towels and surrounded by his appreciative audience, he would then smoke another cigarette and drink a glass of vermouth, before striding back to his hut.

On Boxing Day, 1915, Spicer's fast, manoeuvrable craft captured the smallest of the German steamers, the *Kingani*. Three Germans were blown to pieces by shells, spattering blood all over the ship. The boat was brought back in to shore and trophies were taken. Spicer had the Captain's ring; Petty Officer Flynn bottled some blood clots from the Captain's body and asked Doctor Hanschell for disinfectant to preserve them; another petty officer had half a human finger in his bottle. The Congolese *askaris* wanted to eat the bodies, but Spicer drew the line at this.

A few days later, a wireless message was received: 'His Majesty's congratulations to his most remote expedition.' Over the next few weeks, the *Kingani* was reconditioned and armed with quick-firing Belgian twelve-pounders. Spicer renamed the ship *Fifi*, with typical whimsicality: Fifi is the French for 'Tweet Tweet', he told his men.

On February 9, the three boats sank the 570-ton *Hedwig von Wissman* in a joint operation. And with that Spicer thought his work was done. He had even managed to capture a German naval flag: the first of the whole war. What the Commander didn't know, in the exhilarated aftermath of these victories, was that even as he had been making his practice runs in *Mimi* and *Tou-Tou* back on the Thames in June of the previous year, the *Graf von Götzen* was already sailing up and down Lake Tanganyika. The mighty German warship would make a mockery of his toy navy.

The *Liemba* cast her anchor. At about three in the morning, with the same attendant chaos as before, my own station had arrived at last. I climbed down into the whaler that would take me to dry land. I feared for my footing as I leaped into the rocking black hole. The driver gunned up the engine and we sped off into the night. Then, as the lights of the *Liemba* receded into the distance, we began to struggle against larger and larger waves.

Each time we whacked down on to the lake, water spurted in through cracks in the gunwale. A veil of grey-black clouds rolled in. Moonlight, its intensity rapidly decreasing, provided the only illumination. A storm was coming in, and I was in a leaky boat in the middle of a very large lake.

The rain came down fast and hard. The driver's assistant, a boy in a spotted bandanna, was feverishly bailing away in the depths of the boat with a cut-out plastic bucket. Either side of him, through the driving spray, I could just make out my fellow passengers. They included a bearded Afrikaans brewery manager and his family, three village women in shawls, two bespectacled Japanese tourists on their way to a chimpanzee reserve, and a sullen young Tanzanian soldier in full camouflage and slouch cap. In one hand the soldier held his AK-47, its magazine bound with gaffer tape, in the other a pineapple.

It was two hours before we approached the military sub-station at Mirambo, the soldier's destination. By now I was soaked to the skin. The storm was at its roughest; the driver could hardly control the boat as, swinging from side to side between ten-foot waves, he tried to hold steady by the shore but not run aground. All around us, protruding another ten feet above the waves, were large tussocks of leafy cane. Their shaggy shapes had a fierce and occult aspect, as if they were sentinels of the kind of lost city in search of which Rider Haggard's explorer Allan Quatermain set out, leaving the placid English countryside behind him. 'The thirst for the wilderness was on me; I could tolerate this place no more...'

Putting the pineapple in his pocket, holding the rifle over his head, the soldier pitched over the edge. The black water covered him up to his shoulders. He staggered forward. I could not see the land he was heading for, just darkness and the vicious storm. The wind gusted down between my freezing ears and wet hair, hellhound loud. At one point the whaler seemed to squat in a trough of water, like a fat man going down on his haunches.

Before the soldier could be consumed by the dark places of the night, while his outline was still visible to us, struggling through the

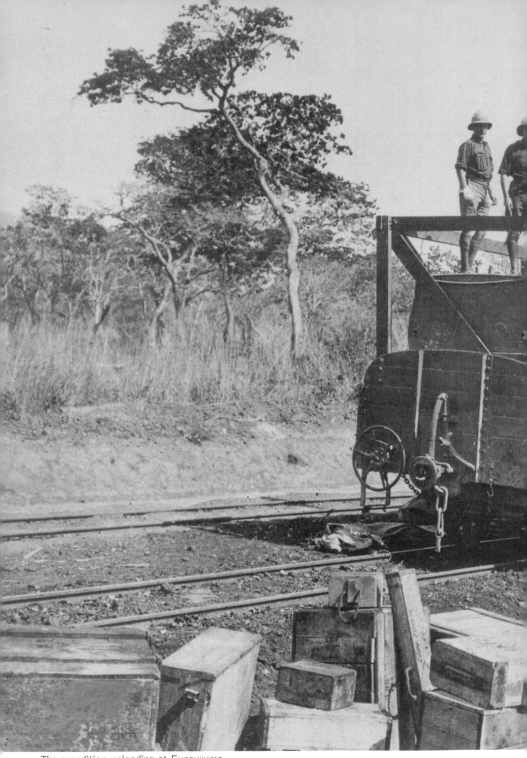

The expedition unloading at Fungurume

water, the boat turned and we headed out once more into the interminable lake. I began to worry about my own landfall, whenever it might be.

By the time I arrived, a further two hours later, the sun had risen. I could see the campsite that would be my base for the next few days. From here I would make my forays to villages up and down the shore of the lake, enquiring after Spicer and the Holo-Holo.

The storm had knocked the stuffing out of me. But sitting on the sand drinking coffee, facing the Congo over the water, with the towering shape of Mount Kungwe behind me, I began to feel confident again. For a moment, surrounded by stunted acacias on the stooping lakeshore, the leafy ones looking like 'umbrellas in a crowd', as Burton wrote of the same place in 1860, I could even imagine myself one of the those old-time explorers.

Dawn became day. I looked out at the lake, sipped some coffee, then made some more, spooning in the powdered milk straight from the tin. It was a taste from childhood that I had forgotten. Caffeine notwithstanding (and there isn't much in African coffee, all the good stuff being exported), I turned in and slept for most of the new day. It had been a long journey. Tomorrow I would begin scouring up and down the lake in a boat with an outboard, interviewing the oldest man in each village about his memories of the war between *Uingereza* and *Ujerumani*. The First World War, as we call it. The Great War, of which Spicer's expedition was only the smallest of sideshows.

Rising sheer from the lake, Mount Kungwe is the mountain that Spicer saw when he arrived on the opposite side. It is home to Mkungwe, spirit of a local sacrificial cult. If you dare to climb Mkungwe and sit on his head, you will die (there are several instances of this happening). If you want good fortune, you must sacrifice something to Mkungwe. Maybe Spicer should have done this. It was near here, through Kungwe Bay, that he watched the *Götzen* through his binoculars and refused to go out and fight. It was under this mountain that he metamorphosed from hero back to eccentric failure. In spite of the urgings of the Belgians, and of his own junior officers, Spicer would not give chase. He gave no reason, but maybe he believed that he had fulfilled his orders in sinking the *Kingani* and the *Hedwig* and that it was foolish to pitch *Mimi* and *Tou-Tou* against such odds.

By early 1916, approaching armies of Rhodesians from the south and Belgians from the west were putting the German forces under great pressure. Spicer still quailed at the prospect of meeting the *Götzen* in battle. By that stage, anyway, his self-confidence had nosedived. He was mocked by the Rhodesian soldiers for his skirt. 'Oh la! la!' they would cry out, wolf-whistling as he went past. 'Kiss me Gertie! Chase me Charlie!'

The Rhodesian colonel reprimanded Spicer in the strongest terms for letting a number of German troops escape in dhows. A few weeks later and Spicer was in trouble again, refusing to help the Belgians, who wanted to use his ships to move troops and supplies up and down the lake. His refusal caused great ructions between the Belgian and British governments.

Why did he behave like this? Lord Bellycloth did not want to add more sinkings to a lifetime tally that was already very embarrassing. There was no way he would jeopardize his new- found glory and face the *Götzen*'s big guns.

After what seems to have been a nervous breakdown, Spicer disappeared into the Congo for a while, leaving the crew of *Mimi* and *Tou-Tou* to fend for themselves. Eventually, in September 1916, he was sent home with a medical certificate citing acute nervous debility. Reaching London, he faced a mixed reaction. He was both reprimanded by the Navy and given the DSO. The Belgians awarded him their Commander of the Order of the Crown.

Spicer claimed prize money for the *Kingani*, and his story ran as a feature in many newspapers. He was 'The Hero of the Gunboats' whose 'Nelson Touch on the African Lake' had rightly earned him medals. He had persuaded history of his own self-image. But the Navy never let him have a command again. 'His tactless behaviour might have contributed to a serious disaster,' wrote the admiral charged with investigating the incident. In the last year of the war Spicer was once again given a desk job, as Assistant Director of Naval Intelligence at the Admiralty.

With the help of local guides, I pursued my search for old men who might remember something—anything at all—of the First World War. We had been walking in single file for a couple of miles inland, towards the village of Kalumbe, when we entered a forest of palms. I had my notebook under my arm and a pair of binoculars round my neck. I was being stung by insects, but the astonishing palms made up for it all. As sturdy as English oaks—almost as wide as those trees at the base, but tapering at the neck—they marched towards one in a steady stream. There must have been thousands of them, and the sight was a hopeful one—it was good to see they had not yet been cut down.

My guides promised it was not much further. Every now and then the forest opened up to reveal human dwellings. Black and scarlet chickens would strut across the path, heralding the revelation of a hamlet or small village. Here was a woman crouched in her hut— stirring a basin of *ugali*, stirring maize meal, stirring the coarse white porridge with a wooden spoon. Here were three other women, peering into a drum of boiling palm oil. Always the women, working. The men just sat around—but still they had the power, gripping on to it like the palm nuts encircling the slender necks of the trees that give them shade.

All the same, the man I came to see at Kalumbe could tell me nothing. He shook his head sadly. No, he did not know any history. Too long ago. Everywhere it is the same. The oral tradition is in crisis in Africa, a trauma brought about by the advent of modern technology, the growth of towns, and the spread of Aids, which has struck a thick black line through two generations of Africans now. In every town, you see the coffins piled up in the marketplace, their newly planed red wood still wet with sap. Of the young men that remain, few want to listen to tales of the past. They want computers and radios and mobile phones. And they want to leave: to accelerate into the global future. Nairobi! New York! Cardiff!

It is—I grumbled to myself, tramping back through the forest to the lake—not so very different back in Britain. How many young Britons know anything about the First World War, or even think of it at all?

I strode through a village full of pye-dogs. They all had foxlike ears and the most amazing patterns in their coats. Black and white and chocolate. Yapping away ten to the dozen, they seemed to be the village's only occupants.

We came out of the palms into open country, and immediately the temperature rose. There is a difference, a discernible difference—

I said to myself, I *told* myself, wiping my face. It is that we in the west have been writing down our history for centuries. Most Africans have no access to books at all, and in most cases the right books do not exist anyway. The living history Africa is losing was once passed down by voice, structured on the genealogy of the tribe and on records of military victories and migrations. It lived in the telling, not in the solid object of a book; and now that the habit of telling has gone, the history is passing away.

From the boat, on the way back to the campsite, I saw bushbuck on the beach, hippopotamus in the water. A croc slid off a rock. At one point I went onshore to look at a place where a Belgian barge carrying cement sank in the 1950s. The cement bags had petrified. They looked like strange rock formations now. Clambering about among them, I found a lump of quartz about the size of a football. It was full of veins of gold, or so I reckoned. I carried the quartz back to the boat, stumbling on the faux-rocks, wondering whether my gold was genuine.

We set off again, with the lump of quartz in the bottom of the boat. The outboard spewed its wake behind—chaotic white foam, but in some kind of process. I looked back at it and realized I was in the most remote place I had ever been to; it was as if it were remote in time as well as in geography. As we made our way back to the campsite, and the mountains of which Kungwe is chief, the landscape grew greener and more populous. Splinters of quartz and granite gave way to lush expanses of bush and occasional village.

I was watching one of these groups of thick mud huts roll past in the distance, when the outboard motor started to spit out puffs of blue smoke. There was a series of puttering coughs, and then one great big puff followed a last valedictory cough. And then there was silence. The motor had conked out.

As the boat boy tried to fix it, I read my copy of Burton's *Lake Regions of Central Africa*. Only the passage of a large ship marked the difference between his time and my own. It was not the *Liemba*, but a freighter taking fuel to Burundi. There has been fighting there this week, the radio had said. The wake of the freighter sent us back, rocking to and fro. At that moment something connected, the outboard kicked, and we were on our way again.

The following morning, at the village of Mirambo-Lagosa, I found

Mr Malyamungu. He was ancient, a tiny man in a flowing red robe underneath which was a dirty T-shirt with the words CHIMP HAVEN printed on it. Moustaches—long, thin and twirled—poked out either side of his nose, exactly in parallel with the drooping straw roof of his hut. He sat under this roof in a deckchair, smoking cheroots. We spoke through two translators. From English into Swahili (mine not being anywhere near good enough for this kind of interview), then from Swahili into Tongwe, a local language.

As a young boy, Mr Malyamungu had narrowly escaped conscription by the Germans. 'My father was a powerful chief and he avoided it,' he told me through the translator. He cut a cheroot with his penknife. 'Yes, during that time I heard of some small boats that chase the *Liemba*. But they never catched her. They were sinking two other boats of the *Kijerumani*.

'I was growing up at this time, and I cut wood for *sitima* [steamer].' He collected timber for the *Götzen's* wood-burning engine. 'The *Kijerumani* and after the *Kingereza* would ring a bell on the cable and we would go out into the forest with our machetes and bring bundles of wood to the station.' He said there was great competition to get the wood-cutting contracts. 'Sometimes there was fighting between groups and people were killed.'

Had he ever heard of Bwana Chifunga-Tumbo, the Englishman in a skirt? 'I have heard of that man, but I never saw him.' Later another white man came and told them not to be afraid, the war was over and the *Kijerumani* could not hang them any more. Did the Germans really hang them? 'Yes, they hung us and they whipped us and were very cruel.'

More cruel than the British? He put out his cheroot by crushing its glow between finger and thumb. 'Yes, but the Holo-Holo were the cruellest.'

The Holo-Holo were the tribe, mainly based on the Congo side, who helped Spicer on his journey. It was they who made the little statue of him. 'Those people who made those statues are gone away now,' Mr Malyamungu told me.

In 1915 there were thousands of Holo-Holo settled along the Tanganyikan shore of the lake. They had originally sailed over in canoes and established discrete family units down the lake. Now there are hardly any on either side of the lake. In his book *Aux Rives du*

Tanganyika, published in 1913, Bishop Adolphe Lechaptois argues that the depopulation was in part caused by the Holo-Holo practice of killing newborn babies. 'Since the Europeans took over the government of this land, this custom has disappeared to a large extent. But in the remote villages, too far away or too small to be visited by the authorities or the missionaries, the practice continues in secret, only instead of throwing the babies into the lake or exposing them in the bush, they are made to disappear by the simple process of sticking a needle into the brain.' A later Bishop, James Holmes-Siedle—writing in 1948 about a trip down the lake in the *Liemba*—calls the Holo-Holo country the Southern Wilderness, 'because the whole place is practically uninhabited'. He adds that there had been recent cases of ordeal by poison among the tribe. A census taken in the same year as Holmes-Siedle was writing listed 4,410 Holo-Holo in Tanganyika.

'Their language is very old,' said Hamidu, a researcher into chimpanzees who hitched a lift in my boat on the return journey. 'They came here long ago, before the railway was built. They enslaved people for the Arabs, and then they worked for the Germans and the British.' He revealed that his grandfather was Holo-Holo. 'Now they have been absorbed into the Tongwe. There are very few pure Holo-Holo left. They were very good fighters. In those days if you did not move off your lands when the Holo-Holo came, he would kill you. But if you obeyed them and left the land they would not kill you.'

Have any words of Holo-Holo come into Tongwe? 'Only one I know. It is *msampwe*. Prisoner.'

We made our way back to camp again. Mist sat on Mount Kungwe above. I spotted a refugee camp on the shoreline, its tents of green polythene torn and flapping. I went in to investigate, but soldiers waved me away. Through my binoculars I watched a tall naked man with a stomach like a drum stoop down to the water, cupping his hand to drink.

The following day I went to Kalilani. A village full of Congolese refugees from the 1960s, it was noticeably poorer than the Tongwe villages nearby. Here, I had been told, lived one of the last pure Holo-Holo along this side of the lake. His name was Sefu Luseza and he came out to greet me smiling, the sun gleaming on the beads of his Muslim skullcap.

Now about sixty-eight (he couldn't remember the exact year of his birth), he had paddled over here from the Congo in 1964. His wife, four children and a chicken came with him in the canoe. We sat on stools in the middle of the village as I asked him why he had left.

'There was too much fighting. There were Belgian mercenaries there.'

Sefu and his family had set off in the morning and arrived at three the following afternoon. There was no village before he came. Now there were about 500 people, mainly Congolese from the Bembe tribe. He speaks to them in Swahili or their own language, having mostly forgotten his Holo-Holo.

Was he always a Muslim? 'No. On the other side we Holo-Holo worshipped a spirit called Migabo. Then they came here and switched to Mkungwe, and then they became either Christian or Muslim. But I am the only Holo-Holo left now.'

Round us, children were beginning to gather, draping themselves over an old tree-trunk. I pressed him on the old-time religion, even though it made him uncomfortable to talk about it.

'There was a hut where the *waganga* [witch-doctors] would call down the spirit. They would smear white soil on their face. Like suntan cream you whites put. They were members of a spirit society and you went inside the hut to see him, and they bring the spirit down into you.'

The children were terrified; he told them that he himself saw this ceremony as a child. 'They don't know any of these stories,' he informed me. 'They cannot capture it any more. In the old days they would sit round and listen.' I suddenly realized that in coming here, researching the oral tradition, I was precipitating a rare instance of it.

I asked Sefu if he could remember anything about the ceremony. Could he show it to me? At first he was reluctant, putting his head in his hands and saying it hurt to remember. Then he sent one of his wives to fetch a cloth. He put the cloth over his head and started to shake, putting out his arms.

'They shook gourds with stones inside,' he said through the cloth, 'and they sang.'

He began to sing in Holo-Holo, dredging ancient words from his memory: '*Nangisane babo, nangisane kulingamira, nanjata kulugo...*' It was the spirit-possession song of the Migabo cult, and hearing it chilled me a little, though the translation was innocuous enough. 'I am coming to you, I am coming to see, I am going home...'

Why call down this *nzimu*, this spirit? Sefu pulled on his fingers, making the list. 'It is to make a sick person better, to explain something that has happened in the past, or to say what is going to happen in the future. And it is also to kill somebody.'

I wrote Sefu's answers down as carefully as he had given them to me. As I was doing so, a motor boat buzzed across the bay. I took out my binoculars and looked. It was one of the boats from the chimpanzee reserve, donated by the Frankfurt Zoological Society, whose logo was printed on the side.

I thanked Sefu for his help and tried to give him some money for his efforts. He refused it, pointing at my binoculars. 'When you come back, bring me some of those.'

After the war, Spicer worked for the International Hydrographic Bureau in Monte Carlo as its first Secretary General. A note in the autobiography of Baroness Orczy, author of *The Scarlet Pimpernel*, talks about him in glowing terms and mentions a lecture he gave to the town's *Société des Conferences* about his mission. The Baroness clearly enjoyed Spicer's talk. 'He showed us some wonderful magic-lantern slides that he had taken and developed himself.' Later in the season the Baroness also tackled Literary Frauds as a subject for a lecture. Had her friend the Commander told the whole story in his own lectures? It seems unlikely, given his past record of fabrication and elaboration. For one thing it was Frank Magee, the journalist and 'Petty Officer Writer', who took the pictures, not Spicer.

In 1937, as the storm clouds of another war approached, the man who had been Bwana Chifunga-Tumbo resigned his post in Monaco. He went to live in Courtenay, British Columbia, where he died on January 29, 1947, at the age of seventy-one. He was survived by his wife Amy.

The *Götzen* had been twice sunk and twice raised by the time Spicer died. A few months before Spicer left Africa with his medical certificate in 1916, the Belgians had taken receipt of four Short seaplanes equipped with bombs. They had been packed in crates in Britain and were reassembled by the lakeside, as the *Götzen* itself had been three years earlier. The pilots had practised. In June they bombed the *Götzen*, doing the job that Spicer shirked. Whether or not the bombs hit the target is disputed but the Germans knew the game was up, for the time being at any rate.

When General Tombeur, the senior Belgian officer, captured the railway and took Kigoma on July 26, 1916, the *Götzen* was nowhere to be seen. Or so it first appeared. Then some masts were spotted, sticking out of the water at the mouth of the Malagarasi river. The ship had been filled with cement and scuttled. Her engines had been greased to preserve them and allow her to be sailed when and if she were raised.

The Germans never got the chance to come back and fulfil their plan. After the war, it was the Belgians who raised the *Götzen* and towed her back to Kigoma harbour. She sank again at her moorings during a storm not long afterwards. In 1921, back in the job of First Lord of the Admiralty in the postwar Liberal government, Winston Churchill ordered that she be raised once more and reconditioned under the auspices of Britain's new territory of Tanganyika. On Monday, May 16, 1927, she sailed again, registered as the *Liemba*. A luncheon of seven or eight courses was served to the dignitaries on board, with Champagne Pommery and liqueurs.

As for *Mimi* and *Tou-Tou*, nobody knows what happened to them. On my return to Kigoma, I received permission to look for them in the military docks, where the old German railway still comes right up to the quay. There were lots of iron hulks there, and a few old wooden boats. I didn't think any of them could be *Mimi* or *Tou-Tou*. With their mahogany hulls, they surely would have rotted away by now.

But just as I was leaving, Musa Hathemani, chief executive of the port authority, called me into his office and said that he had once been told that the wreck of HMS *Tou-Tou* (he called her 'Tow-Tow') was submerged off a village called Kabalangabo. I took a whaler taxi there, thinking it was too good to be true. Surely this was not the gold I had been looking for—a physical historical connection to the British expedition, just as the *Liemba* was to the Germans?

A fisherman directed me to an area of pea-green water about twenty feet offshore. Stripping off, I dived down—swimming as hard as I could into the soup. It was a waste of breath. It was too murky to see; I could not stay down; I got nowhere near the bottom. I came up spluttering, and returned to the shore. Pulling back on my T-shirt, I quizzed the villagers, who had lined up along the beach to watch my ridiculous diving antics. They knew nothing about anything called *Tou-Tou*. But yes, a boat could be seen there until a few years ago—a boat from the Great War. Apparently some part of the superstructure used to stick up, but it was now covered by sand. Whether the craft that had disappeared belonged to *Ujerumani* or *Uingereza*, they did not know. It was just the boat of some white men who had once fought near here, long ago. ☐

FEMME FATALE
T. Coraghessan Boyle

Department of sexology at Indiana University, 1952.
Professor Kinsey second row, far right

Looking back on it now, I don't think I was ever actually 'sex shy' (to use one of Prok's pet phrases), but I'll admit I was pretty naive when I first came to him, not to mention hopelessly dull and conventional. I don't know what he saw in me, really—or perhaps I do. If you'll forgive me a moment of vanity, my wife Iris claims I was something of a heart-throb on campus, though I would have been the last to know of it because I wasn't dating and had always been uncomfortable with the sort of small talk that leads up to the casual enquiry about after-class plans or what you might or might not be doing on Saturday after the game. I had a pretty fair physique in those days, with a matching set of fullback's shoulders and a thirty-inch waist (I was first string on my high school team till I suffered a concussion midway through my junior season and my mother put a premature end to my career), and unlike most men at college, I was conscientious about keeping myself in trim—I still am—but that's neither here nor there. To complete the portrait, because already I've managed to get myself out on a limb here, I was blessed with what Iris calls 'sensitive' eyes, whatever that might mean, and a thatch of wheat-coloured hair with a natural curl that defeated any cream or pomade I'd ever come across. As for sex, I was eager, but inexperienced, and shy in the usual way—unsure of myself and just about as uninformed as anyone you could imagine.

In fact, the first time I developed anything more than a theoretical grasp of what it involved—the mechanics of the act, that is—was during my senior year at IU, in the fall of 1939, when I found myself sitting in a lecture hall jammed to the rafters with silent, dry-mouthed students of both sexes as Prok's colour slides played hugely across the screen. I was there at the instigation of a girl named Laura Feeney, one of the campus *femmes fatales* who never seemed to go anywhere without an arm looped through some letterman's. Laura had the reputation of being 'fast', though I can assure you I was never the beneficiary of her sexual largesse (if, in fact, the rumours were true: as I was later to learn, the steamiest-looking women often have the most repressed sex lives, and vice versa). I remember being distinctly flattered when she stopped me in the corridor one day during fall registration, took hold of my arm at the muscle and pecked a kiss to my cheek.

'Oh, hi, John,' she breathed. 'I was just thinking about you. How was your summer?'

My summer had been spent back home in Michigan City, stocking shelves and bagging groceries, and if I had five minutes to myself my mother had me pruning the trees, re-shingling the roof and pulling weeds in the vegetable garden. I was lonely, bored to tears, masturbating twice a day in my attic room that was like a sweat-box in a penal institution. My only relief derived from books. I came under the spell of John Donne and Andrew Marvell that summer, and I reread Sir Philip Sidney's 'Astrophel and Stella' three times in preparation for an English Literature course I was looking forward to in the fall. But I couldn't tell Laura Feeney all this—or any of it. She would have thought me a washout. Which I was. So I just shrugged and said, 'All right, I guess.'

Voices reverberated in the stairwell, boomed in the corners and fled all the way down the corridor to where the registration tables had been set up in the gymnasium. 'Yeah,' Laura said, and her smile went cold a moment, 'I know how you feel. With me it was work, work, work— my father owns a lunch counter in Fort Wayne, did you know that?'

I didn't know. I shook my head and felt a whole shining loop of my hair fall loose though I must have used half a bottle of creme oil on it. I was wearing one of the stiff new Arrow shirts my grandmother had sent me from Chicago and a glen-plaid tie I think I wore to class every day that year in the hope of making a good impression, my briefcase was in one hand, a stack of library books in the other. As I've said, the gift of small talk eluded me. I think I said something like, 'Fort Wayne, huh?'

In the event, it didn't matter what I said, because she let her turquoise eyes go wide (she was a redhead, or strawberry blonde, actually, with skin so white you'd think it had never seen the sun), gave my muscle a squeeze and lowered her voice. 'Listen,' she said, 'I just wanted to know if you'd mind getting engaged to me—'

Her words hung there between us, closing out everything else— the chatter of the group of freshmen materializing suddenly from the men's room, the sound of an automobile horn out on the street— and I can only imagine the look I must have given her in response. This was long before Prok taught me to tuck all the loose strands of my emotions behind a mask of impassivity, and everything I was thinking routinely rushed to my face along with the blood that settled in my cheeks like a barometer of confusion.

'John, you're not blushing, are you?'

'No,' I said, 'not at all. I'm just—'

She held my eyes, enjoying the moment. 'Just what?'

I shrugged. 'We were out in the sun—yesterday it was, yesterday afternoon. Moving furniture. So I guess, well—'

Someone brushed by me, an undergraduate who looked vaguely familiar—had he been in my psych class last year?—and then she let the other shoe drop. 'I mean just for the semester. For pretend.' She looked away and her hair rose and fell in an ebbing wave. When she turned back to me, she lifted her face till it was like a satellite of my own, pale and glowing in the infusion of light from the windows at the end of the corridor. 'You know,' she said, 'for the marriage course?'

I said, 'Yes.' I said, 'Yes, all right,' and Laura Feeney smiled and before I knew it I was on my way to becoming an initiate in the science of sex, abandoning the ideal for the actual, the dream of Stella ('True, that true beauty virtue is indeed') for anatomy, physiology and an intimate knowledge of Bartholin's gland and the labia minora. All of it—all the years of research, the thousands of miles travelled, the histories taken, the delving and rooting and pioneering—spun out like thread from an infinite spool held in the milk-white palm of Laura Feeney on an otherwise ordinary morning in the autumn of 1939.

But I don't want to make too much of it—we all have our defining moments. And I don't mean to keep you in the dark here either. The 'marriage course' to which Laura Feeney was referring—'Marriage and the Family', properly—was being offered by Professor Kinsey of the Zoology Department and half a dozen of his colleagues from other disciplines, and it was the sensation of the campus. The course was open only to faculty and staff, students who were married or engaged, and seniors of both sexes. There were eleven lectures in all, five of them covering the sociological, psychological, economic, legal and religious facets of marriage, these to be delivered by faculty outside of the Zoology Department, and they were to prove to be informative enough, I suppose, and necessary, but if truth be told they were nothing more than window dressing for the six unexpurgated lectures (with audio-visual aids) Professor Kinsey—Prok—was scheduled to give on the physiology of intra-marital relations.

Word was out on campus, and I suspect there were any number of junior girls like Laura Feeney shopping at the five-and-dime for rhinestone rings—maybe even sophomores and freshmen too. My guess is that Laura's lettermen were engaged to their fall sports, and, by extension, their coaches, and so she cast me in the role of prospective bridegroom. I didn't mind. I would say she wasn't my type, but then all women are every man's type under the right circumstances. She was popular, she was pretty, and if for an hour or two a week people took her to be mine, so much the better. To this point, I'd been immersed in my studies—I made Dean's List five out of the first six semesters—and I barely knew any girls, either on campus or back at home, and to have her there at my side as other couples strolled by and the late-blooming sun ladled syrup over the trees and the apparent world stood still for whole minutes at a time was like no feeling I'd ever had. Was it love? I don't know. It was certainly something, and it stirred me—I could always hope, couldn't I?

At any rate, as I say, word was out, and the lecture hall was full to overflowing when we got there the first day. I remember being surprised at the number of younger faculty crowding the front rows with their prim and upright wives and how many of them I didn't recognize. There was a sprinkling of older faculty too, looking lost and even vaguely queasy, and their presence was a real puzzle—you would have thought people in their forties and fifties with grown children should be acquainted with the basic facts of life, but there they were. ('Maybe they need a refresher course,' Laura said with half a grin and very much *sotto voce*, and even that, even the barest mention of what those couples must have done in private—or once have done—made me go hot all over.) And of course the real multitude was composed of students—there must have been 300 or more of us there, crowded in shoulder to shoulder, all waiting to be scandalized, to hear the forbidden words spoken aloud and see the very act itself depicted in living colour.

Dr Hoenig, the Dean of Women, had been stationed at the door as we filed in, ready to pounce on anyone who wasn't on her list of registered students. She was a short, top-heavy woman in a dowdy dress and a grey cloche hat that seemed like an extension of her pinned-up hair, and though she must have been in her forties then she seemed to us as ancient and vigilant as the Sphinx, her spectacles shining as she bent to check names against the list and scrutinize the ring fingers of all the girls who claimed to be engaged. We passed muster, and sat through the preliminary lectures, biding our time until Professor Kinsey took the stage. We'd seen him at the outset—he'd electrified us all in his introductory lecture by claiming that there were no abnormalities when it came to sex, save for abstinence, celibacy and delayed marriage—but then he'd been succeeded by a doctor from the medical school whose voice was perfectly pitched to the frequency of sleep, and then a Methodist minister and a pinched little man from the Psychology Department who spoke ad nauseam on Freud's *Three Essays on the Theory of Sexuality*.

It was raining, I remember, on the day we'd all been waiting for— the day of the slide presentation—and as Laura Feeney and I stepped into the ante-room with the mob of other students divesting themselves of umbrellas and slickers, I was struck by the deep working odour of all that massed and anointed flesh. Laura must have noticed it too, because the minute she ducked demurely past Dean Hoenig, she wrinkled up her nose and whispered, 'Smells like somebody let all the tomcats loose.'

I didn't know what to say to that, so I gave her a faint smile—it wouldn't do at all to look as if I were enjoying myself, because this was education, after all, this was science, and every face had been ironed sober—and allowed my right hand to rest lightly at her waist as I guided her through the crush and into the semi-darkened hall. We were fifteen minutes early, but already all the aisle seats had been taken and we had to edge awkwardly through a picket of folded knees, book bags and umbrellas to reach the middle of one of the back rows. Laura settled in, shook out her hair, waved to thirty or forty people I didn't recognize, then bent forward over her compact and stealthily reapplied her lipstick. She came up compressing her lips and giving me the sort of look she might have reserved for a little brother or maybe the family dog—she was a junior from Fort Wayne and I was a senior from Michigan City and no matter how much I wanted to believe otherwise there was nothing, absolutely nothing, between us.

I gazed down the row. Nearly all the girls were glancing round them with shining eyes while the men fumbled with loose-leaf binders and worried over the nubs of their pencils. A man from my rooming house—Dick Martone—happened to glance up then and our eyes met briefly. Both of us looked away, but not before I could read his excitement. Here we were—he wedged in between two other senior men, I with Laura Feeney preening at my side—about to see and engage what we'd been hungering after for the better part of our lives. I can't begin to describe the frisson that ran through that hall, communicated from seat to seat, elbow to elbow, through the whole yearning mass of us. Over the course of the past weeks we'd been instructed in the history and customs of marriage, heard about the emotions evoked, the legal ramifications of the nuptial bond and even the anatomy of the structures involved in reproduction, heard the words 'penis', 'nipple', 'vagina' and 'clitoris' spoken aloud in mixed company, and now we were going to see for ourselves. I could feel the blood pounding in my extremities.

Then the side door swung open and Professor Kinsey was there, striding purposefully to the podium. Though a moment before he'd been slogging across campus in galoshes and sou'wester, you would have thought he'd just stepped out of a sunlit meadow, the sheaf of his bristling flat-topped pompadour standing upright from the crown of his head as if it had been pressed from a mould, his dark suit, white shirt and bow tie impeccable, his face relaxed and youthful. He was in his mid-forties then, a looming tall presence with an oversized head, curiously narrowed shoulders and a slight stoop— the result of the rickets he'd suffered as a child—and he never wasted a motion or a single minute of anybody's time either. The anticipatory murmur fell off abruptly as he stepped up to the podium and raised his head to look out on the audience. Silence. Absolute. We all became aware of the sound of the rain then, a steady sizzle like static in the background.

'Today we shall discuss the physiology of sexual response and orgasm in the human animal,' he began, without preliminary, without notes, and as his equable, matter-of-fact tones penetrated the audience, I could feel Laura Feeney go tense beside me. I stole a glance at her. Her face was rapt, her white blouse glowing in the dimness of the lecture hall as if it were the single radiant point in the concave sweep of the audience. She was wearing knee socks and a pleated skirt that pulled tight to reveal the swell of the long muscles of her thighs. Her perfume took hold of me like a vice.

Professor Kinsey—Prok—went on, with the help of the overhead projector, to document how the penis enlarges through vasocongestion and at orgasm releases between two and five million spermatozoa, depending on the individual, and then turned his attention to the female reproductive organs. He talked at length about vaginal secretions and their function in easing intromission of the penis, spoke of the corresponding importance of the cervical secretions, which, in some cases, may serve to loosen the mucous plug that ordinarily lies in the opening—the os—of the cervix, and can prevent fertilization by blocking movement of the sperm into the uterus and subsequently the Fallopian tubes. We bowed our heads, scribbled furiously in our notebooks. Laura Feeney swelled beside me till she was the size of one of the balloons they floated overhead during the Macy's parade. Everyone in the place was breathing as one.

And then, abruptly, the first of the slides appeared, a full-colour, close-up photograph of an erect, circumcised phallus, followed by a shot of the moist and glistening vagina awaiting it. 'The vagina must be spread open as the erect male organ penetrates,' Professor Kinsey went on, as the next slide dominated the screen behind him, 'and thus the female has employed two fingers to this end. You will observe that the clitoris is stimulated at this point, thus providing the erotic stimulation necessary for the completion of the act on the part of the female.' There was more—a very detailed and mechanical account of the various positions the human animal employs in engaging in coitus, as well as techniques of foreplay—and a teaser (as if we needed one) for the next lecture, which was to focus on fertilization and (here the whispers broke out) how to circumvent it.

I heard it all. I even took notes, though afterwards I could make no sense of them. Once the slides appeared I lost all consciousness of the moment (and I can't overemphasize the jolt they gave me, the immediate and intensely physical sensation that was like nothing so much as plunging into a cold stream or being slapped across the face—here it was, here it was at long last!). I might have been sitting there upright in the chair, Laura Feeney swelling at my side, and I drew breath and blinked my eyes and the blood circulated through my veins, but for all intents and purposes I wasn't there at all.

Afterwards—and I can't for the life of me recall how the lecture concluded—people collected their things in silence and moved up the aisles in a sombre processional. There was none of the jostling and joking you would normally expect from a mob of undergraduates set loose after an hour's confinement. Instead, the crowd shuffled forward listlessly, shoulders slumped, eyes averted, for all the world like refugees escaping some disaster. I couldn't look at Laura Feeney. I couldn't guide her with a hand to her waist either—I was on fire, aflame, and I was afraid the merest touch would incinerate her. I studied the back of her head, her hair, her shoulders, as we made our way through the crowd towards the smell of the rain beyond the big flung-open doors at the end of the hallway. We were delayed a moment on the doorstep, a traffic jam there on the landing as the rain lashed down and people squared their hats and fumbled with umbrellas, and then I had my own umbrella open and Laura and I were down the steps and out into the rain.

We must have gone a hundred yards, the trees flailing in the wind, the umbrella streaming, before I found something to say. 'Do you— would you like to take a walk? Or do you need to, perhaps—because I could take you back to the dorm if that's what you—'

Her face was drawn and bloodless and she walked stiffly beside me, avoiding body contact as much as was possible under the circumstances. She stopped suddenly and I stopped too, awkwardly struggling to keep the crown of the umbrella above her. 'A walk?' she repeated. 'In this? You've got the wrong species here, I'm afraid—I'm a *human animal*, not a duck.' And then we were laughing, both of us, and it was all right.

'Well, how about a cup of coffee then—and maybe a piece of, I don't know, pie? Or a drink?' I hesitated. The rain glistened in her hair and her eyes were bright. 'I could use a stiff one after that. I was—what I mean is, I never—'

She touched my arm at the elbow and her smile suddenly bloomed and then faded just as quickly. 'No,' she said, and her voice had gone soft, 'me neither.'

I took her to a tavern crowded with undergraduates seeking a respite from the weather, and the first thing she did when we settled into a booth by the window was twist the rhinestone band off her finger and secrete it in the inside compartment of her purse. Then she unpinned her hat, patted down her hair and turned away from me to reapply her lipstick. I hadn't thought past the moment, and once we agreed on where we were going, we hadn't talked much either, the rain providing background music on the timpani of the umbrella and plucking the strings of the ragged trees as if that were all the distraction we could bear. Now, as I braced my elbows on the table and leaned towards her to ask what she wanted to drink, I realized that this was something very like a date and blessed my luck because I had two and a half dollars left in my wallet after paying out room and board from my scant weekly pay cheque (I was working at the university library then, pushing a broom and re-shelving books five evenings a week). 'Oh, I don't know,' she said, and I could see she wasn't quite herself yet. 'What are you having?'

'Bourbon. And a beer chaser.'

She made a moue of her lips.

'I can get you a soft drink, if you prefer—ginger ale, maybe?'

'A Tom Collins,' she said, 'I'll have a Tom Collins,' and her eyes began to sweep the room.

The lower legs and cuffs of my trousers were wet and my socks squished in my shoes as I rose to make my way to the bar. The place was close and steaming, shoulders and elbows looming up everywhere, the sawdust on the floor darkly compacted by the impressions of a hundred wet heels. When I got back to the table with our drinks, there was another couple sitting opposite Laura, the girl in a green velvet hat that brought out the colour of her eyes, the man in a wet overcoat buttoned up over his collar and the knot of his tie. He had a long nose with a bump in it and two little pincushion eyes set too close together. I don't remember his name— or hers either, not at this remove. Call them Sally and Bill, and identify them as fellow students in the marriage course, sweethearts certainly—worlds more than Laura and I were to each other— though not yet actually engaged.

Laura made the introductions. I nodded and said I was pleased to meet them both.

Bill had a pitcher of beer in front of him, the carbonation rising up from its depths in a rich, golden display, and I watched in silence as he tucked his tongue in the corner of his mouth and meticulously poured out half a glass for Sally and a full one for himself. The golden liquid swirled in the glass and the head rose and steadied before composing itself in a perfect white disc. 'You look like you've done that before,' I said.

'You bet I have,' he replied, then lifted his glass and grinned. 'A toast,' he proposed. He waited till we'd raised our glasses. 'To Professor Kinsey!' he cried. 'Who else?'

This was greeted with a snicker from the booth behind us, but we laughed—all four of us—as a way of defeating our embarrassment. There was one thing only on our minds, one subject we all were burning to talk of, and though Bill had alluded to it, we weren't quite comfortable with it yet. We were silent a moment, studying the faces of the people shuffling damply through the door. 'I like your ring, Sally,' Laura said finally. 'Was it terribly expensive?'

And then they were both giggling and Bill and I were laughing along with them, laughing immoderately, laughing for the sheer joy and release of it. I could feel the bourbon settling in my stomach and sending out feelers to the distant tendrils of my nerves, and my face shone and so did theirs. We were in on a secret together, the four of us—we'd put one over on Dean Hoenig—and we'd just gone through a rite of initiation in a darkened hall in the Biology building. It took a minute. Bill lit a cigarette. The girls searched each other's eyes. 'Jeeze,' Bill said finally, 'did you ever in your life see anything like that?'

'I thought I was going to die,' Sally said. She threw a glance at me, then studied the pattern of wet rings her beer glass had made on the table. 'If my mother—' she began, but couldn't finish the thought.

'God,' Laura snorted, making a drawn-out bleat of it, 'my mother would've gone through the roof.' She'd lit a cigarette too, and it smouldered now in the ashtray, the white of the paper flecked red from the touch of her lips. She picked it up distractedly, took a quick puff, exhaled. 'Because we never, in my family, I mean never, discussed, you know, where little boys and girls come from.'

Sally raised a confidential hand to her mouth. 'They call him "Dr Sex", did you know that?'

'Who does?' I felt as if I were floating above the table, all my tethers cut and the ground fast fading below me. This was heady stuff, naughty, wicked, like when a child first learns the *verboten* words Professor Kinsey had pronounced so distinctly and disinterestedly for us just an hour before.

Sally raised her eyebrows till they met the brim of her hat. 'People. Around campus.'

'Not to mention town,' Bill put in. He dropped his voice. 'He makes you do interviews, you know. About your sex life'—he laughed—'or lack of it.'

'I would hate that,' Sally said. 'It's so...*personal*. And it's not as if he's a medical doctor. Or a minister even.'

I felt overheated suddenly, though the place was as dank as the dripping alley out back. 'Histories,' I said, surprising myself. 'Case histories. He's explained all that—how else are we going to know what people—'

'The human animal, you mean,' Laura said.

'—what people do when they, when they mate, if we don't look at it scientifically? And frankly. I don't know about you, but I applaud what Kinsey's doing, and if it's shocking, I think we should ask ourselves why, because isn't a, a...a *function* as universal as reproductive behaviour just as logical a cause for study as the circulation of the blood or the way the cornea works or any other medical knowledge we've accumulated over the centuries?' It might have been the bourbon talking, but there I was defending Prok before I ever even knew him.

'Yes, but,' Bill said, and we all leaned into the table and talked till our glasses were empty and then we filled them and emptied them again, the rain tracing patterns in the dirt of the window, then the window going dark and the tide of undergraduates ebbing and flowing as people went home to dinner and their books. It was seven o'clock. I was out of money. My head throbbed but I'd never been so excited in my life. When Bill and Sally excused themselves and shrugged out the door and into the wafting dampness of the night, I lingered a moment, half drunk, and put an arm round Laura's shoulders. 'So we're still engaged, aren't we?' I murmured.

Her smile spread softly from her lips to her eyes. She plucked the maraschino cherry from her glass and rotated it between her fingers before gently pressing it into my mouth. 'Sure,' she said.

'Then shouldn't we—or don't we have an obligation, to, to—'

'Sure,' she said, and she leaned forward and gave me a kiss, a kiss that was sweetened by the syrup of the cherry and the smell of her perfume and the proximity of her body that was warm now and languid. It was a long kiss, the longest I'd ever experienced, and it was deepened and complicated by what we'd seen up there on the screen in the lecture hall, by the visual memory of those corresponding organs designed for sensory gratification and the reproduction of the species, mutually receptive, self-lubricated, cohesive and natural. I came up for air encouraged, emboldened, and though there was nothing between us and we both knew it, I whispered, 'Come home with me.'

The look of Laura's face transformed suddenly. Her eyes sharpened and her features came into focus as if I'd never really seen them before, as if this wasn't the girl I'd just kissed in a moment of sweet oblivion. We were both absolutely still, our breath commingling, hands poised at the edge of the table as if we didn't know what to do with them, till she turned away from me and began to gather up her purse, her raincoat, her hat. I became aware of the voices at the bar then, someone singing in a creaking baritone, the hiss of a newly tapped keg. 'I don't know what you're thinking, John,' she said, and I was getting to my feet now too, rattled suddenly, flushing red for all I knew. What kind of a girl was she? Not that kind of girl, she said. □

PUT NOT THY TRUST IN CHARIOTS

Jonathan Tel

D avid had nothing against Arabs personally. This despite the fact
he was religious (he wore a blue-and-white *kippa* which had
been knitted by his wife, Devorah, as an engagement present; if one
looked carefully one could see their linked initials—*dalèd* and
dalèd—embroidered near the edge) and politically he was on the
right. In fact the colleague of his with whom he got on best was an
Arab, Daoud. Perhaps the fact that they shared the same name—in
its Hebrew and Arabic versions—had something to do with it. But
more to the point: they did the same job; they were roughly the same
age; it so happened they were both married with two children and
one on the way; they had a similar practical temperament; they even
looked quite alike—two men in dark suits, short rather than tall,
sturdy, with a steady gaze.

David and Daoud worked in the Jerusalem office. They were bank
tellers, and spent their days taking shekels in and giving shekels out.
They had been employed there for several years, and had every
expectation of staying on until retirement. The job was boring and
not well paid, but neither man defined himself in terms of it, and so
they were reasonably happy.

Since their bank was located near the King David Hotel, they
often talked about visiting the famous terrace for a sundowner—a
gathering of Davids, so to speak—but they never did, because for
one thing the hotel was outside their price range, and for another
there was always the possibility Daoud might be stopped by Security,
which would lead to embarrassment and unpleasantness all round.

What they did instead, however, was head to a local cafe during
their lunch break. (A strictly kosher establishment, of course.) The
owner and the waitresses would greet them when they came in. 'Oh,
it's you two again. Shalom!' Then the tellers would state their regular
order, for a cappuccino and a ciabatta sandwich apiece. If, on a
Monday, David picked up the tab, then on Tuesday it would be
Daoud's turn.

Since politics and religion were not available for discussion
(whatever Daoud's views were, he kept them to himself; given his
profession, and given that he was Christian, one could rule out
violent extremism, at least), and there is only so much to be said
about family: that left money as the obvious topic. Neither man had
enough. Their wives could not work, what with the children to look

after, and it's hard to support a growing family on a teller's salary alone. Ah, if only a tiny percentage of what passed through their hands could find its way into their pockets!

Money—it's astonishing how dirty you can get from handling used banknotes and coins. Before eating lunch David and Daoud would stand side by side in the washroom, cleansing their fingers with liquid soap and a nail file.

Of course David thought long and hard about economizing. But how could he? What was there left to cut back on, without sinking into a life of miserliness? He had already given up smoking, a year previously, at his wife's insistence. Nothing he spent his money on now could be called an extravagance. He and his family rented an apartment in Mekor Chaim (a respectable neighbourhood, neither poor nor rich, neither wholly religious nor wholly secular, a few kilometres to the south). He owned a Mazda Lantis, cream coloured, in excellent working condition, three years old and not brand new when he'd bought it. He allowed himself a new suit twice a year, at Rosh Hashanah and at Passover, but that was necessary for work. His children were fed and clothed as they should be; his wife was dressed in the manner that befits an attractive young religious woman, modest but not fanatically so, in shades of lime or turquoise with a matching cloche hat.

Of course, the obvious saving would be to move out of Jerusalem. He could relocate to one of the nearby settlements, where the rents are lower. For example, what was wrong with Efrat, conveniently linked to Jerusalem by the tunnel road, just about half an hour's commute away if the traffic is flowing smoothly? His wife's brother lived there; David and Devorah and the children had visited many times over Shabbat. Certainly people were friendly in Efrat, and the air was sweeter. In fact Devorah had dropped heavy hints she wouldn't at all mind making her home there, in one of the comparatively spacious new apartments with a view across the hills. And politically, of course, just by taking up residence, he and his family would be doing their bit. But David couldn't bring himself to give up on Jerusalem. He was born in this city. It was his. True, it was not as if he partook much of the urban entertainments, or prayed often at the Wall, but he loved knowing it was all on his doorstep. Wouldn't any Jew desire that he, his wife and his children should live here rather than anywhere else?

Or he could sell his car. Logically, he could do without it. He calculated he saved about twenty minutes per commute by driving as opposed to taking the bus; and then when you take into account the time spent parking, and the general hassle, it was hardly worth it. True, the car was handy for picking up groceries at the Hypernetto, but not essential. Sometimes the family would drive farther afield, but it would be more economical to rent a car for those special occasions. Besides, a car is a dangerous form of transport. Every year more Israelis die in traffic accidents than in acts of terrorism.

On the other hand, if you kept thinking about all the risks involved in daily life, you'd never get out of bed in the morning. David had aspired to this as a young man fresh out of the Army: a wife, children, a home, a job, a car. He was reluctant to give anything up.

Now, one lunch-time David had been discussing, in general terms, his financial situation with Daoud.

Daoud cleared his throat. In his fluent but somehow unnatural Hebrew, he said: 'David, you are habituated never to use your car on your Sabbath, right?'

'Of course not. That would be against my religion.'

'And not on your Jewish holidays, either?'

'No.'

'Now, have I told you about my sister, Danielle?'

'I don't think so.'

'She's divorced with a couple of kids.'

'I'm sorry to hear that.'

'Ah, that husband of hers was a bastard. She's better off without him. She should find herself a new man, you know. She is of pleasant appearance. Honey-brown hair. She works as a translator in the courts. She does numerous child custody cases. The stories she tells me about what goes in some families, it would make your blood boil.'

'Is that so?'

'Now, Danielle would benefit from her own transport. Not on weekdays: the children can walk to school, and she is happy to catch the bus to work—the number eighteen will whisk her right there. But, you know how it is, on Saturdays the children get bored. She'd like to take them to the beach, and to visit our parents in the north.'

David nodded. He could see where this conversation was heading. He interrupted his colleague. 'So what you're saying, Daoud, is that your sister and myself, we could co-own a car. Is that right?'

'Yes. No. It's not a question of ownership. The car is still yours, but she would have sole use of it part-time. It makes sense, no? You need it when she doesn't. She needs it when you don't.' He coughed for emphasis. 'Of course the financial side...'

'Wait a minute, Daoud. There's more to this than money. The Mazda is *my* car.'

'Danielle understands this. She is a very careful driver. Never had an accident. She'd pay for her own gasoline, of course. The idea is that she picks the car up on Friday afternoon, and drops it off at your place by Saturday night. And I was thinking that as an appropriate percentage of the fixed costs—the insurance, and so forth...she might pay you twenty-five per cent...thirty?'

'It's really not as simple as that.'

'In fact, converting the percentage to hard cash...' Daoud snapped open his PDA, and showed David his calculations. 'See. According to my estimate, Danielle should pay you sixty shekels per diem. Does that sound reasonable?'

David was reminded of a meeting seven years previously. Itchy in a brand new suit, he'd been standing in the study room of Rabbi Zalman Altschuler of blessed memory, asking for the hand in marriage of his youngest daughter, Devorah. The Rabbi had discoursed at great length, praising marriage in the abstract, incorporating quotes from the Song of Songs, and listing the dowry he'd be prepared to offer—leaving David uncertain until the very end whether his proposal would be accepted or not.

'Your sister, Danielle—is this her idea?'

'Not at all,' said Daoud. 'It is my suggestion entirely. I wouldn't dream of mentioning it to Danielle, until you and I have come to a complete agreement.'

David murmured the prayer one says after eating a sandwich.

He and his colleague rose, ready to return to work. A moment of thoughtful silence. Then the two of them strolled along Keren Hayesod Street together.

'I really don't think so,' David said, as he tapped in the security code to re-enter the bank office. 'But I'll mention it to my wife. Who knows what she'll say?'

That evening, as David drove home, accelerating and decelerating to cope with the choppy rush-hour traffic, he thought back to his Army days. As a conscript, he had chosen the programme whereby you undergo basic training while simultaneously learning Torah, so in his memory soldiery tended to blur with religion. His driving instructor—a sergeant with a hoarse voice and hay fever—had kept repeating: 'The wise general knows his retreat route.' Quite what this had to with gear-shifting a jeep, David was unsure, but it had seemed a useful principle. How does that quote from the Psalms go? Something about chariots, how you can't rely on them. Well, if it applies to a chariot, then all the more so to a Mazda Lantis. It's only an object after all, a thing, a purchase, imported from Japan.

And money would be needed. He had no prospect of promotion for several years. There was every likelihood his family would keep increasing. Two children now; soon a third. Certainly, three is a fine round number. But suppose he had four, or more? Where would he put them all? How would he feed them?

Personally he wouldn't rule out contraception. He knew what his Rabbi would say. It is the first commandment in the first book of the Bible: 'Be fruitful and multiply.' So in principle contraception is forbidden—except of course when having another child might endanger the mother's health. Or when it's her mental health that might suffer—now that was the catch-all exemption. Devorah would simply have to tell the Rabbi that if she became pregnant again she'd be depressed. But Devorah would never say that. She loved babies, loved children, loved pregnancy. She'd joyfully have five children or six...ten...twenty...

After the children, Yedidyah and Yirmiyahu, had been put to bed, David and Devorah sat in their living room, talking things over. Their apartment was one entire floor of a house which had been subdivided horizontally into three. Faintly they could hear noises from above and from below, of other families with their own children. Small feet running over the ceiling. Voices calling from beneath the floor.

Devorah was six months pregnant. She was enthroned in the big golden armchair—that was 'David's chair' where he would sit and study the newspaper, in the periods when his wife was not pregnant.

'Put your hand here,' she said. 'Can you feel her kicking?'

David did as he was told, placing his palm against his wife's firm belly. 'I think so,' he said. He wasn't sure if the sensation he felt was due to the baby or some motion within the mother. 'Yes, definitely.'

'She's strong,' Devorah said. Devorah always referred to the foetus as 'she'—though in truth the ultrasound had been ambiguous. They already had two sons, and Devorah had decided it was time for a daughter.

'Talking of babies,' David said. 'Er, do you want a coffee? A decaf?'

'I really shouldn't. But go ahead, if you want to.'

'It's all right. I don't really need it.'

'What shall we call her? How about Sarah, after your grandmother and my great-great-grandmother? Or I do think Bracha's a pretty name...'

'I was wondering about the Mazda...'

Then David pulled a hardback wooden chair in front of the armchair, and sat up facing his wife, like a businessman having an interview with the bank manager, and in straightforward terms he explained the scheme Daoud had suggested.

Devorah was aghast. 'But, David, you don't know anything about this woman!'

'I know her brother, Daoud.'

'Daoud *shmaoud*! Even if she was Jewish this wouldn't be appropriate.'

'She's divorced with two children. She works as a translator.'

'She could be anybody!'

'She's offering sixty shekels per day.'

'Sixty shekels! That's quite a large amount of money...' A pause, while Devorah thought about this. '...Suspiciously large, don't you think? Listen, David. We don't know anything about her. She could be a drug smuggler, for all we know. I'm not saying anything bad about her personally, God forbid, but she could have a boyfriend who belongs to Hamas!'

'She only wants the car on Shabbat and holidays, when we don't use it anyway.'

'If she damaged the car, we'd lose our no-claims bonus!'

'Yes, yes. We'd put all that into the agreement. She's responsible for all losses. Put everything in writing, that's best.'

'And suppose the police stop her at a checkpoint, and she does something funny, then they'd take the car to pieces!'

'She's respectable. An Israeli citizen. I really don't think—'

'And when the police arrest her, think of the scandal!'

David sighed. 'No, you're quite right, Devorah. It is taking too much of a gamble. For the sake of our children, we really should be extra cautious.'

Devorah looked into her husband's eyes. 'Of course I trust you, David. I know you wouldn't do anything stupid.'

'Well, I could carry out some more checks on her...'

'And whatever you do, ask for seventy-five shekels, at least.'

The more David thought about it, the more he wondered if his wife was right. This woman—this Danielle—just because her brother was courteous and responsible, it didn't follow that she was too. (And even the brother—did David really know what Daoud got up to when he was away from the bank?) He decided the thing to do was to get more information.

Now, he had a contact from his Army days: Shammai, a big man with a loud laugh. He was now in the Border Police. They had trained together, but they had never been friends. Shammai was living in Ramat Hasharon. They kept in touch once a year, via emailed Rosh Hashanah greetings. David tried to recall what he knew about Shammai. That he told off-colour stories. That his parents came from Iran. That once at their base, when the Israel Defence Force's official magician had put on a show of conjuring tricks, Shammai, clapping super-hard afterwards, had said to David, 'Let's pretend a Palestinian's head is between my hands.' (A joke; but in terrible taste—especially given his current job. And not even funny.) Anyway, David could think of nobody else to ask.

He found Shammai's cellphone number in an old diary. He called him up the following day and, rather to his surprise, he got straight through. There were sounds of traffic in the background. He visualized Shammai in his police car, speeding to the scene of a crime.

'How can I help you, David?'

'Er, it's about a woman...'

Jonathan Tel

'A woman...'

He could hear Shammai chuckling at the other end. 'Tell me more, David.' Shammai didn't sound like he was in any hurry to get back to duty.

'No. It's not what you think. An Arab woman...'

'An Arab woman... My good friend, David, I thought you liked only Jewish women.'

David did manage to explain the situation. And Shammai agreed to put Danielle's name through the police computer.

Ten minutes later, while David was eating a hard-boiled egg, he was called back. 'Yeah. She's clear. Why didn't you say she worked at the courthouse, David? Of course she's clear! They vet them there like nobody's business. She's what we call a good Arab. She's safe. You can do anything you want with her.'

The sound of a police siren, coming loud through the telephone.

'Any other favours I can do you, David?'

He swallowed down the last of the egg. 'No. It's all right.'

'Any time, David. Any time.'

A deep chuckle, then Shammai switched off the phone. And David remembered why he had always disliked that man.

David could not logically oppose the arrangement now. He thought of asking his Rabbi's advice—but what was there to ask? Lending a car to a non-Jew to drive on Shabbat, there's no prohibition against that; provided the contract is worded with care, that is.

He and Daoud drew up a detailed contract. They haggled a little about the payment, and compromised on seventy shekels per Shabbat/holiday. All that remained was for David to get Danielle's signature on the contract and to give her a copy of the keys.

This could have been accomplished via Daoud—but the brother suggested David should deal with his sister in person—and when he thought about it, David realized it was proper he should meet, if only briefly, the one who would henceforth be sharing his car.

So the next lunch-time, instead of eating a ciabatta sandwich with Daoud in their usual cafe, he walked over to Yoel Salomon Street, and sat down at an outside table of one of the cafes there. Hardly any other customers were present. Strange that lingering over a coffee and sandwich in public should count as an act of bravery; you have

214

to at least try to live a normal life. The sun was shining full on him, and he was sweating in his suit, but he didn't feel it would be right to unbutton or loosen anything.

Sure enough, a woman sat down at the chair opposite—no doubt she had been given his description.

'Shalom, Danielle.'

'Shalom, David.'

David avoided looking at the woman face-on. He was a married man, after all. He had a sense of a short dark person (a female version of Daoud, let's say) but with longer, lighter hair, and wearing a green dress.

He put two copies of the contract on the table.

A minute or so later, they were pushed back towards him, signed.

The rendezvous seemed like something out of a spy story. He felt called upon to utter some mysterious code phrase... 'Pigeons are cooing on Yoel Salomon Street,' he said.

'Yes, they are,' she said. Her voice was low, with no discernible accent.

He kept one copy of the contract for himself, tucking it safely into his briefcase. The other he left on the table, placing on it her set of the car keys.

David recalled his first encounter with Devorah. It had taken place on a Shabbat afternoon in the Jewish Quarter of the Old City, at the home of Rabbi and Mrs Mamet, amateur matchmakers, who kept extensive files on suitable single young men and women of proper background and decent personal qualities, on their home computer. (In fact it was the third time the hard-working Mamets had attempted to find David a wife. The previous two would-be matches were pleasant enough, but he had felt no bond.) The Mamets had performed the introduction. David and Devorah, both rather shy, had mumbled a few words and not known what to make of each other. Afterwards they both agreed with the Mamets' suggestion that a second meeting, with greater privacy, would be appropriate. They met the following Saturday night, after Shabbat had ended, in the lobby of the Hilton Hotel—which was favoured for this purpose by religious singles, it being public and formal and brightly lit, without any danger of undue intimacy. They sat down, and made some comment about the weather or traffic, and suddenly they were talking and talking as if they had known each other for years. Ah, Devorah—he could scarcely believe he might be matched with anyone so beautiful.

David and Danielle rose, and left separately. Were David to come across the Arab woman again, he doubted he would recognize her.

The meeting had taken place on Sunday. There were four and a half workdays to go until the car would be borrowed. In advance, David considerately removed his blue-on-white bumper sticker: THE LAND OF ISRAEL FOR THE PEOPLE OF ISRAEL! Although this slogan represented his sincerely held belief (he voted regularly for the National Religious Party, and he held himself to be on its right wing), he didn't wish to offend Danielle. As for the other stickers: the picture of Mickey Mouse in sorcerer's costume which Yedidyah had attached above the left headlight could not possibly upset anyone. And the one in purple lettering on a glittery orange background: LORD OF THE UNIVERSE, WE LOVE YOU! which Yirmiyahu had brought home from nursery school— well, Christians worship the same God as us, don't they? How could she object to that sentiment? After some careful thought, he decided to leave it in place. (Mind you, it would look a little odd for a vehicle with that particular sticker to be seen driving about on Shabbat. The Mazda Lantis would have some explaining to do.)

No doubt the car went off on its own just before dusk on Friday, but David and his family were praying then, and by the time they came home from shul it was well after dark and he and Devorah were busy with the children. It was only the following morning, as David hurried to get to shul on time, that he was aware of the fact that the Mazda was not parked outside his apartment. A moment of sickening loss (had it been stolen?) and then the realization that this was entirely in order. Everything was just as it should be.

David recalled the time he'd broken his canine, as a consequence of biting into a raw carrot. There had been no pain, and eventually the dentist had fixed it, building an artificial tooth on top of the original stump—but that sense of utter strangeness and desolation as his tongue had swept over the otherwise familiar toothscape— this was what it was like to be car-less, even on the day when he had no use for it.

Meeting his wife after shul, he remarked, 'You know, the car's gone.'

'Yes, of course, David... That's what you wanted, isn't it?'

Nor was its return noticed either. At some point on Saturday night, after the Havdalah candle had been extinguished and Shabbat was over, and the children had been put to bed, David looked out of the window and noticed the Mazda was back, parked just where it had been. He ran downstairs, and inspected his car. Devorah came down and stood beside her husband.

Certainly it appeared unaltered, whatever experiences it might have undergone. The two bumper stickers were in place, also the slight scuff over the left front door; the Friday edition of the *Yediot Aharonot* newspaper was rolled up and abandoned between the two child car-seats, as it had been when the vehicle had last been sighted. All the same, just as people who suffer severe but temporary injury to their limbs sometimes have the delusion the healed limb is not their own but an impostor—so David wondered for a second, irrationally, if Danielle had replaced his Mazda with a changeling. He turned the key in the door lock. There on the dashboard was a sealed envelope. It contained the agreed sum. David sniffed the air in the car but could detect nothing unusual. Perhaps the slightest whiff of an alien scent.

Sunday, David drove off to the bank as usual. The first day of the working week, when God created Heaven and Earth, and bank tellers have to sit behind their window and cash customers' cheques.

David had purchased a special beaded mat that hooked over his driving seat, below and behind him. It was designed to keep him alert and cool. As he drove up Bethlehem Way, jolting slowly forward in the line of traffic heading into the heart of the city, he thought to himself that the Arab woman had sat, just twenty-four hours previously, where he was sitting now. He envisioned her on the driving seat: her bottom overlapping with his, her breasts jutting out a few precious centimetres beyond the surface of his own chest.

When the car came back, the next Saturday night, it was parked in an odd way. Nothing the casual observer would have noticed. But look how the front wheels were angled in slightly towards the curb— he would never have left it quite like that. No doubt Danielle's technique for parking was subtly different from his—some exotic procedure inculcated by Palestinian driving instructors.

'There's something wrong,' Devorah said.

'What?'

'You tell me.'

'I've looked in the trunk, Devorah. I've looked under the seat. I've looked at the engine. I've even looked underneath the car. It all seems normal to me.'

'I just know something's not right. Call it my intuition. Please, David, just for my sake, find out what's going on. What's she using the car for? Where does she take it? How can I enjoy my Shabbat when I'm worried about the car?'

'I'll take care of it.' David hugged Devorah. Then there was a yell from within. Yirmiyahu and Yedidyah were quarrelling about nothing in particular, and the parents had to go in to sort it out.

David phoned Shammai. They met at the Paz station on the Hebron Road.

It was a brief assignation. Shammai was in the city on business, he said, and could only spare a few minutes.

His unmarked vehicle—a Mitsubishi Magnum—was parked next to the Mazda, in front of the pumps for regular and unleaded.

Shammai handed over a black object. It resembled a small Walkman. It was labelled in English: PLAY, RECORD, REWIND, PAUSE, STOP/EJECT.

David was a little disappointed. 'I somehow thought it would be, I don't know, different.'

Shammai laughed. 'You mean you thought it would be disguised as a pack of cigarettes or something? Who am I, James Bond? This is just an Olympus Pearlcorder. You can buy it at Tower Records on Hillel Street. Here, have it. I have plenty more. Give it back to me when you're done. What are old friends for?'

Shammai explained to David how it worked. There was nothing much to it. 'Set it on "Voice Activated"—see. That way you save the battery and the tape. You don't have to listen to hours of silence.'

Shammai punched David on the shoulder, by way of an amicable farewell, and drove off.

Then David got into his own car. He hid the Pearlcorder deep in the glove compartment, underneath a map of Haifa. (When had he been in Haifa? Oh, years ago. He had a faint visual memory of the city—Mount Carmel rising above the Mediterranean—but no recollection of why on earth he had visited it. While he had nothing against the place, to the best of his knowledge he knew nobody there and there was nothing there he desired. He had no plans ever to go to Haifa again in this life.)

After breakfast the next Sunday morning, before going to work, David fished the Pearlcorder out from its hiding place. He sat in the driving seat, and played back the tape.

Some odd random street sounds had set off the voice-activated recorder for a few seconds. Brief blurts of engine noise. And then he heard a recording of the radio. (Of course the machine can't tell the difference between a live voice and one coming through the ether. It's not so easy to be a spy.) A phone-in programme in Arabic. Then the Jordanian news. He understood just enough to know he didn't need to understand more.

Next she must have switched channels. The recording was in Hebrew now. The regular Israeli radio news—from the one day of the week when he never listened to the news. Yesterday's news—how fraught with significance it seemed, preserved in this way. A statement by a Minister, concerning corruption. A woman shot in Samaria, while driving to a settlement. The US president denounces terrorism. *Yesterday*. And the weather forecast: hot by day, but becoming cooler at night. *Yesterday*. Next the sports news: soccer results from European fixtures. Borussia Münchengladbach had beaten Red Star Belgrade. AC Milan had suffered a surprise loss at the hands of Glasgow Rangers. *Yesterday, yesterday*. He didn't know why, but this unexpected defeat made him want to cry. And finally, near the end of the tape, when he had almost given up hope of hearing what had actually taken place within the car—the sound of an infant babbling. And a female voice saying a word or two of comfort in Arabic.

David said nothing about this to his wife. (What was there to say?) But he could hardly wait for the next Saturday. This time, he plunged into his Mazda as soon as he decently could, after Havdalah. There was little of significance. He did overhear some snatches of conversation between Danielle and her two children. His Arabic was minimal, and he couldn't understand, but it didn't seem to matter. At one point the mother and the children sang what must be a Palestinian nursery rhyme. Then, just as he was hoping for more—the Pearlcorder (triggered, no doubt, by random street noises) gave him only electronic crackle and engine buzz.

Jonathan Tel

For the next few weeks, he listened eagerly to the secret recordings. Not that he unearthed any revealing information, but he felt he was tunnelling through to a world so unlike, and so like, his own.

There was nobody he could talk to about this. He could hardly mention his obsession to his wife. As for Daoud, David observed him with greater respect and interest, but their lunch-time conversations were on the usual subjects of work and money. Once, though, as he was tucking his younger son, Yirmiyahu, up in bed, he sang him a song whose lyrics were 'La la la' and whose tune was that of Danielle's nursery rhyme.

But just around the High Holidays, he neglected to check the recordings—for on Rosh Hashanah Devorah went into labour, and she and David now had another beautiful child to treasure—Yehoshua.

Yehoshua was circumcised a week later. Then came Yom Kippur. Then, in quick succession, the festivals of Succot and Simchat Torah.

And it was fall already—the first drizzle actually fell on the city—when David realized that almost a month had gone by without his listening to his Pearlcorder.

It wasn't his usual day for it, either. Just a random Wednesday afternoon, after work. He sat in his car, which was parked on King David Street, watching the raindrops fall on the windshield. Something about the wistfulness of it, the craving for it—rain in a dry land: how it is longed for, and then when it comes it falls on the dusty earth and disappears in an instant—this made him realize there was something he had left undone.

Yes, his Arab woman.

He took the Pearlcorder out of the glove compartment, set it on the dashboard, and pressed REWIND. Then PLAY. He heard: soft music from a radio, or a cassette—it was the singer, Fairuz, crooning her famous song 'Al Quds'. Then loud traffic noise. Horns blaring. Then engine murmur. And then Danielle's voice. He had to replay it twice to make out some of her words, in Hebrew. *'Oh, you're so... Oh you're such a... You're all man...'* A shy, almost girlish laugh. Then silence.

David sat alone in the car, hearing only the sound of the rain. It occurred to him that this recording had probably taken place weeks before. (Once the tape was full, it would register nothing more.) How keenly he waited for the next Shabbat.

That Friday, Devorah (she always was intuitive) asked him, 'Oh, talking of the car. Have you done anything about the Palestinian woman yet?'

'No. Not yet,' he white-lied.

And on Saturday night, he played the next instalment.

In between irrelevant noises, he heard what was definitely Danielle's voice. She was cooing to some inaudible person. *'You're mine... You're my only man... Yes, you're mine...'*

He felt he shouldn't listen to this. It was private, and besides it was improper for him to be thinking about these matters. But how could he resist? It crossed his mind that he might have misunderstood: maybe she was talking to her children? But nobody talks to children in that tone of voice.

Suddenly the opposite door opened and shut, and his wife had joined him. He was in the passenger seat; she occupied the driving seat, without asking. He stuffed the Pearlcorder into his pocket. She turned the key in the ignition. They both fastened their seatbelts, and away they went. Devorah's mother was babysitting. They had arranged to visit a discount furniture store on Pierre Koenig Street, just a few minutes' drive from their home, to choose a new crib. He could only wonder how they would have managed without the car.

For the next couple of months, week after week he listened to the tapes. Some weeks there was nothing of interest. Traffic noises, and children at play. But sometimes—more often than not—he would hear the Arab woman speaking of love.

She was divorced. She was a Christian. She was allowed to go on dates. The rules are different for them.

Of course he would never have eavesdropped on a Jewish woman—but this wasn't at all the same. Her life had no connection with his, other than this one frail link. What he was doing was no worse than tuning in to a radio phone-in programme—so he justified his actions to himself.

He began to build up an image of her in his head. And troubling questions arose. For one thing, why was she speaking in Hebrew? Did she have a Jewish boyfriend, then? So what was going on? He absolutely could not countenance any relationship of that kind. My God, the two of them might marry. A Jew might be about to marry out of the faith. His Mazda would be held personally responsible!

Or maybe he had got it the wrong way around. Maybe she was so drawn to this boyfriend that she was about to convert to Judaism herself? Such things have been known. But if so, then what? He most certainly could not permit a Jewess to drive a car on Shabbat. The car-sharing would have to come to an end.

And for another thing, how come he could hear her voice but never that of the man? Did he just have a very quiet voice, then? Was he the strong, silent type? Was he a deaf mute? Or was it simply that women do talk more than men, while making love? (Though what did David know about this? The only woman he'd ever made love to—in the full sense; not counting certain flirty episodes in his Army days—was Devorah.) *Oh you big man, you. You're so wonderful.*

'There's something I've been meaning to tell you...'

'But first *I* have some news for *you*. Guess what?'

'I don't know, Devorah.'

'Go on, David. I'll give you three guesses.'

David looked into his wife's eyes. The big boys had been put to bed, and little Yehoshua was clutched to her breast, one evening in early December. He didn't have to guess. He had seen that look before, three times.

'We're going to have another baby,' he said.

'Isn't it wonderful!' she said.

'But I thought...' He gestured at her nipple, at Yehoshua's mouth, greedily sucking on it. 'I thought it was impossible to become pregnant when you're...' (He was reluctant to say out loud 'breast-feeding'—as if the word itself were somehow indecent.)

'Not impossible, no. Nothing is impossible if God really wants it.'

'Well, all I can say,' David said, 'is that it's the best news I ever heard.' He hugged his wife. His mouth pressed against her cheek, and warm neck, and glided down. Through her dress he sensed the texture of the maternity bra. He felt her hand gently stroking his hair and forehead. She smelled of milk. 'Who's my little boy?' she murmured. 'Who's my favourite little boy?'

During lunch break the following day, he announced the news to Daoud.

'Well, congratulations,' Daoud said. 'Though how on earth you're going to find the wherewithal for another child...'

222

'God will provide,' David said sententiously.

'Yes. Well, God had better start providing for me as well as you, pretty damn quick. I can't borrow any money from my in-laws; the whole family is doing badly now, because of...' But the conversation was about to stray into the forbidden area of politics. Daoud caught himself. 'I wouldn't be at all surprised if you have another son again.'

'I'll take it as it comes.'

Daoud himself had three daughters. 'Personally I like girls,' he said. 'But you know what my parents say: What's wrong with that wife of yours? How come she never gives us any grandsons?'

'Girls are just as good as boys.'

'Easy for you to say.'

And the following morning a miracle took place. As David was driving to work, a flurry of actual snow descended on Jerusalem! He switched on his wipers, and watched the little fragile flakes being shunted aside. By lunchtime there was just slush in the gutters. And during the drive home at dusk, there was no snow at all. No sign it had ever been.

One Sunday evening during Hanukkah, Devorah came angrily into the living room, where David was sitting in the armchair, reading the economics section of *Ma'ariv*. 'Yehoshua lost the button of his romper suit!'

'Oh dear.'

'It caught on the strap of the car-seat! I found it in the car!'

'Well, that's good news, isn't it?'

'But look what else I found in the car...'

Devorah was holding up, with distaste, a women's magazine in Arabic. 'It must have come from your Palestinian woman.'

He glanced at the cover, and flicked through it. Judging by the pictures, the magazine dealt with fashion. There were photographs of models—Spanish-looking, or Italian—wearing beaded evening dresses. A little cleavage was showing here and there. It was at least as modest as some of the Israeli magazines his wife glanced at on the news-rack, though of course she didn't actually buy them.

'Yes. Shocking,' he said.

A heavy pause.

'I'll, er...tell her not to.'

Another pause.

'Do you want me to…?' he said.

He wondered if this was the crunch.

But instead of forbidding him to share his car, Devorah said: 'She's not paying you enough, is she? Does she realize how much insurance costs these days? Demand eighty shekels a day, minimum.'

'I'll try, but… Well, that's a lot to ask for.'

'If she pays up, then we'll know she has an ulterior motive.'

'And if she doesn't pay?'

'Then good riddance.'

David thought about this. It seemed like the old test for witches. 'If they swim, they're guilty. If they sink, they're dead.' He went to get a cup of coffee, and when he returned, his wife was seated immovably—her legs slightly apart, and her hands on her knees—in the golden armchair.

David conducted the renegotiation with Daoud, the following lunch-time. 'About money…' he began. And he tried to explain his position.

'But we already have a contract,' Daoud said.

'The changing situation…' David said vaguely, waving the ciabatta around. 'The new realities…the facts on the ground.'

Daoud set down his cappuccino. He wore a moustache of milk froth. He frowned. 'Has Danielle done…anything inappropriate?'

David hardly felt he could mention the tapes, or the magazine. 'Oh no.'

'And she has looked after your car in a satisfactory manner, David?'

'Yes.'

'Well, now that we are reopening negotiations, you do understand her financial situation? Frankly, she's been urgently requesting me to mention this to you. She really cannot manage more than fifty shekels per diem.'

David took a bite out of his sandwich. He chewed quickly. 'Fifty! But I was hoping for—'

Daoud held up his hand. 'It's all my sister can afford. Take it or leave it.'

What was David to do? He couldn't tell Danielle the deal was off. He would have no money coming in at all then. And besides, he was addicted to the tapes. He needed to find out more. So if he only got paid fifty shekels, and his wife wanted eighty...then he'd have to find thirty shekels per week out of his own pocket. If he cut down on cappuccinos, and had his hair cut more rarely...

When, a few days later, she asked him if he'd dealt with the Arab woman, he mumbled, 'Oh yes. That's all been sorted out.'

That night Devorah, feeling an obscure pressure, had trouble sleeping. She woke in the small hours and spoke her husband's name. He, fumbling to wakefulness, grunted some word beginning with *dalèd*. They possessed twin beds which were pushed apart during her impure time of the month; during the pure time, they were together. Currently the beds were separated. Logically she couldn't be impure now—but according to the Laws of Family Purity you have to observe the Days of Anticipation during the first three months of pregnancy, just in case. David knew for a fact that many pious husbands and wives thought nothing of kissing and cuddling during the Days of Anticipation—but Devorah, daughter of an eminent rabbi, believed in being stringent about such matters. He didn't disagree: this was her domain.

It was only one Sunday morning in February, as he sat outside his home in Mekor Chaim, pulling out the clutch, trying to get the engine to warm up, that he understood what had been happening. Nothing he could articulate prompted the revelation; it simply came to him. He thought back over the sequence of tapes. The mystery of the inaudible lover. How come she always spoke in Hebrew.

He felt his way into the glove compartment. He peeled back the layers of maps and documents, careful and delicate as an archaeologist digging into a *tel*. He was almost down to the stratum of the Pearlcorder. Just the map of Haifa lay on top of it.

He could have sworn he had placed the map face-down, with the name of the city underneath. But now it was inverted!

Danielle had known about his spying all along! (Or ever since she'd left the first message for him, anyway.) She'd been teasing him!

It was easy enough to imagine. No doubt months ago she'd looked in the glove compartment herself, seeking some other map perhaps. She'd discovered his secret. Instead of confronting him, she'd used her feminine wiles to gain power over him.

His face flushed. His bottom stirred on the beaded seat-mat.

He pressed REWIND, and listened to this week's instalment. He played it three times over. How could he have been so foolish? The panting, one-sided lovemaking sounds—how artificial it all was. She had no lover! A divorcee with a couple of brats—she was probably overweight and hideous—no man would ever want her!

He could scarcely wait for the next Shabbat. He attached a Post-it note to the Pearlcorder. 'For Danielle.' Then he recorded his own message on the machine.

He couldn't decide how to put it. He tried several different versions, erasing, and re-recording. Rewinding and recording on top of the previous version.

Finally, his voice just said: 'Shalom, Danielle...Er, Salaam...'

The following Saturday night, he unlocked his own car, and entered, and found the Pearlcorder in full view, placed squarely on the dashboard. He pressed PLAY.

'David. Thank you for your many kindnesses. My father has bought me my own car, so in future I will no longer be needing yours. Payment in full is in the envelope. Thank you once more. Goodbye. Danielle.'

He sank back, shocked. How else could their relationship have concluded? Yet somehow he had never thought it would happen like this, so absolutely, so unilaterally. In a fit of irrationality he thought: maybe if he pleaded with her, maybe if he pleaded with Daoud, then she would change her mind? But of course not. This was the end.

Did he credit her story? Not that it was so important whether she was lying or not, but just out of curiosity, was she? *'My father has bought me my own car.'* So suddenly? Why now and not earlier? Where would her father have obtained the money? Perhaps 'father' was a euphemism. Perhaps she now had a wealthy lover—an Arab or a Jew—who was bestowing largesse on her?

But after all, this was no concern of his. He erased the message for the last time. He slid the Pearlcorder into a padded envelope he had brought along for this purpose, already addressed to Shammai.

What really mattered was the Mazda. How could he keep up the car, on his own? *'Lord of the Universe, we love you!'* he whispered to himself.

He went back into the apartment. Everything seemed quite normal. Yedidyah and Yirmiyahu had juxtaposed some stools, and were playing a let's-pretend game. They were laughing and chatting together in their secret language.

Devorah, leaning over the crib, was talking nonsense to Yehoshua, who was gurgling. She carried the baby to the dining table, and set about changing him.

David knew the time had come to explain. Delaying the moment, he ruffled Yirmiyahu's hair. Children are proof of God's loving kindness. Compared to them, nothing else is of any account. He cleared his throat. 'Look, Devorah. About that car woman...'

'Oh, her.'

'You know, well...'

A stool fell down with a crash. The two older children scampered over, and hung about beside their parents' feet.

'Yes, her,' said David. He couldn't work out what to say; he had to find something to confess. He let his thoughts come out in a mixture of free association and artful improvisation. 'I met her through her brother. I told you that, didn't I? Well, not him, he's fine, he's a good Arab... No, it's her other brother. Did I tell you about him? No? Well, it turns out he's a follower of Arafat. He belongs to Fatah and—'

'Fatah!' she said. 'And she works in the courthouse! The police should be told!'

'No, no. The police know all about it, of course. They have everything under control, and nobody's saying she's a definite... They're laying a trap.'

Devorah fastened the baby's fresh diaper. She lifted her head. 'But you won't let this woman use our car, of course,' she said.

'Certainly not.'

With dignity, Devorah took her place in the armchair. The five-month-old was propped on her lap, looking wise. Her two older children gathered on either side of her. She rested her right hand against her swollen belly. 'That woman!' she spat out. 'For all we know, she could have left a bomb in the trunk! We could all have been blown up!'

Then Devorah became calm. 'What a narrow escape,' she said, with a strange, fond smile. ☐

PROTESTANT BOY
Geoffrey Beattie

I was going home to Belfast to visit my mother. It was the spring of 1998 and the weather was very good for that time of year. My mother lived on her own in Ligoniel, North Belfast, in the little Protestant enclave where I had grown up. Ligoniel is a mill village that once had a mixed population of both Protestants and Catholics, but with more Protestants towards the bottom of the village and more Catholics towards the top.

We call our neighbourhood the 'turn-of-the-road'. It seems a vague sort of term, like saying that you live at the bus stop on the hill or by the corrugated fence on the way to town, but people in Belfast usually know exactly where you mean, which often surprises me. On television, however, they call this area 'Murder Triangle'. It's a Protestant area with murals on the gable walls in tribute to the local men killed or imprisoned for life while in the service of the paramilitary Protestant organization, the Ulster Volunteer Force, the UVF, who re-formed in 1966 on the fiftieth anniversary of the Battle of the Somme, where so many members of the original UVF lost their lives.

The Somme is a key psychological landmark for the Protestant people of Northern Ireland. In the words of Winston Churchill: 'This was the greatest loss and slaughter sustained in a single day in the whole history of the British army.' That 'loss and slaughter' is one of the main influences on the mindset of the people of Ulster. 'Not a single man turned back' was what I heard when I was a child. 'Not a single one.' A German general—possibly Ludendorff—is reported to have said that the ordinary British soldiers of the First World War were lions led by donkeys, and that the donkeys were the British generals. I heard that saying a hundred times when I was a child.

The area where I hail from is bounded by Ardoyne on one side and Ligoniel on the other, two strong Republican areas, no-go zones for people like me—Protestants, I mean. It is a bleak sort of place; that is the only word that I have to describe it. I had left many years before to go to university and had stayed away. 'You always said that you would come back when you got your degree but I knew you wouldn't,' my mother would say. 'I knew that you were lying to me.'

Going home for a visit was a last-minute decision, a spur-of-the-moment kind of thing. I had rung my mother to tell her the good news.

'Where are you ringing from?' she asked.

'Work,' I replied.

'Can't you afford to ring from home?' she responded. But she sounded excited on the phone, even though she was trying hard not to show it. 'Hire a wee car at the airport and we'll visit your father's grave. Nobody has taken me up there for over eight months.'

I felt guilty already: guilty that I didn't go home more frequently, guilty that she had nobody else to take her to my father's grave, guilty that the grave was not looked after properly.

I arrived at the turn-of-the-road late in the evening in a little blue Corsa, which I had dutifully hired at the airport. I parked outside my mother's front door opposite the library, which resembled a concrete bunker with its wire grilles and the sectarian graffiti daubed on its walls. Some curtains moved next door as I let myself in; there didn't seem to be anybody behind them, just a wizened little hand gripping the frayed edge—probably some other elderly woman who didn't have much mental stimulation. My mother's front door wasn't locked; it was an old habit in a mill village, where everybody had once known everybody else, where there had once been a sense of community.

'Hey,' I shouted into the back room. 'It's me.'

There was no answer. The silence was always telling.

'It's the UDA,' I shouted in a thick Belfast accent. 'It's Mad Dog Adair here. Come out with your fucking hands up.'

Perhaps understandably, there was more silence and no comment, not even on my swearing.

'It's Geoffrey, your wee son,' I said, trying a different approach, but still there was no reply. I cleared my throat to break the uncomfortable stillness and opened the door and went through to the back room. There she sat, with her bad legs up on the blue vinyl chairs in front of the black-and-white television. She hardly bothered to glance my way.

'It's about time,' my mother said. 'Are you sure you can spare the time?' she added sarcastically.

I cleared my throat again and pulled out a chair that felt a little greasy. I sat down and stared at the television just to avoid seeing her expression. She usually didn't bother to mask her displeasure, just her happier moods at other times. We sat there for a few minutes. There had been no kiss, no hug. Nor a smile.

I asked her if she fancied a drink.

'I hope that you've brought your own because the off-licence is shut,' she replied. 'You know rightly what time it closes. I've nothing in the house.'

I knew this was untrue—the whiskey was kept hidden behind her make-up bag in the cupboard—but I didn't want an argument.

'Have you any coffee, then?' I asked helpfully and glanced over at her with what I hoped was a slight, friendly smile.

'You know I don't drink that stuff, so why are you bothering to ask?' my mother said, without reciprocating my smile. 'Do you think that I can just nip down to the shops with these bad ankles of mine? No, there's no coffee, there's just tea, but you don't drink tea. Although when you were a boy there didn't seem to be anything wrong with tea. It was good enough for you once upon a time.'

This was the dig I had been waiting for. I had moved away from here, consciously and deliberately, almost culpably, and 'hardly bothered my arse coming back', as she put it. I wasn't interested in my home any longer, she said, or in my own mother: I was too busy enjoying myself across the water.

'You've turned into one of those English snobs now, you've forgotten all about your home and where you came from. "Have you any coffee?"' She imitated my accent, but it didn't sound like me. 'What's the matter with tea? It was all right for your father and me.' She was crying now without turning her face away from the television. 'I'm pleased that your father isn't alive to see what sort of a man you've become. He would be ashamed of you.'

'I only asked if you had any coffee,' I said, trying to defend myself without attacking her. I understood that she lived a drab, monotonous existence. She had never been intended for a life like this.

'I was always told that I was the best-looking girl in Ligoniel,' she used to tell my brother Bill and me when we were children, but she had been widowed in her forties. My mother was never meant to be alone, with her bad, swollen ankles, crimson and gangrenous-looking, which meant that she couldn't walk anywhere and had to go up the stairs on her hands and knees like a helpless child. I was all that she had left, and in her anger she liked to remind me that I hardly counted.

'You're no good for anything. You only look out for number one. You've forgotten about me and your family and where you come from.'

The television programme was about an orphanage in Kosovo; I could tell that she wasn't interested in the thin shaven-headed boys and girls. She said that she was going to bed early. 'There's no point in staying up.' I wasn't mentioned; it was as if she was talking to herself. I sat there, wondering why I had bothered to visit her. My brother used to say that only I could talk her out of her soot-black moods. But sometimes I didn't like to bother, that was what I told myself. It was better than admitting defeat in the face of it.

We sat in silence as she prepared to go up the stairs. I mentioned my dog to her, I don't know why exactly. I told her how he had got some premature grey hairs on his face. I thought that she might be amused to hear of a boxer with a grey beard. She wasn't or didn't seem to be.

'You love that bloody dog more than you love me,' was her reply.

I was tempted to say, 'Is it any wonder? He never sulks.' But I didn't. I just sat there, thinking of the work piling up at the university in my absence. My mother sighed loudly.

And then, out of the blue, something changed. I don't know why: perhaps even she realized that the sulk was pointless, that it was leading nowhere.

'Go and get me a drink, then—you know where it stays.' She looked over at me. 'And put something else on the TV. Those poor children have no chance in this world, not like the spoilt ones you get over here.'

I got up and went straight to the cupboard.

'You can be the barman,' she said. 'But just remember, don't put too much bloody water in my drink. I like whiskey with a dash of water in it, not the other way round.'

The whiskey looked as if it had been watered down to make the bottle look fuller. She kept her feet up on the stool in front of her. And each time she said, 'How much water have you put in this drink?' I replied, 'Not much'—quite truthfully, because I had no need to water it more than it was. And she said that I seemed to like giving her glasses of water to drink.

'You are no drinker,' she often said. 'You're not a proper Belfast man.'

I laughed at that, and then we began to talk, and talked until the small hours. My mother liked the two of us to talk like that, on our own.

'You only have one mother,' she would say. 'You can have a lot of women, but only one mother. Just remember that.'

As I slowly sipped the whiskey from the glass that had a greasy thumb mark on the side I reflected on the fact that she was wrong in her accusations about me: I have never forgotten where I come from. My family and my working-class background have made me who I am and, in addition, I have always felt myself to be an Ulsterman, a Protestant Ulsterman. But this, I must say, is a private, slightly vague feeling rather than a conscious and clear sense of identity.

I have always wanted a clearer sense of who I am and where I belong. After all, the Troubles had been all about identity and belonging. The Catholics of Northern Ireland seemed to know who they were and what they wanted, even if their evocation of traditional Irish culture did seem hopelessly contrived at times. But we Protestants were the other side of the coin. We just wanted the status quo, we wanted to stay British, and she had called me an English snob, where both 'English' and 'snob' were an integral part of the insult.

'I would never want to be English,' my mother always said. 'Or Scottish, for that matter.'

She occasionally told me stories about my family background, about how we were descended from a famous and wealthy family, but I was always left wanting more.

'I'm not educated like you. Why don't you go and find out?' she said.

I told her that one day I probably would.

'You couldn't stop chasing women long enough to have the time,' she said. In her mind that was what I did all day; she believed that my university job occupied only a small part of my life. Perhaps this was just projection on the part of the best-looking girl in Ligoniel. Or perhaps she understood her son better than most.

'We're very alike,' she said when we got on better.

It's all in the name, anyway—that's what they say. That was what Seamus Heaney was writing about in his famous poem, 'Whatever you say say nothing':

Northern reticence, the tight gag of place
And times: yes, yes. Of the 'wee six' I sing

Where to be saved you only must save face
And whatever you say, you say nothing.

Smoke-signals are loud-mouthed compared with us:
Manoeuvrings to find out name and school,
Subtle discrimination by addresses
With hardly an exception to the rule.

My name says it all, you don't need the school. I love hearing of anyone with the same name, love to think that there may be some connection no matter how vague: Trevor Beattie, the advertiser, James Beattie, the footballer, Admiral Beatty—anyone, no matter how tenuous the link. It's a Protestant name, part of that great Plantation of Ulster in the seventeenth century. My family probably came from the Lowlands of Scotland originally, so my name marks me out as a settler, an interloper, someone who does not really belong in Ireland, or perhaps anywhere else for that matter.

I had a friend from Dublin when I was at Cambridge University. On our first day there we met our tutor, an intelligent and cultured man, who asked us to share a room in the psychology department. 'I'll put the two Irishmen together,' he said as he ushered us into a chalk-dusty room. It was probably just small talk on his part, something to say to fill the silence. He left us alone for a few minutes to unpack our boxes of books.

My new colleague looked at me. 'I hate it when people think in crude categories like that,' he said in his Dublin brogue. 'And he's meant to be a psychologist.' He hastily picked the desk with the window to the side and plopped a box of books down on top of the desk, making the chalk dust rise before I even had a chance to look around and get my bearings. I joined the Dublin man over by the window at his newly claimed desk; I noticed the trees outside already starting to shed their leaves, golden in the sunlight.

'What a great view,' he said with some pleasure.

I had been too slow. I smiled to myself: I knew that I would only have white wall to look at for the next three years.

The Dubliner looked pleased with himself; his lips curled in a self-satisfied sort of way. 'Two Irishmen, indeed,' he chuckled. 'And you're not even Irish.'

I made no acknowledgement; there was no sound except that of brown cardboard boxes being ripped open to expose paperback books with dog-eared corners.

'Perhaps you should point this out to our tutor,' he continued. 'You're just a wee Protestant from the North, one of the "no surrender" brigade.' And we both laughed politely, embarrassed.

Later that week John—that was the Dubliner's name—and I were laughing again, in that same kind of way. 'You don't even think like an Irishman,' he said. 'How could anyone mistake you for the genuine article?'

I was thinking of John the other day. A clear image came into my head and I could hear the resonance of his voice. He was always very serious, always discussing profound topics in the field of the philosophy of language—the views of Wittgenstein, Chomsky and Searle—with no hint of uncertainty in his tone. I found it all slightly intimidating.

A number of years after we had left university I learned that he had drowned while on holiday. He had got tangled up in a pedalo while trying to save his son who couldn't swim. Or perhaps it was John himself who couldn't swim. It seemed like a terribly heroic and yet pointless death. We could never have seen anything like that coming, that golden autumn day in Cambridge.

But my memory of John is always tainted by his words about Irishness to me on the day we met.

At Cambridge in the 1970s, the intellectual elite seemed to have a very narrow interpretation of the Ulster conflict. There were just good guys and bad guys: there were the native Irish, 'driven out of their lands', and then there were the Protestant settlers. The Native Americans were fashionable at the time, so too were the aborigines of Australia, and the Catholic Irish seemed to fall into a similar category in some people's minds. Then there were the problems of civil rights and gerrymandering and discrimination, and Bob Dylan singing about times a-changin' and Joan Baez reminding all radicals that we, or they—yes, they—would overcome difficulty and walk across that great emotional bridge to Martin Luther King and all those downtrodden people everywhere who had a legitimate dream.

Cambridge may have been the bastion of the Establishment—I

saw the Prime Minister and the Archbishop of Canterbury on separate days popping into college for dinner, Rab Butler was Master of my college, and the Butler Education Act was probably responsible for my being there in the first place—but every tutor who dressed in denim and leather somehow saw himself as being the exception to this rule, a free spirit fighting for what was right, fighting for the dreams of others. I had never heard such radical talk before.

And they all had the same predictable position on the Irish question: they were clearly and explicitly anti-Unionist and anti-Protestant. One of my tutor's colleagues wrote a book on the abuses of psychology in the interrogation of political prisoners in Northern Ireland. 'The Protestants will use any means to maintain their position, to keep control of the Catholic population,' my tutor said. I was mainly silent.

'If you like Great Britain so much, why don't you settle on the mainland?' one fellow student at Trinity College asked me in a manner that suggested that he was actually trying to be helpful rather than provocative. 'And let's give Ireland back to the Irish.'

My native city of Belfast was being bombed into some form of submission and I sat in a Junior Common Room high above Great Court and listened to these educated people telling me to leave my home for good. I was feeling trapped and hemmed in by the good fortune that had got me here, while my friends at home battled on the streets to maintain their position. But in my opinion my Cambridge colleagues didn't know much about what that position actually was.

The Protestant ascendancy, that's what they thought. My new friends at college had learned just enough Irish history to know of the Penal Code of 1695 preventing Catholics from bearing arms, educating their children and owning any horse above five pounds in value. They also knew about the final penal law that entered the statute books in 1728 and deprived Catholics of the vote. The words they used were 'discrimination', 'persecution'—'deprivation' on the one side and 'privilege', 'elite' and 'the ascendancy' on the other. But I didn't recognize my own experience in what they said. And I detected no understanding on their side of the psychology of these Protestant interlopers.

I left my own personal history vague, intentionally so. I didn't want anybody to feel sorry for or treat me any differently. They asked me about my school and they filled in the rest themselves. One friend assumed that my father was a judge; I have no idea why—I can only assume that he believed that most Protestants worked in the law or were landowners, and because I didn't shoot or hunt my father's profession must be the law. For years this friend asked me about famous trials and the pressures that 'a person who presided over such trials' might be under. He seemed to assume that my reluctance to talk about it was due to issues of security rather than to the fact that my father, who was dead, had been a motor mechanic. He had been a beautiful, gentle man with broken glasses and oil-stained overalls that were never clean because we didn't have a washing machine. He had worked for the Belfast City Corporation in their Falls Road depot.

I never moved back to Ulster after university. The friend who had suggested that Northern Irish Protestants should move to the mainland got it right when it came to me.

That night at my mother's I did not sleep well. The cheap bed was part of the experience of going home. The mattress was soft and springy and I could pinch its fatness between my finger and thumb. I got a pain in my spine. The pillows were flat and gave me a sore neck. Sometime in the night I got up and fetched a towel from the bathroom and folded it under the pillows to make them more comfortable. But it didn't work: the towel was damp, and this dampness probably made my neck worse. Also, there was no duvet, just a few thin blankets, one made of nylon like something from the early 1960s. True, duvets had started to catch on in Belfast but not everywhere, not yet.

Duvets! I remembered I had visited one of my old mates in prison several years previously. Jim was a member of the UVF who was serving eight life sentences for his part in six sectarian murders and two attempted murders. He had been given a further twenty years for a series of thirteen bombings, and possession of explosives, guns and ammunition. He had made the bombs that were used in a number of terrorist attacks: one was a car bomb that exploded at an IRA funeral in Ardoyne, killing two people; another was a bomb packed with industrial nuts, which killed two men in the Avenue Bar in Union Street in 1976. He had joined the UVF about the time I had left Belfast, when the IRA were trying to blow the guts out of the city; he was going to defend Ulster, to save our Protestant heritage. He said that he was 'fighting a war against the IRA'. But he killed civilians.

I read about Jim on the front page of an English newspaper when he was sentenced. When I went to see him he had just been out for a visit home after fourteen years inside. He told me that when he went into his old bedroom for the first time he thought that his mother had put curtains over the bed because he had never seen a duvet and a valance before. 'They hadn't been invented when I went away,' he said.

That was not all that had changed for him in that time. 'I couldn't get used to money on the outside. I got this taxi one day and the fare was one pound sixty. I was fiddling with these notes, and I could see this taxi driver looking at me. He must have thought that he had a real space cadet in the back.' 'Space cadet' was what we used to call anybody who behaved a little oddly by our standards, who didn't conform to the rules on the street corner.

It was eerie hearing this language from a man now in his mid-thirties. Jim saw other familiar things in a new light. 'I thought that Belfast was the most beautiful place on earth. I thought that all the women were beautiful, and I must have been staring at them. The smell of perfume was overwhelming. In prison your senses get starved. It was lovely just to walk up the stairs and feel the carpet under your feet or to stroke a dog. But my home territory looked really run down. You carry this image of your home all the time you're inside and you're shocked when you see the reality of it.'

This was the home territory that he had been defending by joining the UVF in the first place.

I would ring my mother during the years when I was away and she would keep me up to date with what had been happening back home. She would tell me who else from around there had been arrested or who had been gunned down in the street and who had survived. 'Were you a friend of so-and-so?' she would ask. 'Or was it your brother?' 'It was me,' I would answer. 'Oh, yeah, he was a very quiet wee boy but he's just got life. He did more murders than Billy the Kid—that's what I heard, anyway. And do you remember his brother Davy, the good-looking fella? I think that he's a bit older than you. Anyway, they tried to murder him last week when he was coming out of the wee club. The car drove right up beside him and they just opened up.'

It was odd, having these brutal events relayed to you by your mother who now talked about bombs and bullets as part and parcel of her daily life. She had developed some of the vocabulary for reporting the events.

'Do you remember George Walmsley?' she would ask, and you knew what was coming next; it was never going to be a story about success or good fortune, it was always going to be a tale of despair and probably death, that's how it was around there.

'Well,' she began, 'he was gunned down by the IRA as he left the Orange Hall in Ligoniel. I knew George from when I was a wee girl. He was a lovely, quiet man. He was coming home early because he was worried about his mother's health. She had just lost her husband; I told you about that at the time, but you probably can't remember it, you were probably too busy to listen. They don't know whether George was hit by gunmen from a car or by a sniper.'

'Oh God, I'm sorry to hear it,' I said.

'You're okay, you're out of it,' she replied, sounding angry, peeved at me again. 'That's what we have to live with. Why they picked on George Walmsley is beyond me, except that he was a Protestant. He was such a quiet man.' There was a pause, and then she added, 'The good ones always get taken—auld quiet George, your father, your brother. It's always the bad ones who get away with it.'

I wasn't sure if she was including me in this, and perhaps even herself, I couldn't be sure. But the story about George was a dig at me, I knew that. George cared about his mother; in fact, he cared so much that it cost him his life.

Another time my mother asked me whether I could remember the Youngers from Wolfhill Avenue, 'up near where your Uncle Terence used to live?'

'Vaguely,' I replied.

'Well, they murdered old William Younger in his bed. He was eighty-seven years old. Do you remember his daughter Letitia? The one who was never married, the quiet spinster woman. Well, she was found with a pitchfork stuck right through her neck. She was pinned to the floor with it and then they shot her in the head and in the chest. And she still wasn't dead.'

'Oh goodness,' I said.

'She didn't die until she got to the Mater Hospital. It's desperate in this bloody place.'

An invisible enemy was killing my mother's Protestant neighbours. The killers were a sinister and anonymous group. The locals from the mill village of Ligoniel who were Catholic and who had lived there for generations were trustworthy—'dead on', in her words— but some of the new ones that they'd moved up to Ligoniel in more recent years from elsewhere were not.

'Some of them are a right bad bunch. I've got old neighbours who are Catholic who come to see me week in, week out, and that's what they say about some of these newcomers from Ardoyne or West Belfast.'

It made my mother angry when she heard representatives of Sinn Fein saying that the violence of the IRA, unlike that of the UDA and the UVF, did not have a sectarian element to it.

'What do they call it, then?' she would say. 'It's all sectarian; there's no other word for it. How can Gerry Adams say that it's not sectarian? Why are they targeting people like George Walmsley or Billy Younger? He knows that it's a lie.'

She had lived there all her life, but she knew victims on both sides, and she would store up little incidental details to tell me, little details that captured the reality of the violence around her.

'Did you hear about your man being shot in Clifton Street? He was a Catholic. They'd had a wee party in their house and then they went outside for a snowball fight. He was shot when he was walking to his home with all the snow in his hair and on his coat. He was trying to get back up off the ground when his family found him. It must have been awful to watch. It was like if you've ever seen a dog hit by a car, the way that they try to get on their feet again. And you can see in their face that they know that they're dying, that fear, even auld dogs know it, so imagine what it's like for a human being. It's terrible what they do to ordinary people in this town of ours. And imagine being shot dead because you'd gone outside for a wee snowball fight. How terrible is that? If he'd stayed in that night and just watched the snow fall, he'd be alive today.'

It was hard to look at the houses and the streets and the entries around here in the same kind of way, knowing what had gone on.

'You know that pub near the pet shops in Gresham Street where you used to sell your guinea pigs?' my mother said. 'Well, your man just ran in and shouted "All right, all the Prods get to one side and all the Catholics get to the other." And then he opened up. They killed five men in there, men just out having a quiet wee drink; three of them were Catholic and two of them were Protestant. It was just indiscriminate murder. And,' she added, 'the gunman was a Protestant. We're always shooting our own. Our lot can be just as bad as theirs, and a lot stupider.'

Now in my mother's house it was morning. I had been cold all night. The bedroom was chilly, but I didn't want to complain. 'You've always been a cold crackers,' my mother used to say whenever I did. I didn't know what the phrase meant.

My clothes were piled over the divan and I had two suits hung on top of each other on a single metal hanger on the outside of her wardrobe.

'You've brought too much stuff home with you,' she had said. 'You've too many clothes,' which sounded like a criticism, but wasn't. 'You take after your mother,' she would say. 'I was always a great one for the style.'

When she worked all those years in Ewart's, the linen mill in Ligoniel, everybody, including Mr Ewart himself on his annual visit to the shop floor, would comment on her style, according to my mother. Mr Ewart by all accounts was a dashing-looking man, 'a real film star'. He wore a patch over the eye he had lost in the war.

'He was like Douglas Fairbanks Jr,' my mother always said. 'Your father was more like David Niven.'

I never remembered my father being particularly like David Niven—he'd died when I was thirteen—but my memory of him is mostly from old photographs that show him with his thin hair blowing in the wind on the beach.

The house I now stood in, feeling the cold, was not the house I had grown up in. This was the new Housing Executive place. It was perhaps fifty yards from where the old one had stood. My mother had been born and reared in 15 Legmore Street, as had I. Her father, George Willoughby, had lived there all his life. Before that she had no idea where her family came from. They had always been in Ligoniel as far as she knew. But before the linen industry came to Belfast?

'I've no idea,' she said, 'I wasn't around at the time.'

And what about further back, what about the Plantations and Scotland? She said that she had some second cousins in Scotland, that was all she knew, but their father had moved there from Belfast and 'he had a wee horse and cart business that he drank away'. But what about before that?

'We've always been Irish,' was all she ever said. 'We're not Scottish, they're too bloody mean with their money, and we're certainly not English. Who would want to be English? We're just Irish but Protestants, if you know what I mean. We've always been Church of Ireland too.'

O ccasionally, I had searched for evidence of my family's past in my house. I would look for photographs of a thin man on ice skates, perhaps looking a little like David Niven, or a picture of Dromore Cathedral, or a horse and cart, or a thatched cottage. But there were no remnants of this kind in our house. There were just a few discoloured photos, which were kept in an old chocolate box, mostly of my brother Bill and myself when we were young. My older brother Bill, who was a very pretty child, often wore what looked like girl's dresses, made by my mother on her sewing machine, and he sat in toy cars built for him by my father at work. There were photos of me and Bill in matching duffel coats and grey knee socks with our mother looking glamorous and beautiful in lipstick and light buckskin gloves, standing in front of Father Christmas.

The truth is that we were the kind of family that does not leave much behind. I don't remember my grandparents, and the house we'd all lived in had had to come down. That was how my mother always described it: 'the house had to come down'. It was bulldozed one summer afternoon in the 1980s in the great slum clearance that had finally reached North Belfast. Those old mill houses didn't have bathrooms. You washed in the kitchen in a basin with a drip of water from a spitting, boiling geyzer, there was an outside toilet and in the bedrooms there were damp walls with the wallpaper hanging off and small rivulets of water running down them.

My mother was the last resident in Legmore Street to go. She had nobody, not even me. 'You're across the water,' she would say. 'You've got your own life; you don't care. That university keeps you busy. What time do you start in the morning?' she would ask.

'No set time,' I would say, 'except when I've got lectures.'

'How many of them do you have, then?'

'Oh, about twenty or twenty-two,' I would say, as casually as possible.

'A week?'

'No, a year, but there are tutorials and seminars...'

But she had already stopped listening. 'And you can't help your mother get out of her old house,' she'd say. And she would look at me in that particular way, as if to say: 'What kind of son have I reared?'

I used to think that part of the problem was that my mother never understood the nature of academic work. She was used to shift work and having to clock on and off. I would be sitting in the front room doing my homework as a child and she would ask me to go to the shops for a pint of milk.

'But I'm working,' I would say.

'No, you are not working; you are just bloody sitting there. I've been watching you. You haven't written anything for about ten minutes.'

'But I'm thinking,' I once said. 'I'm doing creative things in my head while I just sit here.'

'Well, do them on the way to the shops instead—we need milk for your breakfast in the morning,' she replied.

So the old house came down one afternoon when I was not there. I was probably busy thinking creative thoughts at the time. I was always ambitious and I sensed that you had to put your ambitions first in order to get anywhere if you are working class. The irony is that I think I picked that up from my mother.

The rest of the houses in the street were all boarded up and crumbling around her. Rats and mice were overrunning the area. She was terrified of them.

'If I see one of them rats I'll die,' she said. 'The mouse was bad enough. Sadie had to come all the way up here to get it for me with a brush.'

She would talk about the move, and the new life that was to be hers, but mostly I thought that she liked to talk about it because she knew that I suffered guilt simply for not being there.

One of the benefits of the Troubles, of course, was that housing in Belfast, neglected for so many decades, had suddenly become a priority in the 1970s and 1980s. Like everyone else, my mother profited from the government's largesse, which had also brought newcomers from further afield to reside in our mill village as they moved from their overcrowded streets.

Our street and the others around it, all mixed, had been condemned for years, condemned ever since I was a boy. The bad housing and the social deprivation that it represented were identified as one of the causes of the conflict in Northern Ireland. We were the poor Protestants—not even fighting to keep our footing on a supposedly higher rung on the social ladder, just pawns in someone else's game. That's what those with a socialist perspective always claimed: the working class in Northern Ireland was divided on religious grounds, and hence easily conquered.

They had a point, that was what I always thought, but my mother told me that I was just talking bloody nonsense. And it irritated her to hear about the poor Catholics all the time. The Rocks in our street were poor, there were eleven of them in a house the same size as ours—but Joey Donaghy next door wasn't impoverished and the fruit shop at the top of the street and the off-licence at the bottom of Lavens Drive and the pub were all owned by Catholics.

We collected bottle tops from Brady's, the off-licence just down the street. I had hundreds of these bright winking buttons kept in cardboard boxes with low sides, like trays, and I can remember the 'shooooo' sound when I tilted the box up and they slid from one end to the other. Kieran's, the fruit shop, gave me their old lettuce and carrots for my guinea pigs, which overran my yard when I was in my early teens. The Catholic Bradys and the Kierans were kind to us, and they were better off than we were. My mother liked pointing this out and also liked to remind me that they had proper families to help them move. She had nobody.

'The workmen had to help me out,' my mother said. 'It's bad when you have to rely on strangers.' And for years after she moved, when I asked what had happened to my grandfather's little black sequined cap, which he'd brought back from India and that always prickled my head when I put it on, or the jigsaw of the Battle of Waterloo or the pop-up book about weasels or even my dozens of school books or the books that were prizes for attendance at Sunday school or church, their disappearance was always blamed on the flight from the old house.

'The workmen were lovely but they never gave me the time to get out,' she said. 'Everything was bulldozed away. They told me that there wasn't much point in bringing the carpet from my old house or most of my clothes. Everything was damp; everything had mould all over it. I left a lot in the old house, including the sewing machine, which I didn't mean to leave. I had to get out in such a hurry in the end. After over sixty years it was such a last-minute thing. I'd been born in that house, but I never looked back when I left, not once. When I got to the new house, I went straight to the bathroom. I bought a new flannel and a sponge. My friend Sadie bought me a brand new back-scrubber. I had some fancy Yardley soap and talcum powder that your Aunt Agnes had bought me for Christmas a few years ago. I'd been keeping it for the new house. The only problem was that it had been sitting getting damp in the old place. I didn't want to unwrap it until I had got a bathroom of my own. By the time I got the packet open, I realized that the talcum powder was damp right through. But I've still got it sitting out, even if it is a funny greeny-blue colour. It's an expensive make, you see.'

I have just one or two photographs from the 1960s of the old house as a backdrop to our lives: my father bending down feeding the pigeons in the street with a fag hanging out of his mouth; or Tommy, one of our neighbours from that time who still lives near my mother, standing there with the big wave in his hair. The front door was always open. The hall, that cramped space between the front door and the inside door, was where we entertained our friends in winter. One of my mother's jokes was about the refined wee Belfast man invited to a posh house for tea who needs the bathroom. 'Where's your yard, missus?' he asked. 'Where's your yard?' my mother would repeat. 'As if your yard could be upstairs.' You could just about turn in our yard to track the sun. 'A lovely wee suntrap,' my mother liked to say. 'There's no wind out there.'

I missed the old house. I never liked the new one in the same way, and occasionally the old house pops into my dreams in one form or another. But it's never cold or damp in the old house of my dreams: it's always just warm and cosy and the whole family are in there, along with my Uncle Terence and Aunt Agnes, and we are all laughing out loud, laughing at something on the telly in the corner, but I don't know what the programme is. I can't imagine what would make us all laugh like that.

The old house was the only embodiment, such as it was, of our family's cultural history. It was the place where my mother was born and where her mother had died one Saturday morning when my brother Bill had been sent upstairs to wake her and returned to tell us that she was dead. It was the place where her father had talked about his days in the British army in South Africa and in India, the small place with no privacy where we had celebrated my father's life and untimely death and my brother's life and even more untimely death in the Himalayas, the place where my Uncle Terence, the big man in our family, hid his tears twice. The only place that we ever knew as a family that could link us to our past.

And now that had gone. □

SHAFT
Anne Enright

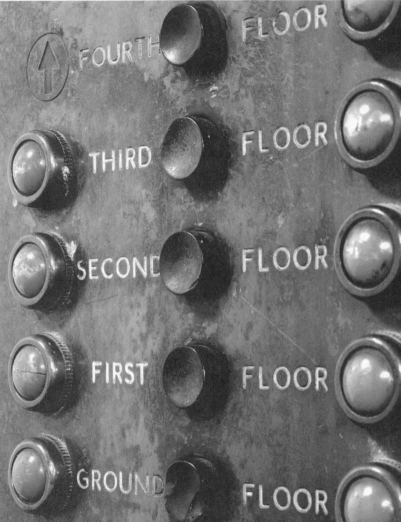

As soon as I walked in, I knew he wanted to touch it. It was a small lift, just a box on a rope really. You could hear the churning of the wheel high above, and the whole thing creaked as it wound you up through the building.

I stood over to give him room—not easy when you are so big. Then, of course, I realized I hadn't pressed the button yet, so I had to swing by him again, almost pivot, my belly like a ball between us. I was sweating already as I reached for the seventh floor.

You know those old bakelite buttons—loose, comfortable things, there's a nice catch to them when they engage. If someone's pushed it before you, of course, they just collapse in an empty sort of way and your finger feels a bit silly. So I always pause a little, before I hit the number seven. And in that pause, I suppose, I get the feeling that this bloody box could go anywhere.

'Oh, I'm sorry,' he said, even though there was no need for it. American. In a suit. Quite tall.

'Oh. Sorry.' I said it too. Well you do, don't you?

The button went in with a soft crunch—wherever he was going, it wasn't to my floor. He eased back into the far corner and we waited for the doors to close.

This blasted lift. Six times a day I go up and down in this box, maybe more, waiting for the machine to make up its mind; waiting for it to finish thinking; checking the building, floor by floor. It's so ancient—it should have those screechy trellis gates, like a murder mystery (I should have an ash blonde permanent wave, the American should be packing a snub little gun). But it doesn't. There are just these two endlessly reluctant doors of metal, that click and surge as though to close, and then change their mind.

I gave a little social sigh—*Well, here we all are*—and flicked a glance his way. He was looking at my stomach, but staring at it— well, people do. So I blinked a bit and smiled my most pregnant smile, all drifty and overwhelmed—*Isn't nature wonderful?* These days, my skin smells of vegetable soup. I mean quite nice soup, but *soup*—you know? I tell you—reproduction, it's a different world.

He looked up at my face then, and smiled. The doors heaved a little in their furrows and then decided against it. Very serious eyelashes. Very bedroom.

'So. When's the happy day then?' he said.

As if it was any of his business. As if we had even been introduced. When you're pregnant, you're public property, you're fair game. 'Well, hello,' they say in shops, 'How are you today.' It's like the whole world has turned American, in a way, and here was the genuine article, corn-fed, free-range; standing there in his nice suit and enquiring after my schedule.

'What do you mean?' I wanted to say. 'I am just suffering from bloat.' Or, 'Who says it's going to be happy? It might be the most miserable day of my life. I might be, for example, screaming in agony, or haemorrhaging, I might be dead.'

'Oh.' I looked down at my belly like I just realized it was there— *What, this old thing?*

'Six weeks,' I said.

'Hey!' he said back. Like a cheerleader. I thought he might reach out and give me a playful little punch on the arm—*Go for it!*

I turned and jabbed the 'doors close' button. At least I thought it was the 'doors close' button, it was actually the 'doors open' button—there is something so confusing about those little triangles— so the doors which were, at that exact moment, closing, caught themselves—*Ooops!*—and slid open again.

We looked out into the small lobby. Still empty.

'Well, good luck!' he said.

And he gave a little 'haha' laugh; rocking back on his heels a bit, while I jabbed at the other button, the correct one this time, the one where the triangles actually point towards each other, and, *Okay,* said the doors—*Now we close.*

Someone got a pot of gloss paint and dickied them up, years ago. Thick paint, you can see the swirl of the brush still in it, a sort of 1970s brown. The doors meet, and sigh a little, and you look at the places where the paint has flaked. You look at the place where the painter left a hair, in a big blonde S. You stand three inches away from another human being, and you think about nothing while the lift thinks about going up, or down.

Decisions decisions.

Good luck with what? The labour? The next forty years?

The lift started to rise.

'I'll need it,' I said.

This building used to be a hotel. I can't think of any other excuse, because there is dark green carpet, actual carpet, on the walls of the lift, up to what might be called the dado line. Above that, there's mirror made of smoked glass, so that everyone in it looks yellow, or at least tanned. Actually, the light is so dim, people can look quite well, and basically you look at them checking themselves in the glass. Or you look at yourself in the glass, and they look at you, as you check yourself in the glass. Or your eyes meet in the glass. But there is very little real looking. I mean the mirror is so hard to resist— there is very little looking that goes straight from one person across space to the other person, in the flesh as it were, as opposed to in the glass.

Or glasses. One reflection begs another, of course, because it is a mirror box—all three walls of it, apart from the doors. So your eyes can meet in any number of reflections, that fan out like wings on either side of you. The American in the corner was surrounded by all my scattered stomachs, but he was staring straight at the real one.

No you can't, I thought. Don't even think about it.

I look so strange anyhow these days. I misjudge distances and my reflection comes at me too fast. I felt like I was tripping over something, just standing there. The American's hands were by his sides. The left one held his document case and the right one was unclenching, softly.

And then, as a mercy, we stopped. The third floor. Ping.

'You'll be fine,' he said, like he was saying goodbye. But when the doors opened, he didn't leave, and there was no one there. They stayed open for a long time while we looked at an empty corridor; then they shut, and it was just me and him, listening to the building outside, listening to our own breathing, while the lift did absolutely nothing for a while.

I always look people in the eye, you know? That is just the way I am. Even if they have a disability, or a strangeness about them, I look them straight in the eye. And if one of their eyes is damaged, then I look at the good eye, because this is where they *are*, somehow. I think it's only polite. But I am not always right. Some people want you to look at their 'thing' and not at them. Some people need you to.

There was that young transvestite I met in the street, once; I used to know his mother, and there were his lovely eyes, still hazel under all that mascara and the kohl. Well I didn't know where else to look at him, except in the eye, but also, I think, I wanted to say hello to him. *Himself.* The boy I used to know. And of course this is not what he wanted at all. He wanted me to admire his dress.

Or Jim, this friend of mine who got MS. I met him one day and I started chatting to him of course—and then I found I was talking faster, like really jabbering, because it was him I wanted to talk to— him and not his disease—and he was sliding down the wall in front of me, jabber jabber jabber jabber, until a complete stranger was saying to him, 'Would you like me to get you a chair?'

I would prefer it if he looked at me, that's all—the American. Even if I was sliding down the mirrored wall in front of him, even if I was giving birth on the floor. I would prefer it if he looked at the person that I am, the person you see in my eyes. That's all. I put my hand on my stomach to steady the baby, who was quiet now, enjoying the ride—and silent, as they always are. But sometimes they leave a bubble of air in there, with their needles and so on. They leave air in there by accident and, because of the air, you can hear the baby cry— really hear it. I read that somewhere. It must be the loneliest sound.

We are all just stuck together. I felt like telling him that too.

Anyway, what the hell. There was this guy looking at my stomach in the lift on the way up to the seventh floor one Tuesday morning when I had very little on my mind. Or everything. I had everything on my mind. I had a whole new person on my mind, for a start, and the fact that we didn't have the money really, for this. I had all this to worry about, a new human being, a whole universe, but of course this is 'Nothing'. *You are worrying about nothing,* my husband says. Everything I think about is too big, for him, or too small.

Of course he is right. I pick the things off the floor because if I don't our life will end up in the gutter. I put the tokens from the supermarket away because if they get lost our child will not be able to afford to go to college. My husband, on the other hand, lives in a place where you don't pick things up off the floor and everything will be just fine. Which must be lovely.

'It's perfectly natural,' he says, when I tell him the trouble I am having with the veins in my legs, or the veins—God help us—in my backside. But sometimes I think he means, *We're just animals, you know.* And sometimes I think he means, *You in particular. You are just an animal.*

By the time we passed the fifth floor I had the sandwich in my mouth. Roast beef, rare, with horseradish sauce. That's why I was in the lift in the first place, I had just waddled out for a little something, and God, it tasted amazing. I lifted my chin up to make the journey down my throat that bit longer and sweeter, and maybe it was this that made him breathe short, like he was laughing, made me look at him finally, sideways, with my mouth full.

'Well, that sure looks good,' he said.

This American laughing at me, because I am helpless with food. And because I look so stupid, and huge, this man I have never met before being able to say to me, 'Would you mind? May I touch?'

I could feel the lift pushing up under my feet. My mouth was still full of roast beef. But he stretched his hand out towards me, anyway. It looked like a hand you might see in an ad—like that old ad for Rothmans cigarettes—slightly too perfect, like he was wearing fake tan. I turned around to him, or I turned the baby round to him, massively. I did not look him in the face. I looked sideways a little, and down at the floor.

I wanted to say to him, Who is going to pay for it? *Or love it.* I wanted to say, *Who is going to love it?* Or, *Do you think it is lonely, in there?* I really wanted to say that. I swallowed and opened my mouth to speak and the lift stopped, and he set his hand down. He touched all my hopes.

'It's asleep,' I said.

The doors opened. So we were standing like that, him touching my belly, me looking at the ground, like some sort of slave woman. Thinking about his eyelashes. Thinking that, no matter what I did these days, no matter what I wore or how I did my hair, I always looked poor. Lumbered.

He said, 'Thank you. You know, this is the most beautiful thing. It's the most beautiful thing in the whole world.'

Well he would say that, wouldn't he. □

NOTES ON CONTRIBUTORS

Diana Athill was one of the most respected editors in British publishing during her fifty-year career at André Deutsch in London. Her books include *Yesterday Morning* (Granta Books) and *Stet: An Editor's Life* (Granta/Grove Atlantic).

Geoffrey Beattie is Professor of Psychology at Manchester University, and the resident psychologist on Channel 4's *Big Brother*. 'Protestant Boy' is taken from his memoir of the same name which is published by Granta Books.

T. C. Boyle's novel, *Drop City* (Bloomsbury/Viking), was a 2003 National Book Award Finalist. 'Femme Fatale' is taken from his forthcoming novel, *The Inner Circle*, which will be published by Viking in the US later this year and in 2005 by Bloomsbury in the UK.

Brian Cathcart is the author of *Rain* (Granta Books) and *The Case of Stephen Lawrence* (Penguin). His latest book is *The Fly in the Cathedral: How a small group of Cambridge scientists won the race to split the atom* (Viking).

Anne Enright's most recent novel is *The Pleasure of Eliza Lynch* (Vintage/Grove Atlantic). Her book of essays, *Making Babies*, will be published in August this year by Jonathan Cape.

Jennie Erdal has worked as a publisher and a translator. Her memoir, *Ghosting*, will be published by Canongate.

Giles Foden was born in Warwickshire in 1967 and grew up in Africa. He is the author of three novels: *Zanzibar* (Faber), *Ladysmith* and *The Last King of Scotland* (Faber/Vintage). He works on the books pages of the *Guardian*.

Jackie Kay's most recent collection of short stories, *Why Don't You Stop Talking*, is published by Picador.

J. Robert Lennon is the author of four novels, most recently *Mailman* (Granta Books/W. W. Norton). Granta Books will publish his collection of very short stories, *Pieces for the Left Hand*, in 2005.

Orhan Pamuk won the International IMPAC Award for *My Name is Red* (Faber/Vintage). 'A Religious Conversation' is taken from his novel, *Snow*, which is published by Faber in the UK and by Alfred A. Knopf in the US.

Daniel Smith's writing has appeared in the *Atlantic Monthly* and he is currently working on a book about the science and history of hearing voices, which will be published by Penguin in the US. He lives in New York.

David J. Spear received the Howard Chapnick Grant in 2000. His book, *Gas Smells But Not Like Skunks,* is published by Strike West Picture Press. He is currently working with young people on the Flathead Reservation in Montana.

Jonathan Tel's story 'Zaghrouda' appeared in *Granta* 78. His novel, *Freud's Alphabet*, is published by Scribner in the UK and by Counterpoint Press in the US. He divides his time between London, New York and Jerusalem.